21ST CENTURY COURAGE:

STIRRING STORIES OF MODERN BRITISH HEROES

TO MY BROTHER BEN
A 21ST CENTURY HERO

21ST CENTURY COURAGE:
STIRRING STORIES OF MODERN BRITISH HEROES

BY

MARK FELTON

Pen & Sword
MILITARY

First published in Great Britain in 2010 by
Pen & Sword Military
An imprint of
Pen & Sword Books Ltd
47 Church Street
Barnsley
South Yorkshire
S70 2AS

Copyright © Mark Felton 2010

ISBN 978 1 84884 073 7

The right of Mark Felton to be identified as Author of this work has been asserted
by him in accordance with the Copyright, Designs and Patents Act 1988.

A CIP catalogue record for this book is
available from the British Library

Typeset by Acredula

Printed and bound in England
By MPG

Pen & Sword Books Ltd incorporates the Imprints of Pen & Sword Aviation,
Pen & Sword Family History, Pen & Sword Maritime, Pen & Sword Military,
Wharncliffe Local History, Pen & Sword Select, Pen & Sword Military Classics,
Leo Cooper, Remember When, Seaforth Publishing and Frontline Publishing

For a complete list of Pen & Sword titles please contact
PEN & SWORD BOOKS LIMITED
47 Church Street, Barnsley, South Yorkshire, S70 2AS, England
E-mail: enquiries@pen-and-sword.co.uk
Website: www.pen-and-sword.co.uk

Contents

Acknowledgements vi
Introduction vii

Chapter 1 – 'Have a Go' Heroes 1
Chapter 2 – Death and Diamonds 18
Chapter 3 – Cops and Robbers 31
Chapter 4 – Courage under Fire 46
Chapter 5 – Fire and Rescue 71
Chapter 6 – Terror on the Streets.................................... 81
Chapter 7 – High Seas Hijack 106
Chapter 8 – Disaster in the Air 112
Chapter 9 – Nerves of Steel.. 124
Chapter 10 – The Last Place on Earth................................ 139

Appendix 1.. 170
Appendix 2.. 179
Appendix 3.. 182
Sources and Selected Bibliography.................................... 184
Index 188

Acknowledgements

This book has been the most immediate that I have written, and the reader will note that the majority of the research material has come from newspaper reports and stories. Many thanks to the British newspapers that have kindly made their stories available and accessible. I should like to thank Shirley Felton for her assistance in gathering background material in Britain, and for kindly sending documents to me in Shanghai; my thanks to Brigadier Henry Wilson, Helen Vodden, Jonathan Wright and the fantastic staff at Pen and Sword Books for helping to make this project a reality, and a special vote of thanks to my editor Martin Middlebrook for all of your hard work. I must thank my wife, Fang Fang, for her incredible support of my work, and for her very valuable and constructive criticism, and lastly my brother Ben Felton, whose heroic story of a daring underwater rescue told to me by others, convinced me that the stories of modern everyday heroes should be told.

Introduction

'People keep talking about the Play Station Generation and saying the youth of today, with their trainers etc, are not up to the task...My soldiers were all young people of today and they were never once found wanting. They were just as brave and robust as their forbears going right back into history.'

Major Nick Calder MC
The Argyll and Sutherland Highlanders,
5th Battalion, The Royal Regiment of Scotland

'I've got your DNA'[1], shouted William Grove as the robber sped away in a car. In his hand Grove held a black balaclava mask that he had just wrenched from the criminal's head as he was in the act of smashing his way through a toughened glass jeweller's window with a sledge hammer on a busy street in Richmond, London in 2008. Grove had single-handedly confronted two young robbers who had set about demolishing the jeweller's front windows in a daring smash and grab raid. What was even more amazing was that Grove was eighty-four-years-old. Grove's bravery caused a great deal of soul-searching in the media about why, out of a large crowd of shoppers and office workers who watched the two men rob the shop, only one very elderly and frail old man had the courage to step forward and intervene. Many editorials came to the conclusion that modern generations of British people are simply no longer possessed of sufficient courage, and that it was an indictment of decades of health and safety legislation, societal breakdown and fear-mongering by the government, police and journalists that had led to a nationwide apathy when it came to 'having a go.' Unsurprisingly, many journalists focused on the fact that Grove was a veteran of the

Second World War, Britain's 'greatest generation', and in stepping forward and doing his civic duty Grove epitomized the generation of Britons who had defeated Hitler and crushed Japan. 'It was a busy day on the high street and there were crowds of shoppers watching,' said thirty-five-year-old Nick Thompson. 'But these days people don't want to have a go in case a robber has a weapon.'[2]

According to a 2005 ICM poll published in the *Daily Mail* the British are a nation of have-a-go heroes rather than people who like to keep themselves to themselves. 'Almost everyone keeps an eye on their neighbour's property while they are away,' said Adrian Grace of Barclays Insurance Services, who commissioned the poll. 'Almost a third of men and a quarter of women said they would go even further and directly intervene if they saw someone behaving suspiciously.' Judging by the stories recounted in this book, probably an equal proportion of British people would also intervene to help someone who was in distress. 'It appears to be a modern myth that there is a lack of community spirit. We just don't talk about it,' said Grace, adding that 'it is reassuring to know that people look out for each other without being asked.'

Modern Britain certainly has its fair share of problems, from youth crime to corrupt politicians, but it is also still a fairly decent society of people who believe that it is one's duty to help others to do the right thing. It is still a gentle land which manages to punch well above its weight on the international stage, a nation confident that being 'British' means more than swearing allegiance to a flag or reciting a National Anthem – it means fair play, good manners, charity and compassion. Where else in the world do strangers greet one another so readily with a jaunty 'good morning': watch how long it takes before two British people smile, laugh or joke in everyday conversation? Watch how freely most British will give of their time to helping the stranger whose car has broken down or who is lost. The British are a welcoming, open and quite often brave and compassionate people, and some of that bravery must be present in every one who believes in the qualities so abundantly found in British society today.

When he was questioned by reporters about his undoubted courage, William Grove said: 'My reaction was natural and instinctive, you can't have this sort of thing going on. I'm not a hero just a responsible citizen, a hero is somebody who jumps into the Thames to rescue a drowning child.'[3]

In writing this book I have discovered that generations of modern Britons are the equal of the Second World War generation. Very little separates them. Bravery has not become devalued, no matter how hard health and safety legislation and the 'nanny state' has tried to devalue the concept, and people will still perform what they see as their human duty to help save the lives of others. It is something instinctual and it is something that spans generations.

Sergeant Stephen McConnell locked his bayonet into place on his SA-80 rifle and, narrowing his eyes against the glare of the harsh Afghan sun, he gave the order to advance. The thirty-two-year-old was commanding 8 Platoon, 1st Battalion, The Royal Irish Regiment, on attachment to 2nd Battalion, The Parachute Regiment. In back of his mind was the thought that this time tomorrow he would be on a military transport plane bound for Britain and some well-deserved leave. Now it looked as though he would be lucky to get out of this situation alive, let alone in one piece to go on leave. The thought made him angry, very angry. O'Connell and his men had been tramping across the tan coloured Afghan landscape for an hour and a half that day in July 2008 when suddenly all hell had been let loose. No. 8 Platoon was suddenly assailed from all sides by up to fifty Taliban insurgents. 'We retaliated and then we fixed bayonets and got our grenades ready and began to advance on them. I went out across an open field to use my bayonet,' recalled O'Connell. 'I remember seeing the plough all around my feet jumping up as the bullets hit it.'[4] The fighting was intense. 'We had just destroyed the third enemy position when they opened up from the rear. We were by now completely surrounded. They had eight positions pouring fire at us and we kept fighting back. I remember charging at them and yelling: 'I'm going on leave tomorrow and you bastards aren't stopping me.'[5] McConnell's citation for the Military Cross contains many phrases that are used to describe the amazing actions made by all of the men and women who appear throughout the pages of this book. Phrases such as 'outstanding bravery' and 'ignoring his own safety' hint at the incredible feats that have been recognized by the British government and society. Without exception, whether military or civilian, the outstanding thing that linked all of these brave men and women together was their concern for others, not themselves, and in many cases they went to such extremes to save other peoples' lives that they willingly forfeited their own.

Reading Major Nick Calder's comments that appear at the beginning of this introduction, one is perhaps struck by how little the British people have changed, rather than by how much, down the generations. Certainly, fashions, musical tastes, values in society and so on have of course changed over the decades following the Second World War. But that indelible strain of innate decency and courage has not diminished in either the soldier or the civilian. Military conflicts in Iraq and Afghanistan, and civilian tragedies such as the London Bombings or the terrorist attack at Glasgow Airport have shown Britons at their very finest. Perhaps no generation is so routinely mocked and derided as the 'Play Station Generation', but what this book hopefully demonstrates are that heroism and bravery are as alive today among the generations who inhabit that 21st Century as at any time in Britain's glorious past.

This book tells the stories of incredible men and women who have risked, and sometimes lost, their lives performing feats of courage worthy of national recognition. They are men and women from varied backgrounds, ages, professions and ethnic groups. They share one thing in common – they are the best examples of modern courage in Britain today. Every story that you read in this book occurred in the 21st century. These are tales of modern courage, and of modern heroes. Their stories should be studied by schoolchildren, in the same way that older generations of Britons looked to Captain Scott or Douglas Bader for inspiration. The faked 'heroics' of the contestants on *I'm a Celebrity* or the vacuousness of *Big Brother* should not stand as indicative of British culture in the early 21st Century. If you pick up a newspaper in modern Britain today you will read article after article deriding modern youth, critique after critique of modern British society, its selfishness, destruction of its institutions and values, and much soul-searching about how preceding generations were somehow 'better' than the Britons of today. 'Young people aren't as bad as they are made out to be,' said William Grove, the pensioner hero from Richmond. 'It had been built up now that everyone is carrying a knife, it's just not true.'[6]

Our perceptions of heroism have certainly changed since the

'Greatest Generation' made their sacrifice in the Second World War. But, if the stories in this book demonstrate anything, it is that when push comes to shove individual Britons are the equal in terms of inbred courage to those of the generations to fought world wars or built an empire or explored and mapped the planet. Perhaps the media has devalued the word 'hero' over the past decades, and it is sometimes unadvisedly used to describe some overpaid footballer's achievements on the soccer pitch or a film star's latest piece of self-promotion.

I was inspired to write this book, somewhat of a different subject from my other publications, by the actions of two people, my brother and my uncle's sister. Both are members of the Metropolitan Police. My brother Ben, a sergeant, saved the life of his diving buddy while the two of them were scuba diving in Leicestershire, and PC Elizabeth Kenworthy saved several lives when she was caught up in the terrible terrorist attacks on the London Underground in 2005. We all know brave people, and I think we are all in awe of their achievements. My brother received commendations from the Metropolitan Police and the Royal Humane Society, and Liz Kenworthy was made an MBE in 2009. This book is in no way the sum total of British courage in the 21st century. The stories that appear here are only the tip of the iceberg, for it would take innumerable volumes just to tell the full story of British heroes in Iraq and Afghanistan, let alone those from the streets of our island nation, and across the world. My apologies to those who stories unfortunately I was unable to include in this book. Their courage has been the equal to all of those who stories are told.

Shanghai
December 2009

1 *'Pensioner foils sledgehammer thief with 'disabling move' learnt in forces'* by Matthew Moore and Lucy Cockcroft, *The Telegraph*, 31 October 2008

2 Ibid.

3 Ibid.

4 *'Bomb disposal expert blown up by Taliban awarded second George Medal as 178 heroes are honoured for bravery'* by Matthew Hickley, *Daily Mail*, 6 March 2009

5 Ibid

6 *'Pensioner foils sledgehammer thief with 'disabling move' learnt in forces'* by Matthew Moore and Lucy Cockcroft, *The Telegraph*, 31 October 2008

CHAPTER 1

'Have a Go' Heroes

'It doesn't matter if you know them or don't know. If someone is in trouble you need to help them. It is wrong to ignore them and walk away.'

Amevi Kouassi, age 30

Commended for tackling a violent mugger, 2009

'Those boys saw a little old lady and thought I was easy pickings, but there was no way I was going to sit there and let them get away with it,'[1] declared sixty-eight-year-old Janet Lane, who single-handedly ran a teenage thief to ground after he had made the mistake of snatching her handbag. The extraordinary events happened in Torquay, Devon, while Mrs. Lane, a retired nurse, was sitting on a park bench waiting to meet a friend near the Riviera International Centre. 'I had my shopping bag with me by my side and I turned around, looking for my friend, Sue, who would be coming around the corner,' recalled Lane. Three boys, dressed in hooded sweaters, approached her and asked her for a cigarette. 'I said no. They must have been checking if I had anything worth stealing. They must have come back and I felt a whooshing movement, and I saw a boy in a grey hooded top take my bag.'[2]

Lane leapt unexpectedly into action. 'There was no way I was going to sit there and let them get away with it,' said Lane. 'I was so angry when they took [my handbag]. I have been to collect my pension and I had water rates to pay with that money.' The thieves had picked on the wrong OAP, for in her youth Lane had been

Yorkshire cross-country running champion and had kept up her fitness with swimming. She set off in pursuit across the park and into the grounds of a nearby hotel. After a 100 metre dash Lane closed in on the youth with her bag, who appeared to be about fifteen years old, and she grabbed him by the collar. At this point the hoodie dropped Lane's handbag and begged to be released before fleeing with his mates empty-handed. Janet Lane made news headlines across Britain after her daring heroics, and her actions demonstrate that intervening to right an injustice has no age limit placed upon it. Devon and Cornwall Police unfortunately issued the usual politically-correct statement straight afterwards ('Generally, for safety reasons, we do not actively encourage this kind of behaviour, as you never know what could happen'[3]) but, as many of the examples in this chapter will demonstrate, the 'walk on by' policy being promulgated by police forces and health and safety gurus has yet to take hold in Britain.

The pistol appeared from nowhere. The Royal Mail investigator holding the small cardboard box full of shiny bullets stared dumbfounded at the weapon that was pointed directly at his chest. It seemed so incongruous – a handgun in the midst of British suburbia, so out of place yet so terrifying. Then the gunman pulled the trigger and murder was done.

Interfering with the Queen's mail is a criminal offence in Britain. The public puts its trust in the Royal Mail to deliver letters safely and parcels on time and without their staff interfering with them in any way. Inevitably, such a huge organisation as the Royal Mail has had its fair share of light-fingered employees over the decades, and it was the job of people like Neil Roberts to catch them. Roberts was a postal investigator, with the power to arrest dishonest employees who were caught stealing mail and parcels. On 3 August 1998 an investigation into missing mail had led Roberts and two of his colleagues to arrest and caution a postman and bring him in for further questioning. The man appeared compliant enough at first, and when he was asked to give his permission to a search being made of his house the postman acquiesced without resistance. It appeared to be another routine case of a postal employee foolishly helping himself to mail that he was supposed to deliver, hunting through envelopes looking for cash sent with birthday cards, new credit cards and cheque books, valuables, and often discovering a veritable treasure trove of temptation for the unscrupulous thief. The Royal Mail has constantly urged people not to send cash and other valuables through the post, but people often do, and it sometimes leads to thefts. Roberts expected to discover plenty of evidence at the postman's house, hopefully enough to bring him up on criminal charges and see him sent to prison.

Roberts and two colleagues drove the postman to his house. After he had let them in, the three investigators began to search the premises. In the bedroom upstairs Roberts discovered an astounding quantity of stolen mail – twelve full black bin bags and twenty-five cloth mail sacks piled high with letters and parcels. The postman had made no effort to hide the results of his crimes, evidently confident that he would not be caught. Further investigation revealed more mail elsewhere in the property as well as a pile of empty mail sacks. During this time, the postman stood in the bedroom doorway watching the investigators in silence. Roberts started to move some of the mail downstairs, where it would later be sent on to the intended recipients. He then returned to the bedroom and opened the wardrobe door where he found it crammed with parcels. No one had noticed that the postman had briefly left the room while everyone else was busy, but now he appeared in the doorway again and stood watching once more, his eyes boring into the investigators.

One of the investigators went through some drawers and turned up an interesting find – a cardboard box full of live pistol bullets. This was clearly an illegal item that would have to be reported to the police, for the possession of controlled ammunition is a serious offence in Britain. He began to ask the postman about the bullets when the handgun suddenly appeared from nowhere. A second later the postman opened fire. A hail of bullets killed one of the investigators instantly, while the other fell to the floor badly wounded. Roberts had been out of view to the gunman behind the wardrobe door. As Roberts' turned the postman fired another shot, the bullet narrowly missing him, embedding itself in the wardrobe. Roberts immediately launched himself at the postman, realising that this was a life or death situation. The two men struggled violently, moving out into the corridor and down the stairs. Finally, in the hallway near the front door, Roberts managed to overpower the postman, he having already wrench the gun away from him on the staircase. Roberts pinned him to the floor and opened the front door of the house and began calling for help. A passerby came running, and he called the police and helped Roberts keep the postman under control until officers arrived to arrest him. The postman was convicted of murder and attempted murder, while Roberts received the Queen's Commendation for Bravery in 2001 for apprehending the gunman[4]. Without his quick and aggressive action Roberts himself would undoubtedly have been killed along with his wounded and helpless colleague who lay injured in the house.

The Queen's Commendation for Bravery is an award that is open to both British subjects and foreigners for bravery entailing risk to life and meriting national recognition where the actions involve British subjects. It consists of a certificate and a spray of laurel leaves, silver for civilians and bronze for military personnel, that is worn on any associated campaign medal, or if no medal was issued, pinned to the left breast of the coat.

Police officers are never really off-duty. They always carry their warrant card with them, and they are expected to be vigilant to crime during rest days. Detective Constables Mark Scott and Stephen Stenson-Pickles were both serving with Suffolk Constabulary and were off-duty in April 2000 when they intervened and prevented a horrific incident was spiralling into a full-blown disaster in the small market town of Bury St. Edmunds. Scott, then thirty-nine, had served for sixteen years with Suffolk Constabulary, though he was originally from Tunstall in Sunderland. Before working in Suffolk, Scott had served for six years in the RAF Police.

A local man, recently jilted by his girlfriend, and clearly unstable, had decided that he was going to take his own life. This is not especially note-worthy as people often kill themselves for a myriad of personal reasons. It was, however, the method which the man had selected that had the potential to cause widespread damage and to have taken many more lives than just his own. He had walked into a Jet service station shop in Bury, poured petrol over himself and declared his intention to end it all while clutching a cigarette lighter in one hand. Self-immolation has to be one of the most painful and public methods of committing suicide, but the man appeared determined. A fire in a petrol station would have resulted in enormous explosions that would have covered surrounding properties in burning fuel and debris and started a major conflagration. DCs Scott and Stenson-Pickles, though off-duty, immediately intervened.

The two police officers tried to reason with the man, but this only made him even crazier. He grabbed bottles of spirits from the shop display counter and smashed them, pouring the liquid over himself, all the time threatening to ignite the cigarette lighter he held in one fist. Scott said that his first instinct was not to become a 'flambéed cop'. The two police officers looked at each other as the hysterical man raved and shouted, and an ever widening pool of petrol and alcohol spread out across the shop floor, dangerously close to the pumps just outside. Both officers realised that further negotiation was a waste of time. Suddenly, Scott and Stenson-Pickles threw themselves at the man, violently wrestling with the lunatic, covering themselves in petrol as they did so, trying to prevent the man from flicking the lighter and killing them all. After a few seconds of thrashing about on the floor, the lighter was taken off of the man and he was restrained and arrested. A terrible disaster had been averted by the quick-witted and extremely courageous actions of two off-duty detectives. Scott and Stenson-Pickles both received a Police Bravery Award from the Home Secretary for their gallantry as well as commendations from Suffolk Constabulary. The man who had tried to kill himself and almost destroyed a petrol station was later sentenced to fifteen months in prison.

An almighty commotion disturbed the usually peaceful small Chinese takeaway shop in Cheltenham, Gloucestershire. A loud bang and much shouting in Cantonese came from the direction of the kitchen. The shop's owner, Kwok Man Fan, glanced at the customer he was serving and then entered the kitchen. His father-in-law was standing with his back to Kwok. He had a large cut in the side of his head and he was bleeding heavily. Because the kitchen was so small, Fan could only see what was going on when his father-in-law stepped back. The cook stood staring at the kitchen helper, in whose hand was a large stainless steel meat cleaver, thin rivulets of blood dripping from its razor sharp edge onto the white tiled floor. For a few seconds the men stood looking at each other in stunned silence.

Mr. Fan sprang into action, scooping up a chair and throwing it at the kitchen helper, who dropped the cleaver with a clatter onto the floor. Next, Fan pushed a metal table up against the kitchen helper's legs, trapping him against the wall, the cook adding his weight to the manoeuvre. Fan's father-in-law managed to escape from the shop at this point, but his wife came down some stairs from the apartment above that connected with the kitchen, alerted by all of the shouting and commotion. She screamed as she saw the kitchen helper grab another long-bladed knife from a counter as Fan and the cook pinned him against the kitchen wall, and she ran into the shop. The man struggled madly to free himself from behind the table, and realising that they could not contain him, Fan and the cook dashed into the shop and slammed the door closed behind them. The kitchen helper began to batter at the door like a lunatic, shouting and cursing at them in Cantonese. Then things suddenly went eerily quiet, an ominous sign, as Fan suddenly remembered that the staircase from the kitchen connected with the upstairs flat where his young son was sleeping.

Fan gingerly opened the kitchen door. The helper was still in the kitchen and he immediately rushed the door, quickly forcing his way into the shop before Fan could prevent him. Playing in the shop was his mother-in-law's granddaughter. Fan tried to restrain the crazed knife-wielding kitchen worker, but he was stabbed in the head and shoulder. Fan managed to break free and ran out of the shop into the street shouting for someone to call the police.

Meanwhile, the kitchen helper attacked the little girl and her grandmother. Fan saw what was happening through his shop window, and picking up a wooden post from the ground, he charged inside and hit the kitchen helper twice. The kitchen helper ran back through into the kitchen pursued by Fan, pausing only to throw a pan of hot cooking oil at Fan. At this point, Fan's young son came down the stairs from the flat above. The kitchen helper took one look at him and stabbed him in the head with the knife. Fan, seeing his son in mortal danger, threw himself at the armed man, but as they struggled the man was able to wound the boy again. Then Fan wrestled the knife from his grasp and threw it out of reach. The two men fought each other across the kitchen, until the kitchen helper gained a sudden advantage and forced Fan's head down towards a lit gas burner. It was like a fight scene from one of the *Die Hard* films. At this point Fan was saved by the cook, who rushed into the kitchen and grabbed the kitchen helper's legs, throwing him off balance and causing him to fall to the floor. Fan jumped on top of him, but the man managed to grab the cleaver once again and he tried repeatedly to hit Fan with it. But Fan held on, and after a few minutes the homicidal kitchen helper tired and went limp. Police officers suddenly burst into the kitchen and arrested the miscreant.

For his amazing bravery in saving the lives of a man and two children Kwok Man Fan was awarded the Queen's Gallantry Medal in 2001. The QGM was instituted in 1974. It is awarded to both civilians and military personnel (for actions not in the face of the enemy) for exemplary acts of bravery. To date, fewer than 600 have been awarded.

The four-foot long sword blade gleamed menacingly under the fluorescent lights of the politician's office. The gleam in the eye of the man holding the weapon was unhinged and leering. Death had come to visit, and this awful realization filled the other two men in the room with a sickening terror. A scene of mundane business was about to be transformed into a butcher's shop of blood, pain and murder.

One of the constitutional duties of British Members of Parliament is to hold regular surgeries in their constituencies so that people living within that area can meet their MP face-to-face and air any grievances, ask for help and support or assistance in resolving a myriad of problems. Local town councillors who are of the same political party as the MP often assist at these surgeries. It is an important part of the British democratic process. However, the MPs do not receive routine police protection unless they are also cabinet ministers, and there is no screening process concerning who gets access to an MP. Open government also means open access to those who govern in the name of the people.

On 28 January 2000 the Liberal Democrat MP for Cheltenham, Nigel Jones, was conducting a surgery in the Gloucestershire town assisted by his close friend and local Lib Dem councillor Andrew Pennington. Jones' receptionist showed a man named Robert Ashman into the office. Jones invited him to sit, but he stiffly declined. He was wearing a full-length overcoat that was buttoned up to the neck. Neither Jones nor Pennington had any reason to feel uneasy in Ashman's presence as he had been a regular visitor to Jones' surgeries, and both politicians had been trying to help him resolve some legal issues. What neither Jones nor Pennington realised that Ashman was insane. Concealed inside his coat he had a razor-sharp fake Japanese *katana* sword of the type wielded by *samurai* warriors in the distant past. As Jones and Ashman chatted, the atmosphere began to take on a rather surreal edge as Ashman's conversation started to veer into nonsense. As Jones and Pennington shared a concerned glance, Ashman reached inside of his coat.

Ashman drew the sword from his coat with a flourish and held it above his head with both hands. Jones stood up, and as he did so Ashman dropped the tip of the blade until it was level with Jones' stomach. Pennington backed away and opened the door to the outer office. He quickly told the secretary to call the police. Back in the office, Jones' efforts to reason with Ashman had come to naught. Suddenly, Ashman jabbed the sword towards Jones, trying to run him through. Jones deflected the blade with his left forearm and then grabbed hold of the razor-sharp sword with both of his hands, causing himself grievous cuts. Blood was soon pouring from the terrible wounds inflicted on his hands. The two men ended up struggling on a sofa for control of the sword. Pennington saw his opportunity and struck Ashman hard from behind and then tried to pull the bigger man off the MP. He managed to drag the lunatic clear and he shouted at Jones to get out, and go and get some help.

Unfortunately Ashman managed to regain control of his sword, but the defenceless Pennington bravely stood his ground and tried to overpower the crazed maniac again. During the fight that followed Pennington was stabbed a total of nine times, including suffering six horrendous wounds that went right through his torso. He died on the floor of the office. Police officers arrived soon afterwards and quickly overpowered and arrested Ashman. Jones was rushed to hospital where he required fifty-seven stitches to one hand and had a severed tendon in the other. He had been lucky to survive the murderous assault, and had done so firstly by grabbing the weapon and fighting with Ashman, and because of Pennington's immense courage in tackling the crazed Ashman when the MP had been badly wounded.

Robert Ashman was committed to a secure mental hospital indefinitely by a judge. For his bravery, Andrew Pennington was posthumously awarded the George Medal. 'He was a giant of a person,' said Jones, 'who devoted his whole adult life to serving the community. Nobody could have worked harder than Andy to help people.'[5] Instituted on the same day as the George Cross, the George Medal is awarded for acts of great civilian bravery, and for military personnel whose courageous acts had not been performed in the face of the enemy. Since 1977 it has also been awarded posthumously. Since 1940, approximately 2,000 have been awarded.

Stephen Nyazika, a student nurse, was driving to work along the Woking to Guildford road in Surrey on 17 April 2001. Suddenly his attention was grabbed by a vicious altercation that was taking place in a bus lay-by. Nyazika pulled over, and being a good citizen, he went to investigate. What he discovered was two men and a woman fighting each other with a pickaxe handle and a seven-inch long kitchen knife. One of the men, thirty-three-year-old Christopher Pearce, was staggering around screaming in pain and clutching his arm, blood pumping from between his fingers in bright red rivulets. Standing opposite him was Own Lynch, a twenty-seven-year-old Liverpudlian, who was holding the knife, now shiny with blood. The woman was with Lynch. Nyazika had stumbled upon an example of 'road rage', the random and sometimes deadly displays of violence shown by drivers towards one another over driving incidents. As a student nurse Nyazika could see that Pearce's wounds were very serious, and that if he did not intervene he could die from blood loss.

The argument between Pearce and Lynch had begun earlier when Pearce, who was on his way to walk his dogs in a local beauty spot with his wife, and became involved in an argument with Lynch. Pearce had smashed Lynch's windscreen with a pickaxe handle. Lynch had then chased Pearce's car down the road, and he 'drove bumper to bumper with his victim before forcing him to pull into a bus layby where he launched a savage onslaught in front of stunned bystanders.'[6] It appeared to many of the onlookers that both men were intent on killing each other.

Bravely, Nyazika approached Lynch and announced that he was a police officer. It seemed a sensible and appropriate ruse. He told him to put down the knife. Lynch was momentarily distracted by a passing vehicle, and seeing that the Liverpudlian had no intention of relinquishing his weapon, Nyazika jumped on him and wrestled him to the ground. The two men struggled furiously until Nyazika managed to get the knife away from Lynch. Taking charge, Nyazika told a bystander to call the police, and then he told Lynch and Pearce to remain where they were. Nyazika took the knife and drove to the nearest police station in Woking to report what had happened.

Pierce had been so badly wounded by Lynch that his arm was amputated by surgeons below the elbow. Lynch was charged with attempted murder, but he was eventually found guilty of the lesser crime of causing grievous bodily harm with intent and was sent to prison for five years. For rescuing Pearce and disarming Lynch, Stephen Nyazika was awarded the Queen's Gallantry Medal.

For Barbara Trussell, working in a service station shop in Skelmersdale, Lancashire, was not supposed to be a life-threatening experience – that was until the middle-aged shop assistant found herself face-to-face with two teenage robbers at 9 pm on the evening of 25 October 2005. It was a nightmare situation, the robbers believing that it would be easy to overpower Mrs. Trussell and make off with the cash from the till. Imran Mahmood, and his partner in crime Rehan Mahmood, both eighteen-years-old, and both from the Wigan area, had donned black masks and armed themselves with a hand gun and large knives. Also working at the garage was Imran Mahmood's girlfriend, nineteen-year-old Marian Zahedi who, unbeknown to Trussell, was also in on setting up the robbery.

The two young Asian youths used extreme violence to try and intimidate Barbara Trussell. 'They threw me to the floor, just picked me up and threw me like a bag of spuds,' she said afterwards. 'I literally could not move'[7]. The two robbers, one of them brandishing the hand gun to intimidate Trussell, rifled through the till while they shouted threats and abuse. They took a quantity of cash from the till, stuffing it into their pockets with haste. Marian Zahedi was also thrown down, the robbers hoping to cover up her involvement in the crime by pretending that she was an innocent bystander.

Trussell genuinely feared for her life. The two young robbers may have been amateur villains, but their adrenaline was pumping hard enough to make them extremely edgy and very violent. Suddenly, local man, Anthony Crompton, walked in through the doors of the shop and everything changed. Crompton, only twenty-one-years-old, had seen what was happening through the plate glass front window. He knew Trussell. 'I saw two women in need of help,' he said later. 'I've known the people there a long time – and I thought I've got to act, I've got to do at least something.'[8] Crompton, who was unarmed, calmly closed the shop door behind him and then charged in and threw himself at the first robber. During the tussle that followed Crompton was stabbed in the chest and suffered a punctured lung. Seemingly unimpeded by his injury, he continued to fight back even when the second robber joined in the fray, trying to pistol-whip Crompton with his handgun. Suddenly, the two robbers, their masks pulled off during the fight, fled from the shop, dropping bank notes as they went. A severely shaken Barbara Trussell helped Crompton to sit down, and the emergency services were soon on their way. 'He saved my life as far as I'm concerned, said Trussell. 'I don't think I'd be here now if he hadn't.'[9]

The fact that Crompton had tackled the robbers and dislodged their masks allowed Lancashire Constabulary to track them down using DNA evidence. 'Without Anthony's intervention…they might have got away with it and gone onto bigger things,'[10] said Detective Inspector Chris Wilde. As it was, the two young men and their female accomplice were arrested and later imprisoned. Imran Mahmood and Rehan Mahmood were each sentenced to six years and eight months imprisonment for robbery and wounding, and Marian Zahedi received a two-year sentence for robbery and attempting to pervert to course of justice.

Perhaps there are no finer examples of bravery than of those ordinary men and women who have thrown themselves directly into the path of great danger to try to help others. Crompton is an excellent example of selfless gallantry performed by people who are not trained to deal with emergency situations, nor equipped to deal with them. They are the 'have a go' heroes of modern Britain.

Anthony Crompton fully recovered from his wounds, and in 2008 he received the Queen's Gallantry Medal from the Queen in a ceremony at Buckingham Palace.

Betting shops are a favourite target of robbers. Large sums of cash are kept on the premises. At Corals in Farnborough one day in 2007 a man walked into the shop, which was deserted apart from the female sales assistants behind the counter and a single customer. The newcomer was determined to rip the place off. What he did not count on was the elderly gentleman who was watching the horse races intervening with a fury and determination no-one thought likely. The robber, who was wearing a motorcycle crash helmet to disguise his features, was armed with a knife. 'It was the screams of the women behind the counter, he had broken down the barrier and I was the only person in there. Women screaming is primordial,'[11] said Michael Seery, a sixty-eight-year old retired soldier and police officer.

Seery, who is blind in one eye, picked up a stool and grappled with the armed man. 'Bravery is nothing to do with it,' he said later. 'I am an ex-soldier and your training comes with it. Somebody is in trouble and you automatically go into overdrive.'[12] Seery certainly went into overdrive himself, fighting with the violent criminal, and getting injured in the process. 'I was stabbed in the groin and the back. I was lucky with the one in the back, it missed a vital organ by centimetres.'[13]

As the robber tried to flee through the front door of the shop, Seery kicked him hard in the back causing his crash helmet to fall off. The sales staff got a good look at the man and recognized him. Police later arrested the robber, and he was tried and sent to prison for seven years. Seery spent five days in hospital recovering from his injuries. 'If the circumstances were the same I would do it again tomorrow,'[14] he said. He was given a National Police Public Bravery Award and in 2009 a Pride of Britain Award for his actions.

When Derek Armiger opened the door to the small convenience store in Frome, Somerset, in July 2008 he received the shock of his life. Standing facing a terrified shop assistant was a young man holding a handgun. 'I opened the door and the bloke turned the gun on me and shouted "Get out",' recalled Armiger, a sixty-five-year-old local bus driver. But Armiger did not leave. 'I had no idea what sort

of gun it was but I thought, "If I bide my time I might get a chance."
I waited and when he turned to the cashier I grabbed it.' A furious
struggled ensued as the pensioner fought with the twenty-year-old
armed robber, Armiger determined to wrestle the gun from his
control.[15] 'I tried to get him in a headlock and as I did so the gun went
off and it just missed my head.'[16] Armiger had no way of knowing
whether the gun was real or not. In this case, it was actually an
imitation pistol that fired ball bearings, though it looked real and
could cause serious injury nonetheless. The ball bearing that was
fired narrowly missed striking Armiger in the head and instead
shattered the shop's plate glass window.

'I managed to get him down before lying across his body,' said
Armiger. 'He started squirming under me complaining that his neck
was hurting.'[17] Police officers arrived shortly afterwards and arrested
the young man. Derek Armiger was awarded the Waley-Cohen
Award from Avon and Somerset Police, which was created in 1965
and recognises members of the public who support the enforcement
of law and order. 'He risked his life to protect the lives of
others…Mr. Armiger's quick thinking could well have prevented
harm coming to the shop assistant as well as any other bystanders
and also helped to bring the offender to justice,'[18] said Deputy Chief
Constable Rob Beckley. In this case 'justice' may be a slight
exaggeration, as the gunman was convicted a Taunton Crown Court
of robbery and possession of an imitation firearm with intent to
cause fear of violence and given a twelve-month suspended sentence
and a two-year supervision order. He was not sent to prison, which,
considering the gravity of his crime, appeared desperately lenient on
the part of the judge. Armiger remained modest about his courage,
saying that 'it was the most natural thing to do.'[19]

Post offices have often been choice targets for armed robbers and
other criminals because of the large amount of cash normally to be
found on the premises. Many sub-post offices are located in rural
areas, and the days of the village bobby are pretty much over, so
criminals know that police response times will be lengthy. A
particularly brutal attempted robbery was carried out by a
Zimbabwean immigrant in the small Hampshire village of Sparsholt
in June 2007. The actions of the elderly postmistress and shop co-

owner, Linda Scorey, were extremely courageous in the face of a disgusting attack committed by eighteen-year-old Admire Masaiti.

Masaiti had entered the post office with his hood up to try and obscure his features from the CCTV surveillance camera. He had browsed for a few minutes, casting around nervous glances, before leaving. A short while later Masaiti had come back into the shop. He walked up to Mrs. Scorey and demanded cash from the till. Scorey flatly refused, and at this point Masaiti pulled out a house brick and smashed it into sixty-seven-year-old Mrs. Scorey's face. Stunned and bleeding, Scorey moved back behind a glass screen that divided the shop, but Masaiti reached down and picked up the brick before hurling it at the glass. He came for Scorey again, this time taking a lead pipe from his pocket, and attacked her. Mrs. Scorey fought back. 'I just reacted and did what I had to do,' she said later. 'I didn't feel brave at all. He was going to hit me with the pipe so I just tried to stop him however I could.' During the violent struggle Scorey managed to trip the shop alarm and pull down Masaiti's hand, fully exposing his face to the security camera. He fled empty handed and took off across fields pursued by a couple of villagers, including one on horseback. Masaiti was later apprehended by the police. Linda Scorey has subsequently sold up following the dreadful assault, and Masaiti has been sent to prison.

The all too familiar figures on Britain's streets today are young men dressed in their ubiquitous hoodies, mooching around aimlessly looking for trouble, or by their very presence hinting at criminality and violence. It is a sad indictment of how the previous Labour Government has failed young people from underprivileged backgrounds, and created a generation hooked on benefits that have scant respect for society. They can expect little in the way of punishment for their crimes, as noted in the case of Derek Armiger and the gunman discussed above, as undermanned police forces find themselves overwhelmed by the sheer scale of the anti-social behaviour problem, and the courts seem incapable of properly punishing those they judge. A wave of criminality has spread far beyond the traditional haven of 'sink-hole estates' and the character of Britain has been changed for the worse. Almost weekly in the newspapers we read of ordinary citizens who have tried to stand up to yobs, but who have been badly beaten and sometimes even murdered in acts of cowardly and pointless violence. Occasionally, however, it is the yobs who find themselves placed squarely onto the back foot, and the ordinary law-abiding citizen can still strike a blow for decency and respect. The sense of decency that has underpinned British society for hundreds of years still finds expression today among those brave 'have-a-go heroes' who refuse to let the dregs of society determine the nation's future. The following two examples demonstrate what can happen when ordinary citizens take a stand against the youths blighting our towns and villages.

Low level vandalism committed by 'disaffected' youths, or hoodies, can make people's lives an absolute misery. We can all relate occasions when someone has kicked off a car wing mirror or scratched the paintwork, other times when small fires have been deliberately started or ugly graffiti scrawled across once pristine public or private spaces. The police normally appear almost indifferent to this low-level criminality that is flourishing in Britain, and the hoodies responsible know that they are unlikely to be punished. Nina Stevens, of Wellington in Somerset, was one such citizen who declared by her actions that 'enough was enough'. One night in August 2008 she heard youths once again vandalizing her car. Stevens' street had been plagued by young hoodies prowling around like wild animals in the early hours of the morning vandalizing residents' cars. 'We'd had our car damaged five times in the last six months,' recalled Miss. Stevens. 'I got really upset about it. My wing mirror had been left hanging on with tape because I couldn't afford to keep getting it repaired,' she said. 'We had guests staying and I suddenly woke up and realised the vandals were destroying their car as well as mine. I legged it out of the back door. It wasn't until I got to the car park that I realised it could be dangerous, but by that point I didn't care. My adrenalin was pumping.' Miss. Stevens confronted two hooded youths, aged twelve and fourteen, and grabbed them both by the scruff of the neck and frog-marched them into her house. 'One of them kept tugging and trying to pull forward, but I had a firm grip and I wasn't letting go. I'm a parent and I acted like a parent. We need to get the message across that we are not standing for this sort of behaviour.'[20] Her boyfriend helped to keep the boys under control until the police arrived and arrested them. They were charged with vandalism and theft.

A more serious situation was confronted by Leslie Shott, a thirty-four-year-old father of one, when he faced down a hooded gunman and rescued an Asian shopkeeper friend. On Sunday 3 March 2009, three hooded youths entered the Staverton Convenience Store in Troubridge, Wiltshire, just as the owner, Mohammed Ullah, was locking up for the day. It had been a difficult day for Ullah as youths had earlier shoplifted from his store. Leslie Shott lived in a flat above the shop with his partner and their eighteen-month-old daughter. The group of yobs confronted Ullah behind the counter, shouting and swearing. Shott heard the commotion and immediately raced downstairs to investigate. 'I ran in and asked what they were doing there and they started shouting and swearing,' recalled Shott. 'One of them said, "you don't know who I am" and after we exchanged a few words one of them pulled out the gun and brought it right up to my face…'[21] Shott had no way of knowing that the pistol was actually an imitation, and in fact an air weapon. However, even air pistols can prove lethal if fired from close range, especially into someone's face.

Shott's first reaction to this dangerous situation was outrage at the temerity of the hooded thug. 'I stepped forward towards him and put my hand over the muzzle and kept it down and then pushed his face down on the floor,' said Shott, who struggled with the nineteen-year-old youth violently. The other hoodies took off as the struggle spilled out into the street in front of Ulla's shop. 'When I had him pinned down at the end and had taken the gun off him I told him, "how dare you pull a gun on me in public.' I told him that he had ruined his life through his actions.' The youth's cockiness soon deserted him as Shott held him face down on the pavement. 'But once I got him on the floor and told him the police were on their way he started begging and crying. It was really pathetic and he was pleading for me to let him go but people need to know they cannot do what they want and get away with it.'[22]

Like many of the heroes whose stories are recounted throughout this book, Leslie Shott was self-effacing regarding his bravery. 'I just acted on instinct and would do it again if I had to. Every man should have the right to protect the area where he lives.' Mohammed Ulla said: 'I don't know what would have happened if my friend had not been there and stepped in like that.'[23] At the time of writing Shott's courage has yet to be recognized by any formal award.

1 'Granny Janet Lane runs teenager to ground over snatched pension' by Simon de Bruxelles, The Times, 15 October 2008

2 Ibid.

3 Ibid.

4 The London Gazette, 30 October 2001, Supplement 2, 12752

5 'Medal for man who died saving MP', BBC News, 30 October 2001

6 'Road rage stab victim loses arm' by Thomas Martin,

7 'Praise for man stabbed by robbers, BBC News, 5 April 2006

8 Ibid.

9 Ibid.

10 'Hero is awarded gallantry medal', BBC News, 13 February 2008

11 'Stabbed man honoured for bravery', BBC News, 9 July 2009

12 Ibid.

13 Ibid.

14 Ibid.

15 'Pictured: The terrifying moment a pensioner wrestled a gun-toting raider to the floor after a shot was fired at his head', The Daily Mail, 31 October 2009

16 Ibid.

17 Ibid.

18 Ibid.

19 Ibid.

20 'Brave mum frogmarches two hoodie vandals to justice – while dressed only in her pyjamas' by Chris Brooke, The Daily Mail, 26 August 2008

21 'How dare you point a gun at me!' Hero father wrestles armed raider to floor…and makes him cry.

22 Ibid.

23 Ibid.

CHAPTER 2

Death and Diamonds

'Jumping over the wall felt like standing on top of a high
diving board only fifty percent sure that there was actually
any water in the pool underneath. For the first few hours the
adrenalin was pumping and we were very relieved to actually
get out of a deadly, bustling market town.'

Major Philip Ashby, Royal Marines

British soldiers, their camouflaged uniforms filthy with dirt and
sweat, hands tied behind them, knelt in the village dirt as rifles were
levelled at their backs by mostly teenage African rebels. An order
was given to fire. The rebels, high on drugs and rot-gut liquor,
laughed as the only sound was the dry click of rifle bolts in empty
weapons. The execution may have been mock, but the intention to
kill the helpless hostages was very real. Sweating profusely, the
bruised and battered British soldiers were hauled back to the hut that
served as their prison by their highly animated and crazy guards to
spend the rest of the day wondering how long their nightmare would
last. Unknown to the soldiers, friendly eyes had witnessed the mock
execution from concealed positions inside the thick green jungle that
bordered the tiny village and, even as the hostages were dragged off
English voices were quietly relaying the news of this latest outrage
back to London. The wheels of a rescue plan were already turning.

Sierra Leone, a small West African country famous for diamonds,
was in a serious state of disorder by 2000. With its fertile soil and
immense mineral wealth, Sierra Leone should have been one of the
richest nations in Africa but by 2000 it was listed by the United

18

Nations as the world's poorest country and one of the most dangerous. The life expectancy for men was only thirty-six-years-old. The former British colony, which had gained independence in 1961, had descended into a state of near anarchy with the established government under concerted rebel attacks, and crime and lawlessness rife on the streets of the capital Freetown and throughout the country. The problems had begun in 1996 when the presidential and legislative elections had been severely marred by widespread rigging in favour of the Sierra Leone Peoples Party (SLPP). International monitors had, however, declared that the elections had been largely fair and free despite the violent tactics employed by Foday Sankoh's Revolutionary United Front (RUF) guerillas. On 25 May 1997 a military coup was staged that deposed President Ahmed Tejan Kabbah, but the resulting junta was not popular with the people of Sierra Leone and in February 1998 the junta was in turn removed by Nigerian-led Economic Community of West African States Monitoring Group (ECOMOG) forces, aided by the Sierra Leone Civil Defence Forces. In March 1998 President Kabbah was restored to power.

The resumption of power by Kabbah did not bring stability to the small nation of 4.8 million people. RUF attacks continued, and by 6 January 1999 the rebel militias had captured most of the capital Freetown, and appeared poised to take control of the government. This was only prevented by ECOMOG forces that battled with the RUF in the streets of the capital and eventually forced them back into the jungle. Some 5,000 people died during the fighting. In May 1999 a ceasefire was declared and in July the Lome Peace Agreement appeared to herald an end to the bloody fighting that had resulted in the deaths of over 75,000 people throughout Sierra Leone. The agreement granted blanket amnesties to all those suspected of having committed war crimes, the ceasefire would be monitored, humanitarian assistance would be provided and four cabinet posts created for the RUF as part of a power-sharing agreement.

In May 2000 the ceasefire dissolved when Koday's RUF launched a concerted drive on the capital. They also made the mistake of taking hostage 500 United Nations peacekeeping troops who were monitoring the ceasefire, and murdering some United Nations personnel and foreign journalists. The RUF also stepped up attacks on neighbouring Guinea. The international community was compelled to act. By late 2000 there were 13,000 UN peacekeepers protecting Freetown and the key towns in the south of the country, and some British observers. After a British officer was taken hostage, Prime Minister Tony Blair authorized the activation of Operation 'Palliser', in which Britain determined to restore peace and democracy to her former colony by force if necessary. The job of the British forces was initially to secure Freetown Airport so that British, European Union and Commonwealth citizens could be evacuated, and allow UN reinforcements to enter the country. To this end the 1st Battalion, The Parachute Regiment deployed on 7 May to Senegal, and the following day seized Freetown Airport and began evacuating British civilians. The Paras formed the spearhead battalion for the new British Rapid Reaction Force, and they would be supported by the Royal Navy's Amphibious Ready Group that was ordered to steam to Sierra Leone from Marseilles, where it had been deployed in the Mediterranean. The ARG consisted of the helicopter carrier HMS *Ocean* which was carrying ten helicopters[1] and the 600 men of 42 Commando, Royal Marines. Air cover was provided by the aircraft carrier HMS *Illustrious* which had aboard seven Fleet Air Arm Sea Harriers and seven Harrier GR7s from the RAF, the frigate HMS *Chatham*, supported by the supply ship RFA *Fort Austin* and two RFA logistic landing ships. Brigadier David Richards took overall command of the Paras battle group that deployed ashore. Operation Palliser represented the largest British military deployment since the 1991 Gulf War.

Within days the evacuation of 299 British nationals had been completed and the Paras extended their mission to patrolling the streets of Freetown and providing logistical support to government forces and loyal militias, backed up by elements of D Squadron, 22nd Special Air Service Regiment (SAS) who, when questioned about their unit by reporters, replied that they were members of the 'Hereford Walking Club'. Preventing the RUF from taking control of Sierra Leone was vital. The RUF traded diamonds from the extensive mines dotted across the nation for arms. The $100 million a year trade in blood diamonds helped to fund the Islamic terrorist groups known collectively as Al-Qaeda who were the main supplier of weapons to the RUF. It was in Britain's interest, especially in the light of subsequent events in New York in 11 September 2001 and in Afghanistan, to stamp out the RUF.

On 17 May the British faced their first test when an RUF militia launched an attack on the airport. Members of 29 Commando Regiment, Royal Artillery, working alongside Nigerian troops, fought off the RUF in a fierce 10-minute gunfight that left four rebels dead. Later that day a British helicopter transported captured RUF leader Sankoh to a secure location. 20 Commando Battery, Royal Artillery also saw action on Pepel Island close to the capital, capturing fifteen rebels along with a quantity of heavy weapons. 1 Para's Pathfinder Platoon was also assaulted by rebels, but the elite airborne soldiers killed twenty rebels for no British loss. Soon afterwards the 1st Battalion, Royal Irish Regiment deployed to Sierra Leone and relieved the 2nd Battalion, Royal Anglian Regiment on 22 July. The Royal Irish began to patrol along the front line. It was a patrol from this regiment that triggered a large-scale battle between the SAS and Paras on the one hand, and the RUF on the other. Some days before the first shots were exchanged in anger between the RUF and British forces, some British officers who had been captured while on UN monitoring duties had staged a dramatic escape from captivity in a bid for freedom from highly unpredictable and unpleasant captors.

Many British and Commonwealth military officers had been working with the UN, assisting in overseeing the disarming of the rebels, when they had suddenly discovered themselves prisoners. The RUF had not hesitated earlier to murder UN personnel, and those British officers held hostage genuinely feared for their lives, trapped a long way from friendly forces and surrounded by hostile jungle swarming with trigger-happy rebels. One such unfortunate was Major Philip Ashby of the Royal Marines.

Phil Ashby was an ideal soldier, in fact rather an all-action hero. A Scotsman from Helensburgh, he was tough, fit, experienced and very determined, and with a healthy streak of aggression honed to a fine point by his extensive commando training, Ashby was thirty-years-old in 2000. He had joined the Royal Marines at the age of seventeen and a half and been commissioned a second lieutenant, becoming the youngest commissioned officer in the forces. He was sponsored to attend Pembroke College, Cambridge and, by the time he found himself an RUF prisoner in Sierra Leone, had served in Alaska, Brunei, Belize, Cyprus, Hong Kong, Northern Ireland and Norway. Ashby had climbed all over the world and survived an epic two-man rowing competition in the Arctic Ocean which had seen the two men row 1,000 miles and complete the only human circumnavigation of the Norwegian island of Spitzbergen. Ashby had survived being trapped in the ice, a polar-bear attack, hurricane force winds and capsizing in the freezing water. He was a Royal Marine Mountain Leader, having passed the longest and hardest specialist infantry course in the forces and served in the Mountain and Arctic Warfare Cadre and in 1999 he had been promoted to major at the age of only twenty-eight, once again being the youngest to hold this rank in the armed forces. To add to his long list of military achievements, Ashby had qualified as a jungle instructor. On top of all this action, Ashby had also found the time to obtain a master's degree in defence technology from Cambridge University.

Ashby and his companions were held hostage in a compound in the small town of Makeni in northern Sierra Leone. They were being held with a party of poorly-armed Kenyan UN peacekeepers. Alongside Ashby were Captain Andrew Samsanoff from The Light Infantry, Lieutenant-Commander Paul Rowland of the Royal Naval Reserve and Major David Lingard, a New Zealander. Ashby and his comrades had decided that it was stupid to just sit in captivity waiting for whatever it was the rebels had planned for them – and they suspected a bullet could well be the result. The party had suffered four days of physical and psychological bombardment from their captors that had included the throwing of the blood-stained uniforms of their fellow UN workers over the compound walls to try and frighten them.

Ashby, with his extensive training and experience of hostile environments and survival training, was the obvious man to lead them to safety. They decided to head for the UN compound at Magburaka, where RUF control was patchy. They had the uniforms they stood up in and a satellite phone that they had managed to hide from the rebels, but little else with which to take to the jungle with. It would require several days of trekking through thick jungle and, once their presence was missed at Makeni, RUF patrols would also be hunting them with orders to shoot first and ask questions later.

Magburaka was south from Makeni, and moving in that direction would also place them closer to British forces in Freetown. A helicopter rescue could then be attempted. The satellite phone was Ashby's and his colleagues' only lifeline to a speedy rescue.

At 2.45 am, with their faces blackened with charcoal, Ashby and his companions carefully scaled the compound wall in a bid for freedom. 'Jumping over the wall felt like standing on top of a high diving board only fifty percent sure that there was actually any water in the pool underneath,' recalled Ashby of the decision to break out of their prison and take to the jungle. 'For the first few hours the adrenalin was pumping and we were very relieved to actually get out of a deadly, bustling market town which, in the middle of the night, with an RUF curfew imposed, it was fair to assume that anyone we saw on the streets was actually in the RUF.' Working their way stealthily past RUF patrols and people on the streets was very difficult. 'We saw several people on the way out,'[2] recalled Ashby. Once clear of Makeni, Ashby and his comrades dived into the jungle and scrub. They moved initially only by night in order to lessen the chances of running into the RUF, who were searching for them. 'We were sleeping in the biggest thickets we could find so that nobody would be able to find us during the day,' said Ashby. 'Our main problem was lack of water. It's still the dry season here and, although there were several rivers marked on our maps, what in practice we were hoping for was for some large jungle rivers that were, in fact, pools of stagnant water.' Ashby and his companions had no choice but to drink this foul standing water, in the process risking a plethora of diseases. 'So we've been drinking unusually coloured water, shall we say, but it was enough to keep us going.'[3] At night time the men, lacking mosquito nets, were assailed by biting insects and by day they were burned by the harsh sun and suffered prickly heat as well as cuts, bruises and scratches as they fought their way through the unfamiliar and difficult landscape. Always present was the fear of running into a heavily-armed RUF patrol, and the fear that any injury could have resulted in being recaptured and facing the consequences of their decision to cut and run.

After three days of living on their nerves, and drinking filthy water, Ashby's party stumbled upon a group of Guinean peacekeepers near the town of Magburaka. Although Ashby had a satellite phone, and had been able to speak to British forces shortly after his escape from Makeni, a problem had arisen. 'They had a satellite phone, so we knew they were on their way,' said Lieutenant Tony Camp at the British HQ in Freetown, 'but the battery packed up after 24 hours.'[4] However, the Guinean soldiers took them to the local town from where they were able to summon help. A helicopter was duly dispatched to pick up Ashby and his men who were flown out to RFA *Sir Percivale* for medical treatment after their jungle odyssey. They were covered in insect bites, suffering from prickly heat and sunburn, and covered in bruises and cuts. Otherwise, they considered themselves very lucky to have managed to walk out of RUF controlled territory without being killed or recaptured. For his tremendous leadership, fortitude and daring Major Ashby was awarded the Queen's Gallantry Medal. The Sierra Leone jungle was not quite through with Major Ashby, for soon after arriving back in Britain he collapsed and discovered that he was paralysed from the waist down. Although movement came back to his lower limbs, Ashby has had to cope with long-term disability caused by a tropical parasite that he picked up during the trek through the jungle to freedom.

No sooner had the saga of Ashby and his colleagues been solved than another group of British soldiers found themselves in dire straits. A ten-man patrol from the Royal Irish Regiment, travelling in two Land Rovers, strayed a bit too far into territory in the Occra Hills controlled by a lawless band of 300 drug-taking and trigger-happy militia associated with the RUF known as the West Side Boys, who were led by Foday Kallay. About 200 members of the Royal Irish were supporting Sierra Leone forces as advisors and training instructors, and their patrol had with them a liaison officer from the local defence force. The British soldiers, under the command of Major Alan Marshall, and their Sierra Leonian colleague, Lieutenant Musa Bangura, had been beaten up and thrown into a rudimentary jail located in a dirty little village on the bank of Rokel Creek deep in the thick jungle of the hinterland. Marshall came in for some criticism from his superiors for having allowed himself and his patrol to be captured, but he was using his initiative and had gone to check out two villages in his role as an intelligence gatherer. It was a calculated risk taken by Marshall that had sadly backfired and resulted in his men's capture by the West Side Boys.

Kallay knew that the British soldiers were valuable to him, so he spared their lives and would attempt to ransom them. In the meantime Lieutenant Bangura, as a Sierra Leonian, was extensively tortured and abused by the West Side Boys and imprisoned separately in a deep hole covered by corrugated iron which the rebels used as an *ad hoc* latrine. The village was called Geberi Bana, and consisted of about twenty ramshackle huts and breeze-block structures built on the north bank of the river. Around 150 heavily-armed West Side Boys were in residence. One and a half miles along Rokel Creek, and on its south bank, was another village, Magbeni, containing a further 100 West Side Boys. They had sufficient machine-guns and mortars to cover Geberi Bana, and they had emplaced four 14.5mm heavy machine-guns around Magbeni for this purpose.

On 3 September Kallay released five of the British soldiers in exchange for a satellite phone and some medical supplies, but further negotiations soon broke down and Kallay threatened to shoot the remaining hostages. After Major Marshall refused to obey Kallay's instructions to call the BBC on the phone, the rebel leader staged a mock execution of the remaining hostages, and it was clear that he might be induced to carry out a real execution within days. 'It became clear that Kallay had no intention of releasing the men,' said a British government spokesman. 'That view was borne out after the raid. The hostages later told us that they were sure they would be executed if we did not rescue them. There was no way they were going to be allowed to walk free.'[5]

Unbeknown to Marshall or the rebels, Geberi Bana was under close observation from observation teams from Britain's crack Special Air Service Regiment. The SAS men had been inserted some days beforehand and had carried out a detailed reconnaissance of both rebel villages, including locating the remaining hostages and carefully recording the conversations of Kallay and the other rebels with special microphones. Based on what the SAS had seen and heard, Tony Blair, acting on the advice of his military commanders, authorized Operation 'Barras', the rescue of the hostages by a special assault force of Paras and SAS. The SAS teams on the ground were ordered to prevent the West Side Boys from executing the prisoners, while the British military in Freetown put together an assault force.

Observation teams from D Squadron, 22 SAS, spent two weeks in the jungle close to Geberi Bana, observing rebel activities around the hostage house from positions to the north. Across the river to the south elements of the Royal Marine's Special Boat Squadron (SBS) did the same. Shortly after 6 am on 10 September the SAS moved into the northern part of Geberi Bana and began to engage the rebels. Simultaneously, SBS frogmen silently crossed the river and infiltrated into the village from the south. Shortly after two Lynx gunships moved up Rokel Creek low and fast with orders to attack the rebels' heavy weapons positions that had been located by the SAS. Mohammed Kamara, one of the West Side Boys in Geberi Bana village looked up at the sudden roar of helicopters at first light. Within seconds the thump of the rotor blades was joined by a cacophony of explosions and bursts of machine-gun fire as the gunships began to engage targets on the ground. 'The helicopters were almost on the water,' recalled Kamara. 'They fired again and again until there was no more shooting.'[6]

Once the Lynx gunships had liberally plastered all the known rebel fixed position, the troop-carrying helicopters arrived. At 6.16 am three giant twin-rotor Chinook helicopters headed for Rokel Creek. Aboard were 147 Paras and several dozen SAS, armed to the teeth and raring to go. Alongside the fighting troops was a Field Surgical Team from 16 Close Support Medical Regiment, Royal Army Medical Corps, and three members of the RAF's Tactical Communications Wing. Another Lynx helicopter from HMS *Chatham* joined the force as it headed inland, the helicopters having been fitted with door mounted machine-guns to provide fire support over the target. The plan called for one Chinook carrying forty-five Paras to put down one third of a mile west of Magbeni, the other two Chinooks would land next to the house in Gebeni Bana where the hostages were being held and in a clearing slightly north of the village respectively.

The downblast as the Chinooks dropped altitude to allow the troops to get off was powerful enough to rip the corrugated-iron roofs off the village huts. At the same time as this was happening SAS and SBS troops opened fire on the huts, blasting them with grenade launchers and automatic fire. At Magbeni the Paras jumped from the tail ramp of the Chinook straight into a deep swamp. 'We waded chest deep through the swamp to the objective,' recalled thirty-year-old Captain Liam Cradden, the deputy assault commander.

As soon as Kallay heard the approach of helicopters, he knew that the game was up. Thinking that he had nothing left to lose, he ordered his men to kill Major Marshall and the other hostages. As a group of West Side Boys ran towards the house in Geberi Bana where Marshall and the others were imprisoned, intending to shoot them, an SAS team suddenly opened fire with their Canadian M16A2 assault rifles, killing them all with double-tap shots to the head and sternum. At 6.40am, Fire Team 1, having alighted from the Chinook, assaulted the hostage house with stun grenades, while eleven other fire teams fanned out from the landing zones, eliminating all rebels who showed themselves. Alongside the house where Major Marshall and his men were being held was another hut containing seventeen Sierra Leonian hostages who had been kidnapped a week earlier. 'There was so much shouting and shooting, it was terrible,' said hostage Emmanuel Fabba. 'We saw a British soldier outside, so we called out, 'Civilian hostages, don't shoot.' They brought us out of the back of the building, tied us up and made us lie face down in case we were West Side Boys. The major [Marshall] confirmed our identity later.'[7] The Paras' assault was so strong that many of the rebels ran off into the jungle, temporarily disorganized and afraid. They later regrouped and counter-attacked.

At the village of Magbeni the Chinook landing zone turned out to be a swamp, which caused some problems for the assaulting Paras. In Gebeni Bana the SAS was tasked with protecting the freed hostages and locating Lieutenant Bangura. They fought off several strong attacks by the regrouped West Side Boys. Down the road in Magbeni the Paras fought hard against strong rebel opposition that included mortars. The battle was not entirely one-sided, and in fact for some time it appeared as though the rebels were gaining the edge, something the British could not believe. Accepted military wisdom regarding African rebels was that they would run away when confronted by properly trained and motivated Western military forces. 'It was, as they say, a damned close-run thing,' said a

Parachute Regiment insider later. 'It was just that far from being a total fuck-up. You've got to ask why we took so many hits. Taking one in ten is fairly serious. We are pretty lucky not to have lost more [men], given the number of wounded.'[8] Captain Liam Cradden, thirty-year-old second-in-command of the troops assaulting Magbeni was shocked by the amount of firepower that the West Side Boys leveled at his men and the teams that assaulted Geberi Bana across the river. Corporal Simon Dawes, a twenty-nine-year-old section commander, was thrust immediately into serious combat. 'It was a very scary experience. I don't like to talk about it too much. But when the battle started the training just took over.'[9] Cradden described the attack on Magbeni as 'a systematic, company level assault on a fixed position.' For all of the members of the 1 Para company assaulting Magbeni and Geberi Bana it was their first experience of combat. 'This is the only firefight I've ever been in,' said Corporal Dawes. 'It's the only experience I had of a two-way, as we call it, when the rounds are coming towards you. This company is a very young company and none of us had ever experienced it before.' Youth was no hindrance when it came to grading the Paras fighting performance. 'There are an awful lot of young guys in our unit and they performed exceptionally professionally,' recalled Cradden. 'We were proud to be asked to take part in this operation.'[10]

The Paras command team at Magbeni was struck by a rebel mortar bomb and most of the senior officers leading the mission were wounded and incapacitated. 'There was a loud explosion and we could hear these agonising screams,'[11] said Private Julian Sheard, aged nineteen. The British found themselves under intense fire from familiar weapons, for the West Side Boys were largely armed with British-manufactured Self-Loading Rifles (SLRs) and General Purpose Machine Guns (GPMGs). The British had sent the Sierra Leonian armed forces 14,000 firearms in June 2000, but many had subsequently fallen into rebel hands. Acting Captain Danny Matthews, aged only twenty-one, took command of the Paras and he led the men in a sweep through the village against dozens of rebel positions, killing many of the enemy and forcing the survivors to flee into the jungle. The fighting was intense, and at close quarters, and were it not for the Paras ingrained aggression and training to take the fight to the enemy the battle could have been in doubt.

At 7 am all of the remaining hostages were evacuated from Geberi Bana by Chinook where they were flown straight out to the RFA *Percivale* for medical treatment. 'They looked as you would expect from people who've spent two weeks in the jungle,' recalled Second Officer Peter Burns aboard RFA *Sir Percivale*, 'very bedraggled, long beards, filthy, but basically OK. We said we're glad to see you and they said not half as glad as we are to see you.'[12] By 10.30 am the last British troops had departed from the two villages, job done. They had killed about twenty-five rebels, though numerous blood trails leading into the jungle suggested several more had been badly wounded, and they had captured eighteen, including their leader Kallay. One British soldier had been killed, and twelve other British soldiers had been wounded. Bombardier Bradley Tinnion, aged twenty-six, was serving a tour with the SAS with the rank of trooper and he had been fatally wounded in the fight around the hostage houses in Geberi Bana. It had been a textbook operation with a happy outcome, and the effects of the operation were far-reaching. Other rebel groups, perhaps fearing that the British would extend their military operations and deal with other militias in a similar fashion, began to surrender and within sixteen months the civil war was over.

For his gallant actions in rallying his men in Magbeni village while under furious rebel fire after the senior officers directing the assault had been felled by mortar fragments, Acting Captain Matthews received the Military Cross. Also receiving Military Crosses were Company Sergeant Major Harry Bartlett, Captain Evan Fuery and Major James Chiswell, all of the Parachute Regiment. Colour Sergeant John Baycroft of the Paras and Squadron Leader Iain MacFarlane of the RAF, who piloted one of the Chinooks under heavy fire, both were awarded Britain's second highest decoration for military bravery, the Conspicuous Gallantry Cross. A Distinguished Service Cross was awarded to Captain George Zambellas, commander of HMS *Chatham*, for his gallant and distinguished services during the operations off Sierra Leone. Distinguished Flying Crosses went to some of the pilots and crew of the Lynx and Chinook helicopters who braved considerable ground fire to get the Paras and SAS in to the two rebel villages: Flight Lieutenant Timothy Burgess, Flight Lieutenant Jonathan Priest and Flight Lieutenant Paul

Shepherd, both of the RAF, and Captain Allan Moyes of the Royal
Marines.

1 Four Royal Navy Sea Kings, two Royal Marine Lynx gunships, two Royal Marine
Gazelles and two RAF Chinooks.

2 '*Marine's Sierra Leone ordeal*', BBC News, 12 May 2000

3 Ibid.

4 '*UN observers escape from rebels*', BBC News, 12 May 2000

5 '*Fire fight in the Occra Hills*' by Philip Sherwell, David Blair and Alastair
McQueen, *The Telegraph*, 17 September 2000

6 Ibid.

7 Ibid.

8 '*Close call in the battle of Rokel Creek*' by Peter Beaumont and Jason Burke, *The
Guardian*, 17 September 2000

9 Ibid.

10 Ibid.

11 '*Fire fight in the Occra Hills*' by Philip Sherwell, David Blair and Alastair
McQueen, *The Telegraph*, 17 September 2000

12 '*Close call in the battle of Rokel Creek*' by Peter Beaumont and Jason Burke, *The
Guardian*

CHAPTER 3

Cops and Robbers

'I jumped over the garden fence from where I had been
hiding to get back to Dave because I realised he had been
shot and, as that stage, I thought he was going to die. He was
lying on the floor and there was blood pouring out of his
head so I took my coat off and put it over him.'

Sergeant Paul Leigh, Lancashire Constabulary

'You can't expect the police to be heroes' ran the newspaper
headline[1]. The Health and Safety Executive's (HSE) latest diktat
stated that the British public has 'unrealistic expectations' that the
police will put themselves in danger to protect ordinary people. The
HSE report went on to say that police officers who are confronted by
dangerous situations 'may choose not to put themselves at
unreasonable risk.' The stories of British police officers' heroic
actions recounted throughout this book demonstrate that for most of
today's officers the exception to the rule is not placing oneself in
danger as part of the job, rather than the rule. Police officers remain
in the vanguard of protecting the public from crime, and also in
rescuing people from life-threatening situations. The HSE's attempts
to change the culture of the British police have been met with
derision by police officers, both serving and retired, and by the
general public at large. Courage never goes out of fashion, and
British police officers are exemplars of courage. Such courage is
daily demonstrated and very often goes unreported or unrewarded.
The following are just a handful of examples of police bravery. To do
the subject justice would require many volumes.

A car suddenly screeched to a halt in front of Police Constables Archer and Woodhouse's patrol vehicle parked on Putney High Street in London. Three men leapt from the vehicle, all of them covered in blood, and screaming and shouting in heavily-accented English at the stunned officers that they had been shot – that men were trying to kill them. Desperate to escape cocaine dealer, Kamran Anwar, and their almost certain assassination, the three Colombian drug dealers had thrown themselves on the mercy of London's finest. PCs Jeremy Archer and Nick Woodhouse found themselves suddenly and unexpectedly thrust into the middle of a dangerous underworld feud between serious villains that had spilled out onto the streets of London at 10pm on 28 May 2001.

The Colombians were all in a bad way. One man was bleeding heavily from a gunshot wound to the stomach. Archer immediately radioed for assistance, calling for an ambulance and some backup, and together the two police officers tried to calm the men down and help them. The story that emerged from the wounded men sounded more like the description of a scene from *Scarface*, than the usual violent incidents that the Metropolitan Police officers dealt with each week. The Colombians had turned up at a house in Putney, little realising that Anwar, and his bodyguard Igor Konopek, were laying in wait for them. Anwar and Konopek were both armed with illegal automatic pistols. Anwar claimed that the Colombians had stolen eighty-five thousand pounds from him and he intended to execute them in revenge. Konopek was a ruthless Serbian hit-man and a former armed response officer from the Belgrade Police. When the Colombians had pulled up outside the house, Anwar and Konopek had immediately opened brisk automatic fire at them. The rattle of pistol shots and the screams of terrified passers-by echoed down the street. The injured Colombians had clambered into their car and sped off at high speed, pursued by their assailants, and driven to the first police officers that they could locate.

Anwar and Konopek drove slowly past the Colombians as PCs Archer and Woodhouse dealt with them. The Colombians panicked and pointed out their would-be assassins and, knowing that help was on the way, the two unarmed officers immediately gave chase. The gunmen's car became mired in heavy traffic, and Konopek alighted and fled on foot. PC Archer jumped from the police car and took off after him. Anwar stayed with his car, trying to bull his way through the traffic, with Woodhouse following close behind, siren howling and blues and two's flashing.

'I chased Konopek down a side street off Putney High Street and into an alleyway,' recalled PC Archer. 'It was a dead end. He put his hand into his top and pulled out a Walther PPK pistol. He pointed the gun at my stomach.'[2] Undeterred, Archer reacted proactively to the threat. 'I grabbed his hand and pushed the gun away.'[3] Konopek dropped the pistol and feigned surrender, evidently realising that the game was up. Archer managed to clamp one handcuff on him before the Serbian suddenly bolted, shoving Archer and taking to his heels back out the alleyway. 'I chased after him and he disappeared into a bush outside a block of flats but a passerby showed me where he was hiding and I arrested him,' said Archer. Later, he reflected on what had happened. 'Looking back I just feel very lucky. I could have been killed,'[4] said the young married officer.

PC Woodhouse continued in his pursuit of Anwar. The drug dealer suddenly abandoned his car and set off on foot into a residential area. Woodhouse, who was married with two children, lost Anwar as he ducked and dived and tried to mingle with the guests at a barbecue party being hosted in one of the back gardens. Woodhouse spotted Anwar and dragged him bodily into an alleyway beside the property in front of the astonished party goers, struggling with him on the ground and eventually cuffing and arresting him.

Konopek was found guilty of grievous bodily harm, attempted grievous bodily harm and possession of two loaded firearms and ammunition. Anwar was found guilty at the Old Bailey of grievous bodily harm, possession of four loaded firearms, possession of controlled ammunition, possession of cocaine and possession of cannabis with intent. Konopek was sentenced to sixteen years imprisonment and Anwar to twenty-three years.[5] Constables Archer and Woodhouse were widely praised for their bravery, not least by the Commissioner of the Metropolitan Police, Sir John Stevens, who said: 'This is just one example of the type of work Met officers perform on a daily basis to ensure the safety of Londoners.'[6] Archer and Woodhouse were both awarded the Queen's Commendation for Bravery in 2004.

It is not only guns that pose a threat to public safety in Britain today, but the ever present risk of knife crime. It is a topic that is never far from the newspapers. They are easy weapons to buy and easy to conceal. The proliferation of knives in crimes is every bit as pernicious as the numbers of firearms being used in robberies and gang-related incidents on Britain's streets. Routinely unarmed police officers are initially expected to deal with both threats until properly armed officers can deploy, sometimes with tragic results. Inspector Michael Tanner pulled up outside his police station next to Finsbury Park bus station in north London on 8 December 2001. It had been a routine shift so far. As he was getting out of the van, a black man with a disheveled appearance and evidently odd demeanour walked up to it, opened his fly and began to urinate over the vehicle's wheels. Tanner immediately confronted the man, thirty-four-year-old Ronald McKoy. Inspector Tanner, of the British Transport Police, demanded an explanation. 'I asked him what he was going. He said 'I will…kill you'. It was the only thing he ever said to me,' recalled Tanner. 'I knew he meant it,'[7] he added.

McKoy suddenly produced a knife, evidently intent on carrying out his threat to kill the policeman. 'It just turned horrible in a matter of seconds,' said Tanner. Tanner drew his baton, but McKoy flew at him and stabbed him in the chest. Tanner turned and ran back a few yards, before he turned around and confronted McKoy again ready with his baton. As Tanner hit McKoy with his baton, McKoy drove his knife into the policeman's arm. Bleeding profusely, Tanner retreated to a parked bus and managed to close the doors before the lunatic McKoy was outside the glass, thrashing wildly with his knife. On one occasion the knife came through the door's rubber trim. Tanner said it was 'like a scene from *The Shining*,'[8] referring to the famous horror film.

As Tanner radioed for assistance, McKoy became even more enraged now that his quarry had escaped. He attacked some members of the public who were standing as a bus stop nearby, and grabbed a fourteen-year-old-girl, putting the knife to her throat. She managed to struggle free but, when he saw what McKoy was doing to bystanders Inspector Tanner, though having been stabbed twice and bleeding heavily, decided to get off the bus and shout at McKoy in the hope of distracting his attention from the crowd, rather in the way one might try to call off a mad dog. The ruse worked. McKoy immediately lost his interest in the bus passengers and instead chased after Inspector Tanner again. After a few yards McKoy appeared to zone out again, losing interest in the policeman and he began to walk away from the scene of the crime as if nothing had occurred. Tanner followed him at a safe distance and soon other police officers arrived to arrest McKoy. He did not submit without further violence. Constable William Morrison, aged forty, and Constable Simon Carver, aged twenty-five, wrestled McKoy to the floor but, before being overpowered, he managed to stab one officer in the leg and pierce the uniform of the other.

It emerged that Ronald McKoy was a paranoid schizophrenic who had been released from a mental institution on licence in 1998. Ten years earlier, McKoy had stabbed a police officer in the throat. In 1992 he had been sent down on an arson charge. Why this man was released into the local community is hard to answer, but the crimes he committed have not been the only ones performed by mentally ill criminals who have been released under current government initiatives. In the past, of course, such a man would have remained firmly under lock and key for the course of his natural life, but the irresistible march of liberalism has meant that the streets of Britain are becoming increasingly unsafe as mental institutions close and the criminally disturbed are allowed to roam free. Although McKoy was sentenced to two life sentences, it is probably a fair comment to say that this man will unfortunately be released again in a few years, perhaps to commit another assault on the police. The judge at McKoy's trial, Gerrald Gordon, commented that: 'Inspector Tanner acted with bravery well beyond the call of duty. Having been stabbed twice with a vicious-looking knife, he deliberately put himself back in danger.' Tanner was off work for nine months recovering from his injuries but he eventually returned to his job. In 2004 Inspector Tanner was awarded the Queen's Gallantry Medal at a ceremony at Buckingham Palace.[9]

As well as dealing with knife-wielding maniacs, as we have seen British police officers are increasingly being confronted by criminals armed with guns. The prevalence of firearms on the streets of British cities has been highlighted repeatedly in the media as approaching a national disgrace, and carrying guns has become something of a status symbol for many of the youths and young men involved in gangs that are turning many of our inner cities into cesspools of criminality. Unless specially trained to do so, the majority of British police officers remain unarmed, posing a huge challenge for their safety as criminals become 'tooled-up'.

On 14 May 2002, at about ten o'clock in the evening, two Metropolitan Police officers out on routine patrol in Ladbroke Grove in West London spotted a car that had been highlighted at a briefing earlier that night. The officers switched on their 'blues and twos' and pulled the suspect car over to the kerb. The lights reflected off the darkened windows of nearby buildings and attracted the glances of passing pedestrians. As one of the officers approached the car, the driver's side door was suddenly flung open and a man bolted from the vehicle and took off like a spooked rabbit. Jermaine James, aged twenty-one, ran along the street, pursued for a short distance by the patrol car, until he ducked down a stairway. The officers immediately radioed for assistance, and Constable Jonathan Davies and a colleague attempted to intercept James as he exited the stairs, but he was too fast and Davies took off after him on foot.

As Davies chased the suspect, James reached into his jacket and drew a .22 calibre automatic pistol. As he ran he turned and fired at the pursuing officer, the bullet flicking through Davies' shirt collar, narrowly missing his neck. Undeterred by the evident life-threatening danger, the unarmed Constable Davies closed the distance between himself and James. Suddenly James turned again and triggered off another shot at the police officer. The small bullet burrowed into Davies' thigh, but the officer only registered that a shot had been fired in his direction and launched himself at James, punching him hard in the face, the two men crashing to the ground in a furious tumble of thrashing arms and legs.[10] Two of Davies' colleagues soon arrived at the fracas, piling in to try to subdue the armed criminal. The gun went off again, but fortunately missed the three policemen, and at one point James tried to aim the pistol at Davies' head, but Davies knocked the weapon from James' hand and kicked it out of reach. After a terrific struggle, James was eventually subdued and handcuffed.

Later, at the police station, Davies complained that he had a 'dead leg.' A medical examination soon revealed that he had been shot, and the bullet was removed later that day by a surgeon. When officers searched James they found a quantity of cannabis in his possession. James was eventually found guilty of the attempted murder of a police officer and for possessing a loaded firearm in a public place. He received a fifteen-year prison sentence on the first count and a further five years on the second. Constable Davies made a full recovery from his injury and returned to work. For his exemplary bravery in facing down an armed criminal and for his extraordinary determination in getting his man, no matter what, Davies received the Queen's Gallantry Medal in 2004.[11]

Police officers are never off-duty. They may hang up their hats at the end of a shift and change out of their uniforms but, even during their leisure time from work, they carry their warrant cards with them at all times, and on innumerable occasions each year off-duty officers intervene in dangerous situations to try and help the public. One officer who was especially vigilant, even when off-duty, was instrumental in preventing a serious armed robbery on the streets of Belfast, even though he was himself unarmed and a reserve policeman. Reserve Constable Robert Moore of the Police Service of Northern Ireland was walking down the street at midday on 17 December 2002 when he saw three men inside a car pull up close to a security van. The guards from the security firm were in the process of making a cash delivery to a bank. Moore immediately realised that a robbery was in progress, so he ran between the van and the car that was parked some distance off. There, he confronted a man who was armed with a handgun and carrying a cash box stolen from the van. The robber immediately levelled his gun at Moore's chest, but the plucky Moore charged him and kicked him in the chest. The robber fell backwards into the street, dropping the container of cash as he did so. The robbers immediately tried to escape from the scene, the car's engine revving wildly. The robber Moore had tackled struggled to his feet and ran towards the car. Moore doggedly pursued the armed criminal, the driver of the car trying to run down the policeman twice, during which Moore was slightly injured. While Moore chased after the armed robber, the criminal kept pointing his gun at the policeman, but he did not fire. Moore was constantly in danger of being gunned down. After a short chase one of the car doors was flung open and the armed man jumped inside and the car tore off down the road. Reserve Constable Moore had successfully disrupted the robbery and saved the bank's cash. He was awarded the Queen's Commendation for Bravery.

PC David Cunnington already had a suspect in mind as he and his colleague drove around to a block of flats in Langton Green, Tunbridge Wells late one February evening in 2004. A burglary had been reported. On arrival at the flats, the two police officers saw the suspect, whom they recognized as he had recently been released from prison, with a rucksack containing what later turned out to be stolen property and carrying a briefcase and a handgun. 'I ran straight into him and grabbed him around the waist to keep his arms down so he couldn't use the gun,' recalled Cunnington. The gun looked like the real thing, though it was effectively an air weapon. 'It was a real gun,' said Cunnington. 'I found out later that it uses compressed gas to fire small lead pellets. Our firearms expert said it could have been lethal if it strikes you in the right place, say through the eye and into the brain.'

'We had a big fight during which he dropped the gun and everything else,' recalled Cunnington of his terrific struggle with the armed man. 'My colleague, who was on the door [of the burgled flat] downstairs, heard the commotion, came running up, and we both tried to keep hold of this man.' The suspect intended to escape and fought the two officers like a madman. 'He is a very big, strong lad, and he managed to drag me down the concrete stairs to the first floor landing before getting free. We had told our colleagues where we were, and that he had escaped, and the man ran out of the flats straight into a van loaded with about four officers, who overpowered him.'

The incident was another example of an unarmed police officer confronting and tackling an armed felon. 'I don't think I was brave,' said Cunnington, 'I just acted on instinct. I knew he was dangerous. He'd previously done an armed robbery on a post office with a machete.' Cunnington, like many fellow police officers, does not, even in the light of this incident, want to carry a gun – though he did think that issuing Taser stun-guns to officers might help. For his actions in tackling a man with a gun, fifty-year-old Cunnington received the Queen's Commendation for Bravery.

A paranoid schizophrenic who had not been taking his medication and who believed that the police and MI5 were persecuting him, Glaister Earl Butler has earlier threatened a council workman at his home and on 21 May 2004, ran wild through the streets of Nechells, in the Aston district of Birmingham, threatening people with a 12-inch long butcher's knife. Police responded quickly to the threat to public safety and Butler was chased onto a canal towpath that ran beneath the M6 motorway. Forty-four-year-old Detective Constable Michael Swindells heard the reports of an armed man being chased by police as he listened to his radio and he decided to assist his colleagues. He and a fellow detective ran towards the towpath and joined in with the pursuit. Shortly afterwards Swindells found himself in the vanguard of the police group and fast catching up to Butler. Swindells raised his baton above his head and shouted 'Stop! Police!'

Swindells had joined the West Midlands Police after serving in the Royal Engineers and was based with the CID at Queen's Road in Alston. He was a highly experienced officer who had previously served with the football intelligence unit and specialist robbery unit. Butler had been born in Jamaica. He was Rolls-Royce's first black design draughtsman until he was made redundant in 1982. Losing his job appears to have caused his paranoia to grow; he believed that he had lost his job because of his colour. Butler was a martial arts fanatic, and increasingly suffering from paranoid schizophrenia.

When Swindells confronted him, Butler lashed out at the police officer with his knife. Swindells was not wearing an anti-stab vest at the time. He managed to dodge the first attack, but Butler attacked Swindells again and the knife was driven into his abdomen and pierced his heart. After stabbing Swindells, Butler ran off and was eventually apprehended by more police more than a mile away down the path. In 2005, after an eight day trial, Butler was found guilty of manslaughter by reason diminished responsibility and sentenced to be held in a secure mental hospital indefinitely.

In 2006 Michael Swindells was posthumously awarded the Queen's Gallantry Medal for his brave actions in trying to arrest Butler.

PC David Lomas knocked hard on the front door of the house in Hardman Avenue, Rawtenstall, Lancashire. Lomas was community beat manager for Rawtenstall and he had arrived at the address of Stephen Hensby intending to arrest him after an allegation of harassment had been made. Two other police officers, PC Lukmann Mulla and PC Matt Walton waited some distance away – the reasoning being that Hensby would come quietly if he did not have half of the Lancashire Constabulary doorstepping him.

As soon as Hensby opened the door he behaved in an aggressive manner in both speech and demeanour. Before Lomas could arrest him, Hensby abruptly slammed the door in the policeman's face. Constable Mulla hastened over to his colleague. Instead of immediately forcing their way into the property, the two officers decided to try and lure Hensby out with a little diplomacy. 'We tried to talk him out but it didn't work,' recalled Mulla, 'after we had exhausted that route we decided to force entry, so we radioed for the battering ram.'[12] Known as an 'enforcer', this mediaeval looking piece of equipment is used by the police to put in doors quickly and efficiently.

Sergeant Paul Leigh responded to Mulla's call and arrived at the scene with the enforcer. The officers smashed in the front door and barrelled into Hensby's hallway. 'I locked his Rottweiler in the living room and we went to the bottom of the staircase, which was barricaded with a wire fence,' said Mulla, who had been in the police force for two years. He added ominously: 'He [Hensby] was expecting someone, I don't know if it was us.'[13] Suddenly, a shadowy figure appeared at the top of the stairs with something in his hands. There was a loud bang and PC Lomas was spun around where he stood. He had been shot. 'Despite his injuries PC Lomas managed to move outside to the side of the house where he collapsed, bleeding heavily and struggling to breathe because of a collapsed right lung.'[14] The shotgun blast had sprayed lethal lead pellets across the right side of Lomas' face, head and chest, but his body armour had probably saved his life by absorbing the brunt of the impact and lead.

A crazed Hensby fired several more shots out of an upstairs window in the general direction of the police officers. He also launched several home-made petrol bombs that flamed with malevolent fury across his tatty front garden. Sergeant Leigh jumped and ran through the line of fire to assist his fallen comrade. Leigh was not wearing body armour, but the thirty-five-year-old father of two disregarded his own safety to help his fellow officer. 'I jumped over the garden fence from where I had been hiding to get back to Dave because I realised he had been shot and, as that stage, I thought he was going to die,'[15] said Leigh later. With shotgun blasts reverberating off the surrounding houses, Leigh and Mulla went to work trying to help Lomas. 'He was lying on the floor and there was blood pouring out of his head so I took my coat off and put it over him as Luke [Lukmann Mulla] went to the car for a first aid kit and radioed for an ambulance,' said Leigh. 'I just tried to keep him calm and get him through it, but we were frightened.' Every movement that the officers made was into the line of fire, with a crazed criminal who was well-armed and motivated by fear of arrest and imprisonment and who was taking random pot shots at them.

Officers from the Armed Response Unit arrived quickly at the scene and, braving Hensby's fire once again, officers dragged PC Lomas clear and eventually he was airlifted to the Royal Preston Hospital where he received emergency treatment. Hensby and his dog were found dead in the house when officers stormed the premises on the following morning – he had committed suicide. 'It is quite clear that the quick-thinking and decisive action shown by these officers prevented a colleague from being more seriously injured,' said Chief Superintendent Jerry Graham, the Division Commander. 'These officers' courageous and selfless actions helped save a life…They showed tremendous commitment to duty and to an injured colleague…' Paul Leigh and Lukmann Mulla were both awarded the Queen's Gallantry Medal for their outstanding bravery.

Richard Coulton and Gary Panther were two young PCs with West Yorkshire Police who, at 5 am one August day in 2005, found themselves sucked into a life-and-death chase with a professional criminal. Coulton and Panther had noticed a van speeding by their position with a flat tyre. The two police officers immediately followed in their patrol car, and they turned on their siren and their blues and twos to signal to the driver to pull over and stop. The chase continued for some minutes at high speed until the suspect suddenly slowed down and pulled over. As soon as the van stopped two men jumped down and ran off. Coulton and Panther immediately gave chase on foot.

As the four men raced down a path, Constable Panther shouted at the two suspects to stop, but they appeared to take no notice. It was only at this point that the policemen realised that one of the men was carrying a long black object in his hands. The second suspect, a hardened criminal named Michael Coe who was out on licence from prison, also revealed something in his hands, which he pointed at the pursuing officers. There was a bang and a puff of smoke, and Coulton and Panther realised that they had just been shot at. Coe then proceeded to throw the gun at the running officers, but Constable Coulton caught up with him and fired CS spray onto the back of Coe's head as he tripped him up. PC Panther then jumped on top of him and attempted to handcuff the powerfully-built Coe. A violent struggle ensued as the crazed Coe thrashed about and tried to reach other weapons that were in his pockets until the policeman managed to restrain him. The driver of the van escaped.

Coe was a London-based criminal who was desperate to avoid being sent back to prison when Coulton and Panther had tried to apprehend him for speeding. He was found guilty of possessing a firearm with intent to resist arrest, possession of a sawn-off shotgun and possession of a loaded shotgun in a public place and was sent back to prison for a further eight years. PCs Coulton and Panther were each awarded the Queen's Commendation for Bravery for their heroic actions in tackling an armed and dangerous man when they themselves were unarmed.[16]

Police Constable Richard Gray, known as "Ricky" to his friends, had had a distinguished record of service to his country. A Scot from Dundee, he had been a soldier – in the famous Black Watch, a Highland regiment – serving in Northern Ireland, Germany and Hong Kong. He had then joined the Cheshire Constabulary in 1997, based at Warrington, before transferring to the West Mercia Police. In August 2006, Gray had married his longtime partner of sixteen years in Venice. A trained firearms officer, Gray had been commended five times for bravery, including a divisional commendation for rescuing a man trying to jump from Shrewsbury's English Bridge into the River Severn. He had been commended for his part in arresting an unstable man armed with a gun, and again for arresting a violent man with an automatic pistol.

Early on Sunday morning, 6 May 2007, Gray and a colleague, PC Matthew Crisp, both of them armed, were called to a disturbance on a residential estate in Shrewsbury, Shropshire. Two unarmed police officers had radioed that they had been confronted with a man armed with a rifle and that they needed urgent armed back-up. Armed officers are always dispatched by the police if a report of firearms is made. In modern Britain today it is extremely difficult to legally possess a firearm. Since the Dunblane Massacre on 13 March 1996, private shooting clubs have dwindled as possession of handguns for sporting purposes has largely been outlawed. The legislation banning private ownership of handguns was driven through on the back of public outrage over Dunblane. Thomas Hamilton killed sixteen children and a teacher at Dunblane Primary School, and wounded fifteen others, before turning one of his guns on himself. He legally owned two 9mm Browning High Power pistols and two Smith & Wesson .357 Magnum revolvers. Some people have argued that law-abiding gun owners have been punished because of the actions of one lone lunatic, but the government successfully made the argument that it could see no reason why private citizens should have guns. It is an argument that has been generally accepted throughout the nation. Exceptions are most obviously professions such as farming, where shotguns are routinely used for controlling wildlife, and the possession of other smoothbore weapons and rifles for sports such as clay pigeon shooting, pheasant and grouse shooting and deer stalking. One other profession that often carries with it the possession of firearms is pest control. When PC Gray and his colleague raced to the scene of the reported firearm on New Park Road in Shrewsbury, they found that it was the owner of a pest control business who had armed himself with a fully licenced .222 rifle.

Initially, the unarmed officers who had first responded to the address had believed that they were dealing with a routine domestic incident. 'However, when the officers arrived they were challenged by a man who held them at gunpoint,'[17] said Detective Chief

Inspector Sheila Thornes of West Mercia Police. That man was Peter Medlicott, the thirty-three-year-old owner of the pest control business. As armed officers Gray and Crisp raced to the scene in their police van at 6.10 am, it came over the radio that a possible gunshot had already been heard from the premises. 'On arrival, they saw two police officers emerge from an alleyway with their hands in the air.' Medlicott was stood with the rifle pointed at the two policemen who, with their arms raised, were backing out of the alleyway.

PC Gray was ahead of Crisp, and he never even hesitated. Raising his weapon, he ran forward and placed himself in front of his two unarmed colleagues. In a commanding voice he shouted at Medlicott: 'Armed police! Put the gun down!' and moved around the corner of the alley out of sight of his partner. The next instant there was a loud gunshot. PC Crisp, his weapon also at the ready, ran around the corner just as Medlicott disappeared out of sight. Gray was slumped against a wall – he had been shot in the head. Crisp then backed away and covered the unarmed officers as they withdrew from the scene.

Reinforcements soon arrived, and PC Gray was carefully removed from the alleyway and rushed to hospital but, tragically, he died from his injury. A police helicopter hovering over the scene later in the day spotted a body lying in the garden. It was Medlicott. He had committed suicide by shooting himself in the head with his own rifle.

Ricky Gray had not hesitated for a second in putting himself into the line of fire to protect his unarmed colleagues, and he had paid the ultimate price for trying to arrest Medlicott. In recognition of his courage, Gray was awarded a posthumous Queen's Commendation for Bravery. PC Crisp also received the same award.

1 '*You can't expect the police to be heroes: Public want too much ran health and safety report*' by Matthew Hickley and Neil Sears, *The Daily Mail*, 8 October 2009

2 '*Courage of Pcs who tackled drug gunmen*' by Justin Davenport, *London Evening Standard*, 9 July 2004

3 Ibid.

4 Ibid.

5 *The London Gazette*, 1 June 2004, Supplement No. 2, 6774

6 '*Courage of Pcs who tackled drug gunmen*' by Justin Davenport, *London Evening Standard*, 9 July 2004

7 '*Stabbed policeman rescued teenager*', BBC News, 11 October 2002

8 Ibid.

9 *London Gazette*, 29 November 2004, Supplement No. 2, 15069

10 '*Medal for officer shot in chase*' by Steve Bird, *The Times*, 2 June 2004

11 *The London Gazette*, 28 May 2004, Supplement No. 2, 6773

12 '*Brave bobbies ran to aid of shot Pc*' by Kelly Livesey, *Manchester Evening News*, 15 July 2005

13 Ibid.

14 '*Gallantry Medals After Officer Shot*', Lancashire Constabulary, 18 January 2007

15 '*Brave bobbies ran to aid of shot Pc*' by Kelly Livesey, *Manchester Evening News*, 15 July 2005

16 '*Four Yorks PCs given Queen's bravery awards after gun attacks*' by David Bruce, *Yorkshire Evening Post*, 18 January 2007

17 '*Tributes paid to shot policeman*', BBC News, 7 May 2007

18 10 Downing Street website, email address www.number10.gov.uk

CHAPTER 4

Courage under Fire

'It's been rather a long time since I've awarded one of these.'

HM The Queen

'Maybe I was brave, I don't know. At the time I was just doing my job, I didn't have time for other thoughts. Some days you the bug, some days you the windshield.'

Private Johnson Beharry VC, The Princess of Wales' Royal Regiment

Nineteen-year-old Private Michelle Norris, inevitably nicknamed "Chuck" by her comrades, jumped down from the Warrior Infantry Fighting Vehicle that she was travelling in and immediately began to climb up its side as bullets slammed into the armour plating all around her and others cracked by her head. One bullet struck Norris' medical rucksack, fortunately not injuring her. On reaching the vehicle's turret, Norris immediately went to work applying emergency first aid to the Warrior's commander, Colour Sergeant Ian Page of the Princess of Wales's Royal Regiment (Queen's and Royal Hampshires), who was bleeding profusely from a bullet wound to his mouth. Norris then helped other soldiers drag Page back into the vehicle, all the while under continuous enemy fire. The five-foot-tall Royal Army Medical Corps orderly was later awarded the Military Cross by the Queen for her bravery that day in Iraq on 11 June 2006. Norris was the first woman ever to receive this decoration. 'At the time I knew someone needed help so I went out there and did what I could,'[1] recalled Norris afterwards. The demands of modern war means that today it is almost normal to find young men and women serving alongside each other in Britain's latest military adventures in Iraq and Afghanistan. Their courage remains as raw and immediate as the bravery and determination shown by previous generations of British soldiers. By every measure, the British soldier of the 21st Century, whether a man or a woman, is the equal of their military forbears.

Operation Telic, the British invasion and occupation of southern Iraq, was one of the biggest military operations mounted by the United Kingdom since the Second World War. At its height in 2003, Telic witnessed the deployment of 42,000 service personnel and a massive array of military hardware to the Gulf region, representing a much bigger deployment than the Falklands War in 1982 or even the British commitment to the Korean War in the 1950s. Only the Gulf War in 1991 had involved more British troops. Although the word 'telic' means a purposeful or defined action, the choice of this word for the operation to support the American deposition of Saddam Hussein carried no political overtones. Unlike the heavily politicized wording of Operation 'Iraqi Freedom' chosen by the Americans for their part of the invasion, Telic was chosen randomly by a computer at the Ministry of Defence in London.

Britain's task was to capture and occupy southern Iraq, particularly the vital port city of Basra. British forces under the overall command of Air Chief Marshal Brian Burridge in Qatar performed superbly, achieving all of their invasion objectives after some stiff fighting with Iraqi and insurgent forces. On the ground, Major General Robin Brims 1st Armoured Division, containing the elite 16th Air Assault Brigade and the famous 7th Armoured Brigade (the 'Desert Rats' of Second World War and Gulf War fame), carried all before them. The Royal Marines of 3 Commando Brigade under Brigadier Jim Dutton made their first assault landing since the Falklands War when they stormed and captured the Al-Faw Peninsula.

By June 2004 the British commitment in Iraq had been drastically reduced as the conventional war fighting element of the operation had ceased, and occupation and reconstruction duties had commenced. Instead of a full division, the British now deployed the 1st Mechanised Brigade in southern Iraq. Major General Andrew

Stuart had taken over as ground forces commander with headquarters in Basra, commanding a new composite division that included troops from many other nations. British forces were to be engaged in continuous low intensity anti-insurgent fighting until the government withdrew them in 2009, in a protracted and bitter campaign to eradicate Islamic extremists who were determined to prevent the rebuilding of Iraq into a prosperous and democratic nation. Total casualties amounted to 179 military personnel killed. The long years of bloody counter-terrorism warfare experience gained by the British Army in Northern Ireland since 1969 was put to good use in Iraq, only on a much bigger scale and against a more numerous, motivated and well-armed enemy. The courage, tenacity and professionalism displayed by British soldiers throughout over six years of combat operations in Iraq won widespread praise, and many were awarded high decorations for their extraordinarily valorous actions.

The paramount British and Commonwealth decoration for courage and valour is the Victoria Cross. To be awarded the VC a serviceman has to have demonstrated almost unparalleled bravery in the face of the enemy, and it is perhaps no surprise that many of the men who have been awarded this simple bronze Maltese cross have either perished in the action for which they were given it, or have come very close to being killed. Since its institution in 1856 during the Crimean War, the VC has only been awarded on 1,357 occasions, making it the rarest gallantry award in the world. The largest number was naturally awarded during the First and Second World Wars, but since 1945 the VC has only been awarded fifteen times, the last occasions to Corporal Bill Apiata of the New Zealand SAS in 2007 for his actions in Iraq and Trooper Mark Thompson of the Australian SAS for valour in Afghanistan in 2008.

The two posthumous awards of the Victoria Cross that were made during the Falklands War in 1982 to Lieutenant-Colonel H. Jones and Sergeant Ian McKay of the Parachute Regiment, were widely believed by many to have been the last occasions when British soldiers would be in the kind of intense combat where the conditions were right to win a VC. Many believed that the Falklands conflict might be Britain's last true conventional war, and the experience of the Gulf War in 1991, with its smart bombs, war by remote control, and air campaign rendering resistance on the ground minimal, appeared to support such a theory. Britain's other commitments throughout the 1990s were, in the main, peacekeeping operations in the former Yugoslavia, counter-insurgency in a much calmer Northern Ireland, and interventions into Sierra Leone, Kosovo and East Timor that witnessed little in the way of conventional war fighting. The events of 9/11 and the Bush Administration's hawkish foreign policy unexpectedly launched British forces into two of the most bloody and protracted military campaigns the nation has experienced since the Korean War in the 1950s. British forces helped to topple the brutal Taliban government in Afghanistan in 2001 and invaded Iraq in 2003.

Once the conventional war fighting was over, the British military found itself bogged down in a seemingly endless counter-insurgency campaign in Iraq until 2009 and one that is currently ongoing in Afghanistan against fanatical enemies and often in extremely inhospitable conditions. The campaigns in Afghanistan and Iraq have resulted in two awards of the VC to British soldiers. Both of the men who won Britain's latest VCs were given this highest honour for more than one outstandingly brave action, and both men gained their VCs for actions during which they saved the lives of their comrades. The two men were Private Johnson Beharry and Corporal Bryan Budd.

Johnson Beharry was born in the former British colony of Grenada in the Caribbean in July 1979. His early years were marked by extreme poverty, and in 1999 he immigrated to Britain. Like many young men from a deprived background, the armed forces offered the promise of a regular salary and opportunities for advancement that were lacking in civilian life, and Beharry enlisted in 2001. After initial training at Catterick in North Yorkshire, Beharry joined one of Britain's most illustrious county regiments, the Princess of Wales's Royal Regiment (Queen's and Royal Hampshire's) or PWRR. Beharry was sent to the 1st Battalion's C Company, where he trained as a Warrior Armoured Fighting Vehicle driver. The PWRR is one of several 'new' regiments created in the British Army by the constant round of amalgamations of older units forced on the army by successive Conservative and Labour governments following each defence review. The PWRR was created in 1992 by the forced marriage of two equally famous regiments, The Queen's Regiment and The Royal Hampshire Regiment. The PWRR – through the Queen's Regiment holds the oldest battle honour in the British Army, 'Tangier 1662', marking an unbroken regimental lineage stretching back hundreds of years in common with all of the other local regiments that form the backbone of the modern army. Today the PWRR recruits from across six southeast English counties including Kent, Sussex and Hampshire, as well as the Isle of Wight and the Channel Islands. The PWRR is further distinguished by being one of only two British Army regiments that has a foreign monarch as its Colonel-in-Chief. Queen Margrethe II of Denmark has fulfilled this role since the death of the Princess of Wales in 1997.

The regiment's 1st Battalion are nicknamed the 'Armoured Tigers' because they operate as armoured infantry, riding into combat aboard their Warriors IFVs. The battalion consists of three Warrior Companies, a Fire Support Company and a Headquarters Company. The Warrior is an impressive weapon, and it has consistently proved itself in combat operations around the world. 'This heavy metal beast is powered by a 17-litre engine, and packs a fearsome punch with its 30mm Rarden cannon and 7.62mm chain gun. In the back of each Warrior, a section of seven highly-trained infantry soldiers sit ready…'[2]

As a part of 1st Mechanized Brigade in Iraq, the PWRR found itself part of a battle group that consisted of a squadron of Challenger 2 main battle tanks from the Queen's Royal Lancers, a company of the Royal Welsh Fusiliers and C and HQ Companies, 1 PWRR. The deployment was between April and October 2004, centered on a former Iraqi Army base at Abu Naji outside Al-Amarah. Y Company (reconnaissance and mortars), 1 PWRR, was stationed 5.5 km away at Al-Amarah. They were there to protect the Coalition Provisional Authority (CPA) based in the CIMIC House, a secure compound in the centre of the town. The battle group's job was to police Maysan Province, and its capital of Al-Amarah, for six months and assist Coalition Forces in maintaining law and order. Private Beharry and his colleagues would find themselves driving their Warrior armoured vehicles in a war zone for the first time. Intelligence estimated that there were around 300 heavily armed militiamen from the insurgent Mahdi Army in and around Al-Amarah. Although they sounded like something last faced by General Gordon in Khartoum, the Mahdi Army was led by another religious fanatic, Muqtader Al-Sadr, and they were considerably better armed than the Sudanese fanatics encountered by the British in the 1880s. Al-Sadr was widely liked by the local population, and he had a long history of resistance to the previous regime of Saddam Hussein, who had murdered his family. Into this stew of local politics and religion was cast the 1 PWRR Battle Group. The British had decided to base their strategy in the region on a previous tour of duty that they had undertaken in the Serbian province of Kosovo in the Balkans. It would consist of a combination of foot patrols, Land Rover patrols and vehicle checkpoints – with the heavy armoured vehicles held in reserve for rapid deployment if the Mahdi Army attacked in force. The city of Al-Amarah was in an unsettled state and, only days before the PWRR advance party had arrived 3,000 Iraqi civilians had rioted on 3 April. The Light Infantry Battle Group, which the PWRR were replacing, was glad to see the back of the place. The base at Abu Naji came under sporadic mortar fire on several nights soon after the PWRR arrived, and it looked as though this was only to be taster of the action to come.

Beharry was his platoon commander's driver, each platoon having a total of six Warrior AFVs. In the dark early morning hours of 1 May Beharry's company received orders to replenish the isolated Y Company outpost that was sited in the centre of Al-Amarah at the CIMIC House. Beharry's platoon was the company reserve force, and was the last to depart from the base. But as the company was making its way through the darkened streets towards the outpost new orders were relayed to it by radio. A foot patrol had become pinned down by sporadic machine gun, rifle and rocket propelled grenade fire. The company was ordered to drive to its rescue with the 30-ton Warriors. Six PWRR soldiers had been wounded from the foot patrol during the course of a long and protracted firefight.

The Rocket-Propelled Grenade or RPG is an old Soviet design that has become 'a staple of insurgents' armouries all over the world.'[3] It is a cheaply produced weapon that is easily portable and can be used by an operator who possesses very limited military training or technical proficiency. The design was actually inspired by another cheap and mass-produced weapon, the German *Panzerfaust* that saw extensive use again Soviet tank regiments during the Battle of Berlin in April-May 1945. The RPG consists of a three-foot long steel tube, flared at one end to allow the rocket blast to be dissipated when fired. The weapon is aimed using a simple iron sight, and activated using a grip and trigger. The rocket weights about ten pounds, and is fired away from the tube using a gunpowder charge. Once in flight the hollow-charge grenade is powered by a small rocket that gives the weapon a range of around 1,000 yards, though it is notoriously inaccurate. As it flies towards its target little fins pop out of the rocket to try and maintain aerial stability, but because it is not directed by the operator, the rocket cannot home in on a target like the much more sophisticated British battlefield missile systems such as Milan and Javelin.

Beharry's platoon, as the reserve, was also ordered to join in with the rescue of the foot patrol. The attack on the patrol was probably a ruse to try and encourage the British to send in armoured reinforcements so that the insurgents could deploy the full gamut of their weapons against them. The insurgents had carefully prepared a killing zone in the city into which Beharry and his comrades unexpectedly stumbled. The platoon's six Warriors, led by Beharry's vehicle, started down a long dusty road in the evening gloom. After crossing a roundabout, something immediately struck the platoon commander as ominous when they started along another street towards the sounds of small-arms fire in the distance. The street was completely deserted – usually a sign that an ambush was imminent.

The convoy halted while the lieutenant tried to assess the route ahead. The road was lined with buildings between which ran many dirty and narrow alleyways that were perfect rat runs for the insurgents who had gathered ready to spring their trap. At some unseen and unheard signal, all hell suddenly broke loose. RPGs hurtled in towards the lead Warrior, exploding with a deafening concussion against the sides and turret. The Warrior was struck repeatedly, the big armoured vehicle rocking on its tracks like a ship in a storm. The platoon commander and the gunner slumped in the turret, both wounded and concussed. All around the convoy blazed the muzzle flashes of AK-47s and light machine-guns as the insurgents fired on the vehicles from the flat rooftops and from the alleyways. When Beharry tried to talk to the lieutenant on the intercom he was met with silence, and when he switched over on the net to speak with the other five Warriors he also heard nothing. Beharry was on his own and would have to act on his own initiative rather than wait for orders that may never come. The multiple RPG strikes had disabled the vehicle's communications completely. In the rear of the Warrior some of the soldiers were also wounded.

Beharry reacted quickly. He reached up and slammed shut his armoured hatch cover. He pressed the accelerator and the Warrior lurched forward, Beharry trying to drive it clear of the ambush before it was destroyed by the storm of anti-tank rockets that were streaming down from all sides. Suddenly, in the dim light, Beharry spotted a makeshift barricade across the road in front of him, and he immediately stopped. The moment the Warrior became stationary another hail of bullets and RPG rockets struck the vehicle. The Warrior caught fire, and soon noxious black smoke began to fill up the interior. Beharry could not see ahead but, realising that inaction would only lead to his death and the deaths of his comrades, he opened his hatch, exposing his helmeted head to the full weight of the ordnance flying around him like enraged hornets. The smoke cleared sufficiently for Beharry to see and, stamping the accelerator once again, he rammed the barricade, heedless of mines or Improvised Explosive Devices (IEDs), and burst through, clearing a path for the other five Warriors to follow.

Suddenly, Beharry glanced up and actually saw a RPG flashing through the air directly towards him. He grabbed the hatch cover handle with one hand and yanked it down, while keeping his other hand on the Warrior's controls. The rocket blew up against the turret, wrenching the hatch cover out of Beharry's hand, and sending gout of flame into the turret where it further wounded the already incapacitated gunner. When Beharry closed the hatch again he discovered that the armoured periscope through which he could have steered the AFV when it was closed up had been smashed beyond repair. He would have to continue to drive with his head sticking out of the vehicle, and fully exposed to the murderous crossfire in the street.

Revving the engine, the Warrior roared on down the road for a further 1,500 metres, the whole time under intense enemy fire. At one point a 7.62mm bullet actually struck Beharry in the head, but his Kevlar helmet saved him from injury as the round lodged in the inner lining. Beharry kept the vehicle moving forwards, even though the weight of enemy fire was enormous and he was constantly exposed to a hail of lead and shrapnel. The rest of his platoon followed closely behind. Suddenly, Beharry spied another Warrior from his company up ahead and, following the vehicle, Beharry and the rest of his platoon arrived outside the CIMIC House outpost, which was also under sporadic small-arms fire.

As bullets cracked through the air around him, and whacked off the armoured sides of the stationary Warrior, Beharry clambered out of the driver's tunnel and climbed up onto the turret. Single-handedly, Private Beharry pulled his wounded platoon commander from the turret and off the vehicle to safety. He then darted back out into the enemy's fire and once more climbed onto the Warrior's turret to rescue the wounded gunner. For a third time, Beharry braved the gunfire to lead the dazed and wounded soldiers out of the back of the Warrior to safety. Then, when all the men had been accounted for, incredibly Beharry turned his attention to saving his vehicle.

Beharry drove the smouldering Warrior through a complex chicane in front of the main gate that was constructed from concrete-filled oil drums and was designed to prevent suicide bombers from crashing vehicles laden with explosives into the front of the CIMIC House. He entered the compound. Once inside, Beharry pulled the fire extinguisher handles and doused the engine. Completely exhausted, Beharry struggled from the IFV and dragged himself into the back of another Warrior where he collapsed, his ordeal finally at an end.

Although Private Beharry had performed feats of bravery worthy of the highest recognition, he was soon back behind the wheel of another Warrior, and once more in the vanguard of his platoon. On 11 June Beharry's platoon roared into action as part of the quick reaction force. An insurgent mortar had opened fire on Coalition troops, and Beharry's platoon was tasked with attempting to cut the insurgents off in the dark streets of Al-Amarah. The Warrior's were being driven at high speed through the empty streets towards where an intelligence assessment had pinpointed the likely origin of the recent mortar fire. Suddenly, in an eerie replay of the events that had so nearly cost him his life the month before, Beharry's platoon drove once again straight into an insurgent ambush.

Lining the street at roof-top level were small groups of insurgents who were hunkered down and armed with RPGs and AK-47s. With a WHOOSH and a blinding flash, a rocket-propelled grenade detonated against Beharry's Warrior only six inches from the young soldier's head. Although his helmet absorbed most of the blast, Beharry was nonetheless badly wounded. Stunned, disorientated and bleeding profusely from his wounds, Beharry's head began to clear as more rockets thumped into the vehicle, wounding and incapacitating the commander and the rest of the crew. Scarcely pausing to think, and with his blood running into his eyes that obscured his vision, Beharry slammed the Warrior into reverse and accelerating wildly, drove out of the ambush zone. Beharry's withdrawal was abruptly terminated by a dusty wall, the Warrior crunching into it and coming to a lurching halt. Within seconds, as the smoke and dust began to clear, other Warrior crewmen were on the scene, and they lifted Beharry and his comrades to safety. Beharry collapsed soon afterwards and fell into a coma. He spent many months in hospital in Britain slowly recovering from his terrible injuries, enduring several difficult operations. In recognition of his two amazingly courageous actions Beharry was awarded the Victoria Cross, the first to a county regiment since Korea. Although he has remained in the army, and was promoted to lance-corporal in 2006, Beharry has continued to suffer from severe pain in his neck and head, as well as having flash-backs to the events in Iraq. In 2006 he published his autobiography entitled *Barefoot Soldier*, netting a one million pound publishing deal. 'Its been rather a long time since I've awarded one of these,' said the Queen to Beharry when she pinned the Victoria Cross onto his tunic at Buckingham Palace. Beharry remained modest about his incredible achievements. 'Maybe I was brave, I don't know,' he said. 'At the time I was just doing my job, I didn't have time for other thoughts.' Summing the whole experience up simply, Beharry said: 'Some days you the bug, some days you the windshield.'[4]

Sometimes death and destruction are sown by one's own Allies. The military use the term 'blue on blue' for contacts between Allied forces, though they are more widely known as 'friendly fire' incidents when reported in the media. Christopher Finney was an eighteen-year-old trooper in the famous Blues and Royals, one of the two regiments, the other being the Life Guards, that form the Household Cavalry. Famous for their mounted squadron that rides at the Queen's Birthday Parade and at the State Opening of Parliament, the Blues and Royals alternate with the Life Guards in providing mounted guards outside Horse Guards in London. They are, along with the five Foot Guard regiments, the most visible symbol of the British Army, but they are also much more than just ceremonial soldiers. The Household Cavalry provides an armoured regiment that has seen action at the forefront of Britain's latest overseas deployments, including the Falklands War in 1982 and the War in Iraq. On 28 March 2003 D Squadron of the Household Cavalry, equipped with Scimitar light tanks, was in the vanguard of the British 16 Air Assault Brigade advance up the Shatt al-Arab waterway north of the Iraqi city of Basra. The Squadron's task was to locate and attack the numerically vastly superior and better equipped Iraqi 6th Armoured Division.

Trooper Finney was from Marple, near Stockport, and he had joined the army in 2000 straight from school. After he had attended the Army Foundation College in Harrogate, Finney had joined the Household Cavalry Regiment at Windsor in January 2002. In March 2003 the regiment was an integral element of the British assault on Basra and the reduction of regular Iraqi Army units blocking the Coalition advance on Baghdad. It was Finney's first operational deployment, and very nearly his last.

D Squadron was probing about thirty kilometres ahead of 16 Air Assault Brigade, the tan coloured tanks moving through flat, almost featureless desert. Finney was driving the leading Scimitar of his troop. For several hours Finney and his comrades had engaged and knocked out several Iraqi armoured vehicles that had tried to stop the British force. The Squadron mopped up pockets of resistance while continuing north, expecting to run into more serious opposition when it encountered the 6th Armoured Division. Finney's tank, along with the Troop Commander's Scimitar, paused beside a levee. The officer scanned the route ahead with binoculars, assessing the ground and any likely opposition. Suddenly, without warning, the two light tanks found themselves under a furious assault. 'When it happened, I heard a bang and I made up my own little story that we had been attacked by a rocket-propelled grenade, but it wasn't,'[5] recalled Finney. Armour-piercing cannon shells ripped through the tanks as the scream of jet engines passed low overhead. Through the confusion and dust of the attack, some of the cavalrymen saw their attackers banking away into the clear blue sky, squat and ugly black planes whose engine noise reverberated off the burning vehicles. They were American A-10 Warthogs, and D Squadron had just been strafed by the most capable tank killing plane in the Allied inventory, firing 30mm depleted uranium shells. The reasons for the attack were unimportant in the shocked aftermath of the assault, as men lay bleeding and screaming inside the wrecked Scimitars and rounds started to cook off inside the gun turrets with loud bangs. Trooper Finney, though shaken by the suddenness and violence of the aerial attack, nonetheless kept his head and managed to haul his wounded gunner off the burning vehicle and dragged him to a safer position close by where he applied a field dressing to his wounds. 'I jumped out and saw Corporal Tudbole, who was my gunner, lying half out of his hatch and I helped him get down and started to sort him out,' said Finney.

Whilst this was going on, Iraqi armour had joined in, and Corporal-of-Horse Mick Flynn, a Falklands War veteran, rallied the remaining British tanks and began fighting back. Looking around for someone to report to, Finney saw that his Troop Commander was wounded, and no-one else was taking command of the situation. Finney knew that he had to inform his own headquarters of the attack, but that would mean going into his burning Scimitar to use the radio. Disregarding his own safety, Finney broke cover and ran over to the light tank and radioed a lucid report to his HQ, despite the risks he faced from a spreading fire and exploding ammunition. After completing his report Finney ran back over to his injured gunner and began to help him walk towards a Spartan armoured recovery vehicle that Staff Sergeant Andrew Sindall of the Royal Engineers had brought forward to assist the stricken Scimitars, moving into the line of fire.

Looking skyward once again, Finney realised to his horror that the two Warthogs were lining up to make another strafing run at the tanks. Finney and his gunner continued to hobble along as the American aircraft fired their cannons, shells ripping into the Scimitars, and tearing up the road surface in great fountains of dirt and debris. One survivor who was there described the terrifying sound of the Warthog cannon: 'That gun - I don't want to ever hear that again, it's like a cross between a moan and a roar.'[6] Finney was wounded in the lower back and both legs, while the gunner received a further wound to his head. Despite being in considerable pain, Finney managed to single-handedly drag Corporal Tudbole to the safety of the Spartan. Turning around, Finney could see that the driver of the other Scimitar was still slumped in his seat inside the burning tank. Finney made his way back to the tank, as ammunition continued to explode all around him and valiantly climbed up onto the Scimitar in an effort to reach the driver, twenty-five-year-old Lance-Corporal of Horse Matty Hull. Unfortunately, the light tank was now well alight, and the heat, smoke and flames confounded Finney's efforts to get to Hull. Finney was beaten back until he collapsed beside the road, and Hull unfortunately perished in the inferno. A party of Royal Engineers recovered Finney from the scene and took him to the Spartan for treatment. 'During these attacks and their horrifying aftermath, Finney displayed clear-headed courage and devotion to his comrades which was out of all proportion to his age and experience,' read his citation. 'Acting with complete disregard for his own safety even when wounded, his bravery was of the highest order throughout.'[7] The British were bitter at the behaviour of the American pilots responsible for the death of one of their comrades. 'Instead of providing air cover while helicopters were drafted in to evacuate the casualties, the planes flew away. The survivors of the attack went on to call the pilots "cowboys".'[8] In 2007, Andrew Walker, Oxfordshire Deputy Assistant Coroner, ruled that the attack on the Blues and Royals was a '"criminal, unlawful act" tantamount to manslaughter.' He went on to say: 'The pilot who opened fire did so with disregard for the rules of engagement and acting outside the protection of the law of armed conflict.'[9] The Pentagon in Washington D.C. rejected the British coroner's findings.

Christopher Finney became the youngest serviceman to be awarded the George Cross at Buckingham Palace in February 2004. He was subsequently promoted to Lance-Corporal-of-Horse.

Corporal-of-Horse Mick Flynn was awarded the Conspicious Gallantry Cross for his efforts in protecting the rescue effort from interference by Iraqi armoured forces. The award covered not only the blue-on-blue incident but his incredible efforts over a sustained period of combat. His citation says he also fought 'over a period of seven days with no consideration for his own safety and under fire from enemy tanks and artillery'.[10] Flynn was later awarded the Military Cross during operations in Afghanistan and is currently the second most decorated soldier serving in the army after Johnson Beharry. Staff Sergeant Andrew Sindall, who brought his Spartan armoured recovery vehicle through the fire to help Finney and Corporal Tudbole received the Queen's Gallantry Medal.

It is often forgotten that the conflict in Iraq has not just been about war fighting, but also about reconstruction and training tasks. Certainly, this is what the politicians earnestly told the people during the course of Britain's involvement in Iraq. Many of these reconstruction projects were placed into the hands of civilian agencies and companies, and many of their personnel, who were not combat-trained soldiers, nonetheless ended up in the front lines in the war against the insurgents. Some have displayed quite extraordinary courage in horrendous situations for which they were completely untrained and unprepared. Their stories have often been overshadowed by the saga of the military war in Iraq, but it a story that should be recorded.

Dr. Andrew Rathmell was a Briton in charge of Planning, Policy and Analysis at the Coalition Provisional Authority (CPA) in Baghdad. The CPA was established by the Americans until they were able to hand over power to a reconstituted Iraqi government. Rathmell had arrived in Baghdad from London, where he lived with his wife and two young children. He had been seconded from the Rand Corporation to the US Department of Defense in August 2003. His job would take him to many of the front-line bases in Iraq, and on 21 January 2004 Rathmell was at the American Forward Operating Base (FOB) Warhorse in the town of Baquba, along with some civilian and military colleagues. With a terrible and unexpected suddenness, the base was attacked by well-armed insurgents, and Rathmell and the other analysts found themselves thrust unexpectedly into the thick of the fighting. Mortar rounds began to land inside the base compound, exploding with huge fountains of dirt, shrapnel and rock, and RPGs hissed overhead to detonate with loud cracks against walls. Everyone was heading for cover when a mortar bomb impacted close to Dr. Rathmell, the blast sucking the air from his lungs and flinging him down in the dust. His hearing was temporarily gone. Rathmell looked around him and saw that his colleague, Colonel Ralph Sabatino of the US Army was also down on the ground and obviously wounded. Rathmell ran over to the soldier and dragged him out of the danger zone and into cover. Not satisfied with this cool display of bravery, Rathmell went out three more times into the heavy enemy fire, as more mortars pounded the base and rockets exploded all around him. On each occasion, Rathmell administered life-saving first aid to injured personnel, and also managed to confirm that two US Army soldiers had been killed.

'Andrew Rathmell is not a professional warrior,' said Paul Bremer, US Ambassador to Iraq, 'but he displayed the courage and coolness under fire to which all warriors aspire.'[11] At a special ceremony in Baghdad, Ambassador Bremer presented Rathmell with the Department of Defense Medal for Valor, an award that was created in 2001 to reward Americans who perform an act of heroism or sacrifice, with voluntary risk of personal safety in the face of danger. Dr. Rathmell was the first foreign recipient of the medal.

Military operations continued in and around Basra long after Private Johnson Beharry was awarded his Victoria Cross. The dangers posed to British forces did not diminish, and the insurgents continued to keep up their pressure with constant attacks on British foot and vehicle patrols throughout the city and in the surrounding towns and villages. As we are currently witnessing almost daily in Afghanistan, one of the insurgents' favoured weapons was the Improvised Explosive Device or IED. Utilising land mines, hand grenades, explosives, and pretty much anything that would cause the maximum damage to vehicles or men on foot patrol, IEDs were a largely unseen threat that reminded military commanders of operations in Northern Ireland during the worst of 'the Troubles'. Insurgents often combined IEDs with a follow-up ambush using AK47s and RPGs. The sum total of all of this mayhem for British forces was the constant stress of unexpected attack when out on patrol, and casualties had been mounting steadily since the conclusion of the conventional war fighting phase in 2003 and the fall of Saddam Hussein. A very good example of the kind of warfare that was faced by British soldiers in Iraq is the story of David Smith, and his incredible valour in the face of sudden destruction and injury.

Fusilier Smith, known as "Smudge" to his mates, had joined the army in order to 'better himself' as he put it. Born in Rochdale, after initial training at the Infantry Training Centre at Catterick, Smith had joined the 2nd Battalion, The Royal Regiment of Fusiliers (2 RRF), one of Britain's foremost regiments. The battalion had just completed a tour of duty in Northern Ireland, but in the peace that reigned in the once troubled province there was little opportunity to test their training for real. The battalion was next stationed in Cyprus, where Britain maintains the Sovereign Base Areas of Akrotiri and Dhekelia, allowing Britain to maintain a sizeable military presence and airbase close to the Middle East. Smith moved into married quarters with his young wife, Joanna. From Cyprus, 2 RRF provided part of a battle group to support British operations in and around troubled Basra.

2 RRF mounted patrols around Basra and the nearby town of Al-Zubaya, showing the flag and trying to maintain stability in a region that was increasingly falling into anarchy as the insurgents grew in confidence and the local population, which had been largely supportive of the British efforts in 2003, began to view the British as an occupying force rather than a liberating army. After the 2003 invasion, Basra had been relatively calm as the British had set to work trying to restore the city's infrastructure, win hearts and minds with humanitarian projects, and train the local Iraqi police and army. It was the revelations of American and British abuse of Iraqi detainees that was one of the roots that led to a breakdown in relations with the local populace and an increase in bombings and shootings throughout the city. The British were forced into the invidious position of trying to maintain order as the province descended slowly into insurgency. As mentioned earlier, al'Sadr's Mahdi Army was one of the biggest insurgent groups in Basra, whipping up anti-British sentiment among the locals and calling for holy war against the infidel. The British had too few men for the task

that they had been assigned and little support for the vague war aims from the authorities back home.

On 5 September 2005, Fusilier Smith and a patrol from 2 RRF were in two Land Rovers driving through the dusty and dirty streets of Al-Zubaya when they ran into trouble. Smith was acting as top cover in the second vehicle. It was hot, the sun beating down relentlessly on his helmet. Dust from the two vehicles billowed up behind them as they passed long cement walls and small shops where the locals eked out a basic living. Here and there patches of vegetation broke up the rather uniformly white and tan shades of the buildings and road. Local men glanced up from their chores as the British vehicles lumbered by, dressed in shirts, trousers and sandals, their faces neither hostile nor friendly. Unbeknown to Smith and his comrades, they were driving slowly into a world of trouble.

The explosion was very loud, shockingly so, jerking the soldiers from heat-induced day-dreaming with an unpleasantly violent lurch. The leading Land Rover had disappeared into a riot of dust and smoke, while pieces of the vehicle rained down onto the road, still smouldering from the heat of the blast. The patrol had fallen victim to an IED – remotely detonated by some unseen watcher as the little convoy had drove by. Smith's vehicle smashed into the one in front with a sickening thud and the sound of breaking glass. The front Land Rover was on fire and more petrol was leaking over the road from jerry cans split wide open by the blast of the bomb. Men were still inside the shattered lead vehicle, grievously injured and helpless. It was chaos.

Smith jumped down from his vehicle and raced over to the burning Land Rover, heedless of any follow-up ambush that the insurgents might have had planned, or any further IEDs that they may have detonated. He wrenched open the broken and bent back doors and was met with a scene of horror. His comrades' lay on the floor of the vehicle, blood splattered around like a butcher's shop, a deep dust haze and smoke from the fuel fire catching in Smith's throat. Smith was a trained medic, and he immediately started pulling his injured comrades out of the Land Rover to safety. 'Fusilier Smith showed outstanding courage far above and beyond his years,'[12] said his commanding officer, Lieutenant-Colonel Ingram, afterwards.

'He's a big lad and we call him the gentle giant,' said Smith's father Gary. 'He always thinks about others before himself.'[13] One of his mates died of his injuries before he made it to the British military hospital in Basra.

Just six days later on 11 September Smith was out on patrol again, this time in Basra city itself. And once again his patrol ran into an IED roadside bomb. A massive explosion completely wrecked the lead vehicle, setting it on fire. Smith, who was again acting as top cover in the second vehicle, once more dashed forward into the danger, intent only on saving the lives of his colleagues. 'With no regard for his own safety and with his focus firmly on saving those in the vehicle, he commenced the evacuation of the casualties from the burning chaos,'[14] wrote Colonel Ingram. His comrades lay moaning in the back of the wrecked vehicle, in agony from multiple blast injuries. Smith immediately set to evacuating them and treating their injuries as best he could before they could be sent to an aid post. 'His actions in trying to save his comrades in Iraq - and one of his best friends died in the bombing - showed just how courageous, determined and professional he was in a very dangerous situation,' said Smith's father. 'He's an inspiring example to all of us and to his country.'[15] Fusilier Smith was awarded one of Britain's highest honours for his bravery and coolness in handling a terrible and dangerous situation on *two* occasions that would have severely tested the resolve and mettle of many people far older than Smith's twenty years. In 2006 Smith received the George Medal from the Queen at Buckingham Palace, second only to the George Cross. 'It's a surprise but a tremendous honour I am going to receive a George Medal,' said Smith when he was informed of the award. 'But my thoughts at this time are more with the families and friends of the soldiers who were lost that day. We were all close mates and they will not be forgotten.' Those words apply to so many of the men and women Britain has sent to the wars in Afghanistan and Iraq.

Incredible courage in many forms has been demonstrated by British forces in Iraq. Another example that stands proudly out from among the many is a story of incredible coolness under fire and bravery exhibited by another young soldier who acted with a maturity and strength of character that would put many older people to shame. Corporal Martin Caines, a twenty-seven-year-old section commander in 1st Battalion, Princess of Wales's Royal Regiment (1 PWRR), had been in the army for eight years when he faced his greatest and deadliest challenge. Married, with two young children at home, Corporal Caines acted with immense bravery to save the young soldiers under his command from almost certain injury or death at the hands of a large and angry Iraqi mob in southern Iraq.

Trouble had begun when a sizeable contingent of Iraqi soldiers had been left without water by their own incompetent commanders. Caines and his patrol confronted the extremely agitated group of Iraqis who were all well-armed and evidently intent on blaming their situation not on the unprofessional behaviour of their own leaders but instead on their British allies. Caines, who comes from Feltham, tried to give the Iraqis what water he could spare from his patrol's own limited supplies, but the Iraqis instead continued to work themselves up into a frenzied state, shouting and waving their arms and ominously cocking their AK47s. Caines ordered his section to take cover, but on no account to open fire. All British soldiers knew that a fight between British soldiers and the Iraqi National Army would badly poison Coalition relations and play directly into the hands of the insurgents.

Suddenly, gunfire erupted as the Iraqi soldiers opened a vigorous fire directed at Caines and his men. Caines shouted at his section to keep their heads down while he reported back to his commander on the radio what was happening. They were in a bad situation, outnumbered and outgunned by their erstwhile allies, bullets cracking overhead and smashing into walls and houses all around them. The leader of the disgruntled Iraqi troops produced a Soviet sniper rifle and coolly fired two shots directly in front of Caines' section – evidently intending to go further and shoot directly at the British troops the next time. Other Iraqis likewise lowered their fire, until Kalashnikov bullets were kicking up spurts in the dirt and Caines was becoming very worried for the safety of his men. It was at this moment that Caines did something incredibly courageous or incredibly stupid, depending how you look at these things.

In a moment of sheer bravado, Corporal Caines suddenly stood up, fully exposing himself to the Iraqi guns. He held his SA80 rifle down by his side in a non-threatening posture, and pulling himself up to his full height he glared directly at the Iraqi leader of the mutinous troops. The firing abruptly stopped, as the Iraqis were no doubt astonished that anyone would willingly expose themselves to automatic rifle fire. Perhaps they thought Caines was mad. The ringleader pointed his sniper rifle at Caines, keeping it levelled at his chest for about twenty seconds, when like two gunslingers in the American West they faced each other across the dusty road.

According to Caines, the situation had been getting totally out of control. 'I was in command and decided to save it,' he said later. 'I had a few new blokes and didn't want them to get involved in something where they might get hurt.'[16] The seconds ticked slowly by, and then suddenly the chief Iraqi lowered his rifle and threw it down into the dirt and stalked off muttering to himself. The tension abruptly relaxed and the Iraqis no longer appeared hostile. 'I realised later it might have been stupid,' said Caines of his heroics, 'but it calmed the situation.'[17] Caines actions prevented bloodshed between the two allies and helped the British cause immeasurably. It was a difficult decision to take, to order his men not to return fire when it looked as though their lives were in mortal danger. Few would have had the courage and sense not to fight back, still fewer the bravery to place themselves into the lion's mouth and risk immediate death to save the lives of others. Those twenty seconds of staring down the barrel of the sniper rifle must have seemed like an eternity to the young British NCO. Corporal Caines, like Fusilier Smith, was also awarded the George Medal. Caines, in common with the other recipients of bravery awards, is not a boastful man. 'I was shocked to be told I was getting it,' said Caines. 'There are lot of blokes out there doing the same sort of thing.'

As we saw earlier, women such as medic Michelle Norris are increasingly entering what was until recently an almost completely male-dominated arena – the battlefield. Most women found in the battle zone today are medical personnel, often attached to frontline fighting battalions. Another way that women are playing a direct role on the battlefield is from above, as pilots with the Royal Air Force. This is also another new innovation. One such RAF pilot proved in Iraq that women can be as technically proficient and courageous as their male counterparts in the finest traditions of the world's oldest air force.

Flight Lieutenant Michelle Goodman joined the RAF in 2000 straight from Manchester University, where she had studied aerospace engineering. By 2004 she was a helicopter pilot, flying the new Merlin aircraft, with 78 Squadron based at RAF Benson in Oxfordshire. On 1 June 2007 Goodman was captain of an Incident Reaction Team (IRT) based at Basra Airbase in Iraq, her job being to airlift casualties to hospital, a dangerous activity as the big Merlins were regularly shot at by insurgents. A call had come through to Goodman at 11.15 pm requesting an IRT sortie into the centre of Basra City where a casualty awaited immediate evacuation. Twenty-year-old Rifleman Stephen Vause of the 4th Battalion, The Rifles, had been badly wounded by an exploding mortar bomb, and as it turned out his wounds were mortal. Every effort would be expended to get Vause to a hospital, even though the city was infested with gunmen. Goodman knew the risks of flying a large military helicopter straight into the centre of a hostile city, and she asked her crew for their thoughts before taking off. 'I wouldn't have done it without asking them,' she said. 'This wasn't going to be a one-woman show. I just told them, "I think this could be a little dodgy." But they all wanted to go, and they were all fantastically professional'. As Goodman said: '[If] it was me lying down there [in Basra] I'd like to think there was someone prepared to come and get me.'[18]

The flight into downtown Basra was to prove extremely tricky. Goodman took the Merlin in very low, skimming across the buildings to present a smaller target to insurgents, moving along at 160 mph. Goodman wore Night Vision Goggles. Goodman had been told before taking off that British intelligence had received a report that Iraqi insurgents were planning a 'spectacular' attack on British forces scheduled for that night, with the possibility of a helicopter being the target. Goodman would also be taking her aircraft into a hot landing site where insurgents were still engaged with British ground forces.

It was Goodman's second tour in Iraq with the Joint Helicopter Force, but the mission to rescue Rifleman Vause was certainly the most hazardous she had yet faced. Goodman was to land her Merlin on an unfamiliar and dangerous zone that was under direct enemy attack. There were numerous obstructions at the landing site that could have proved hazardous and, as well as incoming insurgent fire there was also outgoing friendly fire passing close by intended to assist her in landing and evacuating the casualty. Goodman landed the Merlin in a swirl of dust. 'It was so thick, it was impossible to see where we were going,'[19] she recalled. As the medics and Aviation Reaction Force left the aircraft four mortar bombs impacted to the rear blowing out lethal shrapnel and debris in all directions. 'The crew could see the ground and guided me down,' said Goodman as the big chopper came to rest. An Army Air Corps Lynx helicopter that was flying top cover for the rescue by providing gunfire support to Goodman reported numerous explosions in the vicinity of the landing zone, both mortars and RPGs. 'It sounds odd to say it, but your training just kicks in, and you just get on with it,' said Goodman of the experience of being under fire. 'I guess the adrenaline keeps you going – I felt like my eyes were out on stalks.'[20] Goodman held the Merlin on the ground for five anxious minutes while the evacuation was underway. As Goodman got airborne again, further mortar bombs landed close by the aircraft. Friendly artillery rounds also began to impact close to the landing zone. As the Merlin gained altitude an alarm sounded in the cockpit indicating that the aircraft was being 'painted' by a surface-to-air missile. Flares were automatically discharged and Goodman made good her escape from danger. A missile was not launched, but it was a close-run thing nonetheless. Goodman delivered Vause to the British field hospital only fourteen minutes after departing the hot landing zone.

When it was announced that Goodman had been gazetted a Distinguished Flying Cross, the first ever awarded to a woman, she paid tribute to the heroism and professionalism of all the IRT crews and support personnel operating worldwide: 'I am truly honoured to be awarded a DFC but, without both my crew and all the engineering support personnel, the rescue of the casualty would not have been possible. The helicopter Incident Reaction Team (IRT), whether in Iraq or Afghanistan, is regularly confronted with dangerous casualty extractions and all are dealt with in a professional and timely manner. This is not an award just for me, but recognizes all the soldiers, sailors and airmen, who, day in and day out put their lives on the line for the British public to remain safe.'[21]

Honoured at the same ceremony as Flight Lieutenant Goodman was another RAF hero. Corporal David Hayden was serving in Iraq in August 2007 when he performed an act of astonishing courage in the face of serious insurgent opposition. Hayden had been a member of the RAF Regiment since 1997. He came from a military family – his father had been a Warrant Officer Class 2 in the Queen's Royal Hussars and Hayden had been born in Germany where his father was serving in 1979. Hayden was a section commander in 1 Squadron, based at RAF Honington in Suffolk when the unit deployed to Iraq.

The RAF Regiment is a specialist airfield defence corps established in 1942. It is in effect the RAFs own little army. Currently, the regiment comprises seven field squadrons and three Royal Auxiliary Air Force squadrons, each squadron being considerably larger than a standard infantry company. The RAF Regiment is also famous for its 63 Squadron (Queen's Colour Squadron) whose excellent in drill is on a par with the Guards. The RAF Regiment counters ground based threats to the RAF and are trained to move on foot or mounted in helicopters or Land Rovers to defend airfields. They also often provide Forward Air Controllers with the army. In Iraq, RAF Regiment personnel undertook routine foot patrols as an adjunct to the army.

It was while dismounted and conducting a foot patrol on the outskirts of Basra in August 2007, that Corporal Hayden and his section was ambushed by around fifty well-armed insurgents. The airmen were soon surrounded and a high concentration of automatic fire was plastering their posiition. 'Every time we tried to move, we got hammered from about four or five different places,'[22] recalled Hayden. During the barrage of fire, Leading Aircraftsman Martin Beard was hit and fatally wounded. Hayden was determined to get to Beard and render what first aid he could. The problem was a six-foot dried mud wall separating the two men. Hayden, who stands 6ft 3in tall and is powerfully built, did not let this stop him. There was a steel door set into the wall, but it was locked. 'I just got my head down and ran at the door,' said Hayden. 'It came off its hinges and we ran into the open to get Beard. Me and one of the lads from the section grabbed him and moved him about 20 yards to cover.'[23] During this rescue, Hayden and his companion were under intense fire.

Hayden realised that he had to get Beard out of the ambush and he set about doing so in the most direct way he knew how. He hoisted Beard over his shoulder and ran 200 yards through withering insurgent fire, racing across cesspits, broken sewers and many obstacles. Once Beard had been taken to safety, Hayden turned around and ran back through the fire and brought out the rest of his section. 'Obviously I was gutted because we lost Beardy,' said Hayden. 'The men that were with me that day were fantastic. It's a team effort.'[24] Corporal Hayden was awarded the Military Cross at Buckingham Palace in 2008, the first airman to receive this honour.

Operation Telic, the British military operation in southern Iraq, was formally ended on 30 April 2009 when the last British troops withdrew from Basra Airport and control was handed over to the United States military. Between 2003 and 2009 the British military lost 179 personnel killed and 315 wounded in action.

A note on the Victoria Cross. Australia, New Zealand and Canada now award their own versions of the Victoria Cross. They are identical to the British VC, and are cast from the same Crimean War Chinese gunmetal. The only significant difference is the Canadian version. Because of the bilingual nature of modern Canada, the VC motto 'For Valour' has been altered to the neutral Latin 'Pro Valore'. Australia was the first to stop using the British medal in 1991, followed by Canada in 1993 and New Zealand in 1999. Both New Zealand and Australia have made a single award of the renamed medal, but Canada has yet to.

1 '*The day 5ft Army girl defied enemy guns*' by David Wilkes, *Daily Mail*, 10 August 2006

2 Princess of Wales's Royal Regiment website

3 Patrick Bishop, 3 PARA, (London: Harper Perennial, 2008), 67

4 Chris Hunter, *Eight Lives Down*, (London: Corgi Books, 2008), 304

5 '*Trooper who saved friend in face of friendly fire awarded George Cross*' by Audrey Gillan and Richard Norton-Taylor, *The Guardian*, 31 October 2003

6 Ibid.

7 *The London Gazette*, No. 57100, 30 October 2003

8 '*Trooper who saved friend in face of friendly fire awarded George Cross*' by Audrey Gillan and Richard Norton-Taylor, *The Guardian*, 31 October 2003

9 '*Friendly-fire killing of Matty Hull was criminal and unlawful, says coroner*' by Michael Evans, *The Times*, 17 March 2007

10 '*Trooper who saved friend in face of friendly fire awarded George Cross*' by Audrey Gillan and Richard Norton-Taylor, *The Guardian*, 31 October 2003

11 '*British Civilian Awarded US Bravery Medal*', The Coalition Provisional Authority, 29 April 2004

12 Ministry of Defence website

13 '*We're so proud of our Iraq hero son*' by David Appleton, *Manchester Evening News*, 12 September 2006

14 Ministry of Defence website

15 '*We're so proud of our Iraq hero son*' by David Appleton, *Manchester Evening News*, 12 September 2006

16 '*Standing up for peace*' by Chris Briddon, *Richmond and Twickenham Times*, 27 December 2006

17 Ibid.

18 '*The brown-eyed, blonde RAF hero who is proud to wear her uniform*' by Paul Harris, *The Daily Mail*, 8 March 2008

19 Ibid.

20 Ibid.

21 '*RAF Benson pilot receives top honour*', Royal Air Force, http://www.raf.mod.uk, accessed 21 December 2009

22 '*The brown-eyed, blonde RAF hero who is proud to wear her uniform*' by Paul Harris, *The Daily Mail*, 8 March 2008

23 Ibid.

24 Ibid.

CHAPTER 5

Fire and Rescue

'To go into a flat fire once without support is courageous but
then to go back in again is just incredibly courageous
and brave.'

Christine Wornham on her son Firefighter
Jeffrey Wornham, GM

PC Robert Greenall was the first member of the emergency services
to arrive at a house fire in a two-storey house in Langney, East
Sussex. The forty-three-year-old father of two was told by the owners
that their ten-month old baby girl was still inside her room on the
first floor of the house, trapped by the growing inferno engulfing the
property. Greenall swung immediately into action. He had no fire-
fighting equipment, nor any protective clothing or breathing gear,
but he nonetheless went straight into the burning house and climbed
up the smoke-shrouded stairs. The smoke was thick and acrid, and
Greenall choked as he tried to locate the child. Realising that he
couldn't see anything, he ran back outside to his patrol car and
grabbed a torch before running back inside the burning house. 'The
torch was useless,' said Greenall. 'I could see nothing and could only
hear the crackling of flames. As I fell out of the room I heard the
sound of a baby crying, the cries were quite weak.'

Realising that he had only a few minutes at most in which to save
the child's life before the bedroom was consumed by the growing
conflagration, Greenall dashed downstairs to the kitchen and
grabbed a wet cloth with which to cover his nose and mouth before

he once more climbed the stairs back into the inferno. Flames suddenly shot across the child's room, illuminating a cot for a second through the thick smoke, enabling Greenall to see where the baby was. 'I could see a small pair of legs sticking out of the railings of the cot,' recalled Greenall, 'the flames were practically licking the baby's feet.' Another attempt to reach the child was defeated by the overpowering dense smoke. Greenall refused to give up and he made one last attempt to reach the girl, crawling across the floor to the cot where he managed to pull the child free and into his arms. 'Her cry was dying, it just went and I thought she was dead,' said Greenall, 'I knew I had to go back in, I was going to go back in until I got her.' Once he had managed to pull the child out of the cot, Greenall discovered that 'she was lifeless like a rag doll. There was no movement and I knew then she had died.' Greenall ran outside with the child cradled in his arms. 'I remember holding her in my arms willing her to breathe. Then she spluttered back to life. It was the best noise in the world, it was the best thing I have ever heard, it really was. I don't think I could have lived with myself if I hadn't got her.' Greenall was awarded a Police Bravery Award in 2001. The child and her rescuer both made a full recovery from their ordeal.

Michael Righton was a master at the Dragon School in Oxford. He also coached the rowing team and it was in this capacity that he was supervising a group of children on Dorney Rowing Lake near Eton College in Berkshire, at 4 pm on the afternoon of 4 December 2002. Across from where the children were busy with their water sports, workmen were clearing a flat area at the edge of the lake using a mechanical excavator. Righton's attention was drawn by shouts and from his position he saw the excavator slip into the lake as the platform it was working on gave way. The entire vehicle, along with the driver who was still in the cab, was quickly swallowed up by the freezing waters of the lake.

Righton swung immediately into action. He shouted at the crew of the boat that he was supervising not to move and then he sprinted some sixty metres along the lake shore. He paused to see if the excavator driver emerged from the lake under his own steam. When nothing happened, Righton fished out his mobile phone and alerted the lake reception to what had happened. Help would not arrive before the unfortunate driver drowned and so Righton took it upon himself to save the man. Diving straight into the extremely cold water, Righton swam out to the submerged excavator and climbed onto its roof. Trying in vain to open the vehicle's emergency hatch or smash the windows, Righton shouted at a lorry driver who was watching close by from the shore to throw him something he could use to break the windscreen. The lorry driver tossed Righton a hammer and, with this, Righton was able to smash the windscreen, with an enormous effort, pull the bulky driver out of the cab. The man appeared to be dead, but holding his head clear of the water, Righton shouted for assistance. A construction worker dove into the lake and swam out to help him with the seemingly lifeless body of the driver.

Righton administered mouth-to-mouth resuscitation to the driver whilst in the water and the driver miraculously regained consciousness. Shortly afterwards, an ambulance and the Fire Brigade rolled up and Righton, the driver, and the construction worker were rescued by an emergency launch. If Righton had waited for the emergency services the driver of the excavator would have undoubtedly drowned. For his actions Righton was awarded the Queen's Commendation for Bravery.

Vicky Murray has attributed her coolness under stress and her quick reactions in an emergency to the training she had received as a member of the Army Cadet Force. Murray, a lance-corporal, was only fourteen-years-old when she bravely rescued a woman from a terrible house fire in Birmingham in 2003.

Murray, from Selly Oak, Birmingham, was a proud member of Warwickshire and West Midlands Army Cadet Force. She was on her way to school at 8.20 am on 10 March 2003, accompanied by her brother and two friends, when she noticed a group of adults and children standing around outside a block of flats. A closer inspection soon revealed that one of the ground floor flats was on fire. An elderly couple lived inside the flat. The living room was already fully ablaze and the front window had blown out, causing fire and black smoke to roar through the hole 'in a blowtorch effect.'[1]

Murray sprang immediately and apparently instinctively into action. 'When I got there, people were just standing about and I felt I had to do something,' she said later. Murray could see an elderly women feebly tugging at the curtains in the bedroom and she dashed through the smoke and flames to reach the window. Realising that she had nothing with which to smash the window and rescue the old lady, Murray used her bare hands. She hammered on the glass until it shattered, sustaining lacerations and bruises as she bashed her way through. Murray tried to pull the women out through the opening by herself but the adult was too heavy for a child to manage all on her own. Fortunately at this point, the bystanders, who up until that point had stood transfixed by the drama unfolding before them like people docilely watching television, began to offer their assistance. A couple of men quickly built a platform from loose bricks and then pulled the woman through the broken window to safety. By now the sounds of sirens could be heard fast approaching as a fire engine and an ambulance raced to the scene. Murray, exercising a coolness and authority that went way beyond her years, told the men to carry the old lady out of the smoke, and then she covered her with her jacket as the woman was in shock. 'My training as an Army Cadet helped enormously,' said Murray, 'especially the first aid and taking command of the situation.' In the meantime firefighters managed to rescue the elderly husband from the inferno but the man, who was confined to a wheelchair, had been badly burned and later died from his injuries in hospital.

Murray became the first Army Cadet since 1941 to receive a national honour when she was presented with the Queen's Commendation for Bravery by The Duke of Kent. 'I am so very proud of her,' said Sue Murray, Vicky's mother. 'The Army Cadet training gave her confidence and maturity'.

At about 4 am on 16 July 2003 Sergeant Ian Marshall was on duty at Newquay Police Station in Cornwall. Suddenly, he heard a commotion outside in the street with people shouting and running about. Marshall went out into the street, which was still dark apart from the street lamps. Several people drew his attention to a nearby block of flats above a parade of shop. Marshall could see smoke billowing up against the pre-dawn sky. Someone quickly told Marshall that a woman and her young son were trapped in the burning flat. Marshall and a police colleague dashed across to the building. Inside they called out several times but there was no response. When they moved to the first floor they found that further investigations were blocked by a strong industrial fire door, so both men decided to go back across to their station and collect a police battering ram, known as an enforcer. Just as they were about to leave the building, someone called out to them to stand still and, seconds later a large burning window frame crashed down into the street before them. It was a lucky escape from serious injury.

Time was pressing and, when Marshall was told that the woman was lying on the window ledge of her burning flat in an attempt to escape the heat and flames, he realized that he could gain access to her from another flat. Marshall climbed on to a flat roof and immediately he could see the woman up on the ledge near him, as smoke and flames billowing from the broken windows of her apartment. Marshall quickly located a ladder and propped it under the ledge and began, unsuccessfully, to persuade her to climb down to safety. The woman was afraid of heights and would not budge, so Marshall instead shouted to distract her and then grabbed one of her legs and pulled her onto his shoulder in a crude fireman's carry. With the woman thrown over his shoulder, Marshall started to descent the ladder but, with a loud crack the ladder snapped and the hand he had been using to hold on to the rungs was trapped against the wall, the other wrapped around the terrified woman. Sergeant Marshall began to lose his balance and, as the woman started to lean away from him, his hand was freed but he completely lost his balance and the two of them fell on to the roof. Fortunately, neither of them was badly injured, and more police officers were on hand to drag them both to safety. For his daring actions in saving a woman from a house fire, Sergeant Marshall was awarded the Queen's Commendation for Bravery.

We all know how dangerous and unpredictable the sea can be. Britain is an island, and most of us are never more than a few miles from the coast. Anyone who has watched a cold, stormy sea, with its dark green waters heaving and roiling, and waves smacking onto hard sea-shore rocks, can have felt its enormous power. Every year the sea inevitably claims its victims. Ships get caught in storms and are sunk, people have accidents while enjoying water sports, others are swept away from the land by freakish waves or trapped by rapid and unpredictable tides. It was one of these freakish occurrences that turned an innocent day out at the beach into a life and death struggle for survival.

On 7 February 2004 four young girls aged twelve and thirteen had been happily rock hopping at a place called Seaton Sluice in Collywell Bay on the rocky shore of Northumberland. The winter sea was stormy, with large waves pounding onto the shoreline, but the girls were well above the waterline and considered themselves to be quite safe. Further along the shoreline, men were sea fishing, casting out their long lines into the green water, the slate grey sky low above. The sea was freezing cold and inhospitable at this time of the year in northern England. The four girls sat resting and chatting on a concrete slipway, oblivious to any danger. Suddenly the sea seemed to rear up, and a wall of water crashed down onto the slipway. The girls had been struck by a freak thirty-foot wave that plucked them from their resting place and dragged them out into deeper water in a few frantic, terrifying seconds.

People immediately called the emergency services and, before they arrived, some of the fishermen had managed to pluck two of the girls from the ocean. One of the girls, Emma Douglas, recalled: 'Two fishermen and a woman came into the water with a rope and a harness. I was so numb with cold and shock I could not get the harness over me so I grabbed it with my arm and I was dragged out.'[2]

The first member of the emergency services on the scene was thirty-seven-year-old PC Darren Purvis of Northumbria Police. He could see twelve-year-old Beth Gardner was still close to the shore. Passerby Cath Robins recalled Purvis' determination to save the girls: 'There were people shouting and screaming for ropes. Suddenly one was found and PC Purvis came running down the bank, over a small fence and on to the rocks. He pulled his tunic off, tied the rope around himself and just went straight in. He never hesitated. He is a real hero.'[3] Purvis managed to grab hold of Beth and dragged her back to the rocky shore where passersby pulled her from the sea. Another girl, Jade Anderson, had drifted too far out for Purvis to reach her in the turbulent water. She was motionless and floating face down. A police helicopter was quickly at the scene and the pilot used the rotor's downdraft to push Anderson back towards the shore.[4] Once the distance had been shortened, Purvis once again jumped into the freezing water and pulled the unconscious girl to safety.

An ambulance rushed the four girls to the local hospital but tragically, Jade Anderson died in the early hours of the following morning. The other three were suffering from shock and hypothermia but they were otherwise unharmed. PC Purvis, who is married with a young son, said afterwards: 'You have to think that was your son out there and you wouldn't want people to stand back and simply watch.'[5] Jade's mother, Sandra Bland, said of Purvis: 'We may not have had the outcome we wanted for Jade, but had it not been for his bravery Beth may also have died. He risked his own life trying to save Jade and for that we will be eternally grateful. In our opinion he is a hero.'[6] Constable Purvis' courage was recognized when he was awarded the Queen's Commendation for Bravery in November 2004.

Flames licked from the windows of a flat located on the fourteenth floor of a block in the town of Stevenage in Hertfordshire during the early hours of a cold February morning in 2005. Down below in the street, the first fire appliances had just arrived and firefighters were making their equipment and water sources ready before they tackled the high-rise conflagration. Two of the firefighters, twenty-six-year-old Michael Miller and Jeffrey Wornham, who was twenty-eight, had already climbed up the many flights of stairs towards the source of the blaze to assess the situation. They were in contact with their colleagues down below by radio. Suddenly, from inside the burning flat, came the sound of a man calling for help. Neither Miller nor Wornham had completed dressing in their protective equipment before they had set off on their reconnaissance, and they lacked special breathing apparatus but, hearing the cries, neither man hesitated.

Disregarding their own safety, the two young firemen forced their way through the front door into the smoke-filled flat. There they quickly discovered Nicholas Savage, the thirty-seven-year-old owner, and helped him to safety. But Savage was desperate – telling Miller and Wornham that his girlfriend, Natalie Close, who was the mother of two children, was trapped further inside the flat. Without waiting for backup or the proper equipment to combat the dense, poisonous smoke, the two brave firemen plunged back into the blazing flat to search for Close. 'By then the conditions were deteriorating rapidly with intense heat and zero visibility.' The fire was growing in ferocity, devouring furnishings inside the flat and producing thick, choking, black smoke. Tragically, on this occasion Miller and Wornham did not emerge. Both of them had been overcome by the blaze and perished inside the flat, along with thirty-two-year-old Natalie Close.

Without a question of doubt, if Miller and Wornham had not gone into the burning flat, Nicholas Savage would have died alongside his girlfriend. 'They were both incredibly brave,' said Wornham's mother, Christine, 'To go into a flat fire once without support is courageous but then to go back in again is just incredibly courageous and brave.'[7] Of her son she said: 'He always was a boy that put others in front of himself. He was like that throughout his life.'[8] When it was announced that both Miller and Wornham had been awarded the George Medal[9], Miller's father Howard said: 'It doesn't bring me or, I doubt, the Wornhams any more comfort, but it makes us even more proud than we already were…You can understand why they have been given such a high award. The circumstances were quite incredibly heroic. I would have run a mile, but neither Michael or Jeff did.'[10]

In January 2009 Jason Pardoe, a thirty-four-year-old printer, had been on the night shift at his company in Hereford when he had felt unwell and decided to head home early. He was walking along the bank of the River Wye at 3 am, when he had suddenly heard the frantic cries of a woman coming from the water. Running over to the river bank, Pardoe could make out a young woman thrashing about in the icy river, clearly in considerable distress and trouble, and screaming for help. The temperature of the water was close to only just above freezing, and the current was strong after several days of heavy rain. Pardoe realized that he was the woman's only hope and he decided to act fast to save her from drowning.

Pardoe pulled his mobile phone out of his coat pocket and quickly called the police, reporting where he was and what was happening. Then he dove straight into the freezing water fully clothed and struck out for the woman. He grabbed hold of her, but the current swept them both further downstream. As they floated along, Pardoe managed to reach out and grabbed a tree branch to stop them. For an incredible thirty minutes Pardoe kept the woman's head above water while also holding onto the tree branch, both of them immersed in the freezing water, desperately waiting for help to arrive. 'We were clinging to each other and were both very cold and we were literally praying for the boat to turn up,'[11] recalled Pardoe. Firefighters from Hereford and Worcester Fire Service arrived and rescued the pair. Pardoe and the young woman were treated in hospital for hypothermia, but were otherwise unharmed by their ordeal. A spokesman for the Fire Brigade said of Pardoe: 'I don't think it's any exaggeration to call him a hero. Any person would have known that their life was at risk doing what he did. It was very unusual that anybody would still be alive in water the temperature that it was.' 'I'm not a hero,' said Pardoe. 'The people in the emergency services are the real heroes. Somebody was in trouble and I wanted to help them. I'm OK and I'm just grateful we both came out of the situation alive.' Jason Pardoe was later awarded the Royal Humane Society Certificate for Saving Life.

Another dramatic river rescue that went tragically wrong illustrates the enormous bravery of ordinary passersby. At around 1 am on a cold December night in 2009, builder Sean Griffiths was walking home after a night out in Bideford, Devon when he saw a young man throw himself into the River Torridge. Eighteen-year-old Sean Mason was apparently attempting to commit suicide. Griffiths, age forty and with a young child at home, immediately dived into the black water in an attempt to save Mason's life. Other passersby who saw the two men in the water immediately called the emergency services, while another threw Griffiths a life ring. It was unfortunately too late. Griffiths was unconscious in the water at Bideford Quay when he was spotted by the first police officer on the scene. PC Jeanne Hellyer herself plunged into the freezing water in an attempt to rescue him. She dragged Griffiths back to the shore where firefighters tried to resuscitate him, but it was too late. Ironically, Mason survived and was taken to hospital for treatment. It is hoped and expected that Sean Griffiths outstanding bravery will be recognised in due course, for the selflessness of strangers remains one of the truly extraordinary characteristics of the British people.

1 *The London Gazette*, 30 November 2004, Supplement No. 2, 15070

2 '*Bravery award for sea rescue PC*', BBC News, 30 November 2004

3 '*PC saves girls in wave tragedy*' by fencom, Police999, http://www.police999.com, accessed 31 July 2009

4 *The London Gazette*, 30 November 2004, Supplement No.2, 15070

5 '*Heroic police officer honoured*', *Sunderland Echo*, 8 December 2004

6 Ibid.

7 '*Tragic firefighter honoured for bravery*', *East Anglian Daily Times*, 30 November 2007

8 Ibid.

9 *The London Gazette*, 26 November 2007, Supplement No. 1, 17199

10 '*George Medals for hero firefighters*' by Sara Black, *Hertfordshire Mercury*, 27 October 2007

11 '*Hero plunges into icy river to save drowning woman – and holds her afloat for 30 MINUTES*' by Daily Mail Reporter, The Daily Mail

CHAPTER 6

Terror on the Streets

'We could all stand still or lie down and say, "Oh, it's somebody else's job," doesn't get anybody anywhere. You've got to do something. You don't think about it. If you stop to think about it, you just couldn't do it. You'd be mesmerized and transfixed to the spot.'

Arthur Burton-Garbett

Islamic terrorism has been an ever-present threat in mainland Britain since the tragic September 11, 2001, attacks on the World Trade Center in New York, and especially so since the horrific London transport bombings of 2005. Police officers and vigilant citizens remain the thin blue line of defence against individuals and groups who are determined to perpetrate the most heinous acts of murder and violence against innocent people. The language of the terrorist is the bomb. We read daily in the newspapers of the incredible heroism of British service personnel tackling terrorism at the grass roots level in Afghanistan but, all too often, brave police officers at home are overlooked, sometimes shamefully so, by the government. An especially pertinent story is that of the heroism and untimely death of Stephen Oake in Manchester in 2003.

The police forces of Britain work together to combat terrorist groups wherever they operate throughout the nation. Headed by the Counter Terrorism Command (SO15) of London's Metropolitan Police and, the National Police Intelligence Service, Britain's answer to America's FBI, they hope to prevent terrorist attacks long before the bombs are set off and people are killed or injured. The Security

Service (MI5) also works alongside Britain's police in gathering intelligence and investigating the various groups that are plotting outrages in Britain today. In the end though, it often comes down to the bravery of individual police officers who have to make the actual arrests of terrorist suspects, and this can lead to extremely dangerous situations.

Forty-year-old Detective Constable Stephen Oake was serving with Greater Manchester Police and was part of a raid on a suspected Islamic terrorist named Kamel Bourgass who lived in a flat in the city. When the police broke down Bourgass's front door, Bourgass panicked and, thoroughly determined that he would escape arrest, he quickly snatched up a kitchen knife and began slashing wildly at the officers. 'When Stephen Oake entered that flat Bourgass had already attacked and almost murdered another officer,'[1] said Paul Kelly, chairman of the Greater Manchester Police Federation. Realising that his colleagues were in mortal danger Oake moved immediately to try and disarm Bourgass, although he himself was unarmed. 'When he tackled that evil man he knew he was going to be at the very least seriously injured,' said Kelly. 'He knew he was putting his life on the line.'[2] Tragically, Detective Constable Oake was stabbed in the heart and both lungs by twenty-seven-year-old Bourgass and died at the scene.

Stephen Oake's colleagues submitted a request that their fallen comrade should be awarded Britain's highest award for civilian gallantry, the George Cross. In February 2006 the awards committee caused an huge outcry in police and public circles when it recommended to the government that, astoundingly, Oake should not receive the George Cross – *or any award whatsoever.* 'It is almost 30 years since a police officer received this award,' said Paul Kelly. 'We have lost a number of police officers since then but this is the first time we have felt moved to call for this award to be given.'[3] Mr. Kelly added: 'If Stephen's actions do not warrant a serious consideration then I don't know what would. It is always said that every police officer puts his life on the line when they go out on patrol, but the reality is we don't. What Stephen did was over and above what normal officers do.'[4] It seemed inconceivable that the government could ignore the evident bravery of this police officer, who had saved the lives of his colleagues and, in doing so, forfeited his own in the line of duty.

Many police officers and members of the public suspected that the decision not to recognise Oake's bravery was politically motivated. Tony Blair's government was deeply involved at the time in two unpopular wars in Iraq and Afghanistan, and had stirred up extremism and militancy among many in Britain's own Muslim communities by supporting President Bush's confused foreign policy adventures. Being seen to reward someone for doing their job supporting unpopular government policies, was evidently too much for the bureaucrats in Whitehall. Fortunately for Oake's family and colleagues, the various police associations around the country were not prepared to stand for this insult to the memory of a brave officer. A campaign was organised that eventually resulted in an embarrassing U-turn by the government – a decision that was roundly welcomed by most people as absolutely right.

The pressure exerted on the government eventually led to the grudging award of a posthumous Queen's Gallantry Medal after a five-year campaign. 'It would have been nice had the award been made much earlier,' said Chris Burrows, chairman of the Greater Manchester branch of the Police Federation. Chief Constable Peter Fahy of Greater Manchester Police summed up the feelings of many officers when he wrote:

> We are still one of the few forces in the world that are routinely unarmed. That's a responsibility that British police officers carry and clearly we would hope that the honour system would recognise that and particularly the bravery of British police officers who have to demonstrate their bravery because they are routinely unarmed.[5]

It was not to be the last occasion when the motivations of the government were to be questioned over the distribution of gallantry awards.

It was just another ordinary working day in Europe's biggest city. The main-line stations of London were crowded with commuters piling into the city on trains from the surrounding counties, most of the workers heading straight for the Underground system on the morning of 7 July 2005. Tens of thousands of people stood on escalators that took them smoothly down into the windy labyrinthine depths below the great metropolis, while outside the stations hundreds of other commuters stood patiently in orderly queues waiting to board red double-decker buses or hailed ubiquitous black cabs.

The people of Britain were in a good mood as, only the day before, it had been announced that Britain would host the 2012 Olympic Games, the first time the world's most important sporting event had come to the nation since 1948. The newspapers were full of Olympic triumph, as well as reports from Gleneagles Hotel in Scotland where Prime Minister Tony Blair was about to host the first full day of the important G8 summit of the top industrialized nations. Britain was the focus of world attention that summer morning but unknown to the workers and politicians, it was about to become a focus of the world's horror and disbelief as well. Unbeknown to anyone, moving through the cheerful and polite crowds of commuters that morning were men with evil in their hearts, men who hated everything Britain stood for, and who believed that the outrages they were about to perpetrate would guarantee each of them a special place with their god.

Three Muslim fanatics, each carrying a large bomb concealed inside a backpack, boarded three different Underground trains just at the height of the rush hour. All of the bombs exploded within fifty seconds of each other, around 8.50 am, when the metropolis's transport network was at its most crowded. Not since the dark days of 'The Troubles' in Northern Ireland, which had seen a vicious bombing campaign initiated on the mainland by the IRA, had London faced a more direct threat to its peace and security.

The first explosion occurred on board Circle Line train 204, which was travelling eastbound between Liverpool Street Station and Aldgate. The train had left King's Cross St. Pancras Station only eight minutes earlier. The bomb was detonated in the third carriage when the train was about 100 yards down the tunnel from Liverpool Street. The second bomb went off aboard the westbound Circle Line train 216, which had just pulled away from Platform 4 at Edgware Road headed for Paddington Station. An eastbound Circle Line train was passing next to it when the terrorist blew himself up, damaging this second train as well. Piccadilly Line train 311 was travelling between King's Cross St. Pancras and Russell Square when a bomb exploded at the rear of the first carriage only one minute after the train had left King's Cross Station.

Detective Constable Antonio Silvestro of the British Transport Police, the whose duties included patrolling the London Underground, was the first officer on the scene at Aldgate Station following the explosion. 'I was in my office working on my computer and heard a loud bang and the building really did shake,' said Silvestro afterwards. 'My initial thought was that...something had driven into the building, so I rushed down the stairs and everybody was looking into the station.'[6] Off-duty Metropolitan Police Constable Elizabeth Kenworthy, who was involved in the bombing, initially thought that her train had been involved in an accident. 'There was a bang and the train had smoke coming in,' Kenworthy later recalled. 'I tried to send a text message to inform someone of the accident and that I was ok, but it wouldn't go through. I could hear people shouting. I got out my badge to inform people I was a police officer.'[7] Kenworthy had been with Haringey Police since 1987, and at the time of the bombings she was Safer Schools Officer for Gladesmore Secondary School. She had been on the way to a meeting in Westminster when the explosion occurred. 'I could see people coming towards me shouting and I knew something had happened.'[8] Instead of escaping, Kenworthy instinctively headed instead towards the danger and she began moving through the carriages to the seat of the explosion. A man tried to stop her but she showed him her warrant card and continued on through the smoke. 'At first I thought the train had crashed but when I saw the damage I knew it hadn't,' recalled Kenworthy. She was confronted by, in the words of her Borough Commander, Chief Superintendent Dave Grant, 'scenes of absolute carnage.'[9]

At Aldgate Station, plain clothes officer Antonio Silvestro identified himself as a policeman to the crowds of people milling about the station entrance. He then walked into the smoke-filled tunnel and soon encountered commuters who were slowly walking towards the exit with torn clothes and their hair in disarray. 'You know that Michael Jackson video Thriller? With people walking with their hair sticking out and white eyes? There was people coming through like that. They were like zombies walking out so I just shouted 'police, police, keep going.'[10]

'The carriage had been torn open like a can opener,' said PC Kenworthy when she arrived at the bombed carriage, 'disemboweled, I crawled through the door to get inside.' Chief Superintendent Grant commented: 'She was incredibly brave, when the natural instinct is to run away from horror, Liz went into it...she literally kept people alive by keeping her head and remaining calm and professional. That's a difficult thing to do given the sights she was seeing and the conditions she was faced with.'[11] When DC Silvestro reached the tunnel he found the bomb devastated train carriage. 'The doors were ripped off and there was mangled metal everywhere, and people screaming.' PC Kenworthy set to work trying to help the injured, many of whom were grievously wounded. 'I didn't have a lot of time to think, it was just a case of getting on with it. I found people who were trapped and delivered first aid. I had no communications, all I could do was give first aid and stay with the injured.'[12] Kenworthy saved three of the four very seriously injured, including one man whose legs had been blown off. Without her professionalism, all four would probably have died in the shattered carriage.

Horrific blast injuries had been inflicted on many of the survivors at the three bombings, as the terrorists had deliberately detonated their suicide bombs within the enclosed train carriages while they were inside the tunnel system to concentrate the power of the blasts. 'As I looked into the carriage there was a couple,' recalled Silvestro. 'They were sat down and directly across them there was this female, and she was being kept up by another woman who I eventually found out was a doctor.'[13] The female victim had lost one of her legs.

Fifty-three-year-old teacher Tim Coulson was aboard the eastbound Circle Line train that was damaged by the bomb on Train 216 as the carriages passed each other in the tunnel. Coulson, who had suffered cuts, bruises and temporary hearing loss in the explosion, and would later suffer the effects of smoke inhalation, smashed the window of his carriage, climbed through and crossed over the rail lines to try to help the many injured. He discovered Australian Alison Sayer, who had been blown out of the carriage by the force of the explosion, and gave her first aid and comfort. The father of five, who also has three grandchildren, climbed into the bomb blasted carriage to be met by a scene of utter devastation and horror. Many people had been killed when the bomb went off, and many more were seriously injured. The carriage was completely wrecked. Coulson tried to help Stan Brewster who had lost both of his legs in the blast, but Brewster succumbed to his massive injuries and died in Coulson's arms. Later, Coulson helped an inexperienced emergency services worker who was overcome by the scenes of horror inside the carriage.[14]

Tube train driver David Matthews was taking a meal break when one of the bombs went off. 'The table jumped and I knew something was wrong,' he said. 'But we never suspected a bomb. We were dealing with chaos and we still didn't realise what it was.'[15] Although not members of the emergency services, Matthews and his fellow staff members were at the forefront of helping people. 'We were waiting for the emergency services to arrive. But they were dealing with the other explosions and didn't get to us for 40 minutes,' he recalled. 'So it was left to staff and passengers to get on with it. There were 1,500 people on the train and within 20 minutes we had everyone that could walk evacuated. Only the seriously injured and the dead were still inside.'[16]

Inspector Glen McMunn was one of several British Transport Police officers who were at the site of the Russell Square bomb within minutes. He was two hours into his shift at Tottenham Court Road in central London when the phone rang, and he was informed that there had been a power surge at Liverpool Street Station. Initially, the bomb blasts were reported in the media to have been the results of a power surge blowing up circuits on the Tube system.

When McMunn and a colleague arrived at Liverpool Street he liaised immediately with firefighters, who had responded to a report of a person under a train at Edgware Road tube station. As McMunn headed for Edgware Road he was called again – this time informing him that large numbers of people were emerging from Russell Square Station with what looked like bomb blast injuries. 'I knew there were already people dealing with the Edgware situation so I diverted to Russell Square,' recalled McMunn. 'I got there about 9.20 am; we were the first police vehicle on the scene.'[17] McMunn saw large numbers of commuters, their clothes and faces blackened with soot, stumbling from the station entrance, many bleeding from multiple wounds. 'I originally thought that they had been travelling on the train, but they had just been standing on the platform when they were hit by the bomb blast,' recalled McMunn.

Stephen Hucklesby, a forty-three-year-old policy advisor for the Methodist Church, was in the same carriage as Tim Coulson when his train was damaged by an explosion. He too went to assist the victims of the bomb. 'The blast was enormous,' said Hucklesby, 'and it was a scene of carnage and devastation inside [the carriage]. I jumped into the bombed carriage because I had done a first aid course but nothing prepares you for that sort of carnage. It was obvious people had been killed in the blast carriage. I had to work out who needed attention – who was alive and who wasn't.'[18] Hucklesby worked hard to try to save the injured. 'Largely, it was a question of getting people down on the ground inside the carriage, making them comfortable, and stemming the bleeding,'[19] he said later.

Two other passengers at the Edgware Road bombing behaved with great bravery in trying to help victims. Adrian Heili was traveling on the westbound Circle Line train. When the explosion occurred towards the front of the carriage, Heili saw flames dancing around outside. The train slowed down, and thick choking black smoke filled the carriage. Heili could hear someone calling for help. He went to investigate, leaving the carriage through the connecting door. Whilst he was going this he tried to calm his fellow passengers down by shouting advice and instructions to them. He soon realized that an injured man had been thrown from the train by the blast and was trapped underneath the carriage.

Hurrying towards the two stopped Circle Line trains in the tunnel was train driver Lee Hunt and his colleagues. Hunt had been on a refreshment break in a room above the station when he had heard the explosion. As Hunt and his colleagues hastened across the tracks, they found the lifeless body of a women lying in the dirt. She had been blown off the train. Hunt could hear a man screaming from beneath one of the trains, the same man Adrian Heili was trying to locate.

Heili made his way to the front of the train to meet the driver and explain that he was trained in administering first aid. Heili and Hunt crawled down underneath the train to assist the wounded man, applying tourniquets to both of his legs and dressing a head and other wounds. Heili stayed with the man until paramedics eventually arrived and carefully evacuated him, with Heili's assistance, on a stretcher. 'During this time, a queue of passengers had built up because they were unable to pass between the train and the tunnel wall due to the injured man's position,' read Hunt's citation. 'He attempted to find an alternative route for evacuation but, unable to do so, placated them to remain there until the man was taken out to safety.'

After borrowing some medical equipment from the medics, instead of allowing himself to be evacuated Heili returned to the shattered carriage and started treating more of the wounded passengers. Hunt joined him. The two men stayed on the train working alongside medical staff until the last casualty had been removed. Only then did Heili and Hunt make their own way up to the surface. During his time at the site, Hunt also assisted medical staff by drawing a diagram for the Fire Brigade so that they could arrange more lighting at the scene. For their actions, both Heili and Hunt were awarded the Queen's Commendation for Bravery[1]. Heili received the Royal Humane Society Silver Medal for his efforts to save passengers, and he was further honoured by the RHS when he was given the gold Stanhope Medal, the highest award for bravery, awarded once annually to the most outstanding existing medal winner from Britain, Australia, Canada and New Zealand.[2]

At Russell Square Station, Inspector McMunn and his colleagues from the British Transport Police were trying to work out what had happened. McMunn crossed to the Piccadilly Line platform, where the bombed train had travelled after it had departed from King's Cross St. Pancras. 'When I got down there I saw the driver of the train on the platform. He was hysterical and just waving his arms saying a "bombs gone off, a bombs gone off".'[20] The Piccadilly Line tunnel was one of the deepest on the Underground, and there was little room for emergency services to work in. McMunn quickly explained to four paramedics what had happened. It was obvious that

---

[1] This award is open to both British subjects and foreigners for bravery entailing risk to life and meriting national recognition. It consists of a certificate and a spray of laurel leaves, silver for civilians and bronze for military personnel, worn on any associated medal, or if no medal was issued, pinned to the left breast.
[2] The Royal Humane Society was set up in 1774 to recognize acts of bravery in the saving of human life. They annually award a series of nationally recognized medals to military, emergency services and civilians. The Stanhope Medal was established in 1873, and is the most prestigious award. Below this is the Silver Medal, which dates from 1775, followed by the Police Medal (established 2000) and the Bronze Medal (established 1837).

people must be trapped inside the wrecked train which was about 300 yards down the tunnel. 'We didn't know if there had been a secondary device planted in there or if there were any chemicals down there, but they [the paramedics] all agreed to come down with me,'[21] said McMunn.

By now McMunn had seven British Transport Police and several plain clothes officers with him to begin the search for survivors. The tunnel was the closest any of them would ever see to the second ring of hell. Long, soot-blackened brick walls lit only by weak emergency lights led towards the mangled remains of the train carriage. Thick, choking black smoke filled the tunnel from the fire that had engulfed the carriage after the explosion. Through the gloom, pierced by the police officers' torches, stumbled figures, survivors disorientated wounded who were desperately trying to find their way out of this tomb-like hole in the ground into the light of the world above. When McMunn climbed into the carriage he was confronted by a scene of bloody mayhem. 'It was like Armageddon,' he said later. 'The doors were blown out, there was blood everywhere and body parts. I think 22 people died in that first carriage.'[22]

The first casualty the paramedics encountered inside the destroyed carriage was a man with half of one of his legs missing. McCann and the emergency workers had to treat people as best they could and get them out as quickly as possible. 'Virtually one of the first people we went to was Gill Hicks, she sat up and you could see that she had lost one of her legs. She had lost a lot of blood, you could see one of the legs was literally only attached by a sinew, but she was conscious.'[23]

What Tim Coulson witnessed on the Underground that morning had a profound impact on his life. He suffered from Post Traumatic Stress Disorder and had to take early retirement from his job at Queen Mary's College in Basingstoke. When he was told that he, along with five other people caught up in the London bombings, were to be made a Member of the Order of the British Empire (MBE), he said: 'This reward says to me that I did the right thing. I sometimes wonder if it would have been better to have walked away.'[24] Coulson was also awarded the Bronze Medal from the Royal Humane Society for his efforts to save lives. Others honoured by the

RHS were Alison Macarthy, who saved the lives of two severely injured passengers and received the Silver Medal, as well as Peter Zimonjic and Wing Commander Craig Staniforth, based at RAF Lynham in Norfolk, who received the Bronze Medal for their extraordinary efforts on 7 July.

Incredibly, when Mr. Coulson and the other five people honoured with MBEs in 2009 were initially proposed for awards by friends, colleagues and the emergency services, the government had rejected them. In 2006 twenty-three members of the emergency services and civilians had been honoured by the government for their part in saving lives during the bombings[3], but many had also been overlooked at that time. In a letter to Mrs. Coulson, who had recommended her husband for official recognition, a Cabinet Office civil servant had written that honours could only be given to people 'for meritorious service over a sustained period and not for specifically saving someone's life'[25]. Considering how many actors and sports personalities, not to mention civil servants, receive national honours virtually as part and parcel of their jobs, the deliberate snubbing of the overlooked heroes of 7/7 smacked of hypocrisy. Fortunately this situation was rectified by Prime Minister Gordon Brown in the Queen's Birthday Honours of 2009, four years after the tragic events in London.

'I was lucky that day, I wasn't hurt,' said Elizabeth Kenworthy, who was one of the five overlooked heroes who was made an MBE in 2009. 'seven people were killed on my train. I think I did the right thing, I was very calm, this is what I needed to do.'[26] David Matthews and Antonio Silvestro were also made MBEs, along with Australian-born Gill Hicks, who unfortunately lost both of her legs in the bombings but who went on to found a charity that tries to bring communities together. Stephen Hucklesby said self-effacingly when informed of the award of an MBE, 'A lot of people helped there on that day and I was only one of them…I was only doing what anyone else would do in those circumstances.'[27]

The grim toll of death and destruction was not yet over for London. Less than an hour after the Underground explosions, and while pandemonium reigned beneath London's streets and

[3] See Appendix 2

conflicting news reports tried to provide explanations for what had occurred, another suicide bomber boarded one of London's eponymous red double-decker buses. At 9.47 am a huge explosion tore off the roof of the upper deck and destroyed the back of the No. 30 bus in Tavistock Square, as it plied its route between Marble Arch and Hackney Wick. Probationary police officer PC Ashley Walker, aged twenty-six, was only 100 yards from the bus when the bomb went off as the vehicle passed in front of the British Medical Association headquarters building. PC Walker was on duty in Euston Road, busy putting out traffic bollards and directing traffic following the earlier blast near King's Cross Station. 'I just heard the noise and saw debris flying off,' recalled Walker. 'I knew instantly it was a bomb.'[28] Pandemonium reigned in the street as pedestrians fled towards the only policeman that they could see. 'Hundreds of people were turning and running towards me,' said Walker. 'You don't have time to think or be scared.' Walker ran towards the wrecked bus. 'The roof had been blown off the bus and I ran around to the double doors at the side. [Passengers] were falling and throwing themselves off the top deck while the bottom deck was full of panicking people trying to get off.'[19] Added to the chaos were other people who were trying to get on to the bus to help those still inside. Although Walker was new to the job, he knew that he had to take charge, as he was the only policeman at the scene at that time. People were looking to him for leadership. He did not fail in his duty and, standing just inside the bus, he quickly oversaw the evacuation of those who could walk. He then personally administered first aid to around twenty badly injured passengers before spending the rest of the day on patrol outside the British Medical Association building. One month earlier Walker had demonstrated great courage when he had tackled an armed man in Kentish Town Road who was threatening people with a loaded gun.

Another thirteen people were killed by the bus bomb at Tavistock Square, to add to the thirty-nine who had died earlier that morning on the Underground system. It was the bloodiest day in London since the last German air attacks of the Second World War six decades earlier. PC Walker later received the Commissioner's Commendation, the Metropolitan Police's highest award for bravery, for his courage and leadership in tackling the after effects of the Tavistock Square bomb.

London was targeted for a second time later in July 2005 by another terrorist cell. Once again their targets were to be in London's transport network, where they hoped to cause the maximum loss of life and damage. Repeating the pattern of attacks that had been successfully carried out by suicide bombers on 7 July, a newly emerged terrorist cell that consisted of at least four young Muslims dispersed into the capital on the morning of 21 July. Each was wearing a rucksack that contained a six-and-a-quarter litre clear plastic food container packed with a bomb and armed with a detonator. The homemade explosive that the bombers were using gave off a distinctive and unpleasant odour. Three of the bombers boarded Tube trains, and a fourth a double-decker bus in a repeat of the 7 July attacks. At 12.26 pm an explosion was reported at Shepherd's Bush station in west London on the Hammersmith and City Line. At 12.30 pm a second explosion occurred at Oval Station on the Northern Line, followed by another smaller detonation fifteen minutes later on a Victoria Line train at Warren Street Station.

Off-duty firefighter Angus Campbell was on his way to work on the Northern Line train that was targeted by Somali bomber Ramzi Mohammed. He noticed Mohammed in the carriage, with his large rucksack and the furtive glances that he was nervously casting around him. Mohammed suddenly turned his back to a mother and infant who were sitting opposite him and activated his suicide bomb. There was a loud bang as the detonator exploded and what looked like flour began spilling out onto the floor of the carriage. The train was moving, and the passengers were terrified, screaming and trying to move away from Mohammed, many sure that a terrible explosion was about to follow.

Instinctively, Campbell moved the woman and the child to the back of the carriage and then turned his wrath upon the suicide bomber. 'What's that?' he shouted at Mohammed. 'What the fucking hell is that?' he said as he pointed at the rucksack and the debris on the floor of the carriage. 'What is it? What is it?' bellowed Campbell at the Somali extremist. 'You tell me now what the fuck that is!' Mohammed laughed and shouted back: 'This is flour, this is fucking flour.'[30] Campbell ordered Mohammed to lie down and 'be submissive to me!', but the train had just arrived at the Oval station, and as soon as the doors opened Mohammed fled along the platform. At this point sixty-eight-year-old George Brawley, a retired engineer, grabbed hold of Mohammed but the younger man broke free and continued running 'like Linford Christie. He was really going hell for leather,'[31] recalled Brawley.

Brawley and others were shouting out, 'Stop that man!' but most people were too transfixed by fear or simple bewilderment and they did nothing to stop the fleeing terrorist – all except another pensioner and former journalist, Arthur Burton-Garbett. As Mohammed vaulted up the escalator to the exit, Burton-Garbett tried to grab him. He shouted 'stop that man, he's a bomber,' but Mohammed escaped into the street. Burton-Garbett said later: 'My father and other people's fathers fought for this country in two world wars, and why should these people just try and blow us to bits? I thought the absolute audacity to try and bomb my city, and I wasn't standing for it.'[32] For his bravery in confronting and remonstrating with a crazed bomber armed with a backpack full of explosives and perhaps other concealed weapons, Firefighter Angus Campbell received the Queen's Gallantry Medal. 'Most firefighters would have done exactly what I did,' he said later. 'I was at that time, at that place and hopefully did my best. Would I have done anything different and no I don't think I would.'

At 1.30 pm the last small explosion occurred on the No. 26 bus when it was on Hackney Road at the corner of Columbia Road in Shoreditch in East London as it followed its route from Waterloo Station to Hackney Wick. Muktah Said Ibrahim was sitting on the top deck when he tried to detonate his rucksack bomb. Mark Maybanks, the bus driver, was startled. 'The sound of the bang was…was very loud. I really must admit that I thought I was gonna see the top part of me bus gone.'[33] Maybanks slammed on the brakes and evacuated his passengers into the street, among them Ibrahim who furtively slipped off with the crowd and then fled the scene of the crime.

Fortunately, none of the explosions was any bigger than a large firework. Only the detonator caps fired and the actual bombs had failed to detonate. Police explosives experts later established that the bombs may have failed because of the low quality hydrogen peroxide that had been used in making the devices. If the bombs had exploded, dozens would have been killed and many more horrifically injured in a dreadful second act to the 7 July atrocities.

Police moved quickly to try and capture the bombers who, had all fled the scenes of their failed martyrdoms. At 2.30 pm, loud bangs were heard in University College Hospital after armed police chased a man into the building who was suspected of being a bomber from Warren Street Station. Police later said that the reports were not gunshots, but more bomb detonators exploding. London Underground staff reported seeing one of the bombers trying to detonate his bomb after it failed to explode by firing a handgun into his rucksack. This also failed to cause an explosion and the terrorist ran off.

On 23 July police discovered an abandoned rucksack bomb of the same construction as those used in the London bombings of 7 July in some bushes in Little Wormwood Scrubs just north of White City and Shepherd's Bush in west London. It was destroyed by a controlled explosion, leading police to suspect that there was a fifth bomber at large in the city on 21 July who has never been positively identified.

The massive police effort to capture those responsible for attempting to commit mass murder on London's transport network soon bagged the four failed bombers. Yasin Hassan Omar was arrested in Birmingham on 27 July, followed by Muktor Said Ibrahim and Ramzi Mohammed on the 29th in London, and Osman Hussein in Rome. Hussein was later extradited back to Britain to stand trial. Whabi Mohammed, Ramzi's brother, was arrested on 28 July on suspicion of being the fifth bomber, as well as Manfo Kwaku Asiedu who was charged as well. These men were charged with conspiracy to commit murder. A further nine other suspects were charged by police with withholding information. The four failed suicide bombers, Ibrahim, Omar, Mohammed and Hussein were found guilty and each was sentenced to a minimum of forty years in prison.

It is not just in the UK that British citizens are faced with terrorism – increasingly, British civilians with expert skills are working in the terrorists' backyards. An airfield in Yemen was protected by a group of scruffy and bored looking Yemeni Army guards in dirty uniforms, clutching Soviet-made Kalashnikov AK-47 assault rifles – the Third World's weapon of choice. The guards looked disinterested as David Duguid, a British security operative, escorted his client across the airstrip under the boiling summer sun. Yemen was a nation struggling with internal terrorism and from groups linked to al-Qaeda, and in 2000 this had been graphically illustrated when an American warship, the destroyer USS *Cole*, had been attacked by a suicide boat in Aden harbour as she was refueling. The boat, packed with about 1,000 pounds of explosives, had come along the port side of the warship and been detonated. The blast blew a huge hole in the side of the *Cole*, killed seventeen sailors and injured thirty-nine others. The first ship on the scene to offer help was a British frigate, HMS *Marlborough*.

Duguid, who was unarmed but was accompanied by a driver and an armed escort, waited patiently as his client's aircraft landed and taxied to a halt. Duguid began to move towards the aircraft but suddenly he felt a pain in his arm and heard the distinctive bark of automatic fire. He realized that he had been shot. A terrorist attack was unfolding before his eyes as he sought cover. Several people lay wounded on the dusty tarmac, while a Yemeni soldier fired bursts from his AK-47 at them, and at the plane. The soldier moved out of Duguid's sight around the far side of the plane, still firing bursts of automatic fire. Duguid decided that he was going to overpower the gunman before he murdered dozens of people, and he quickly broke cover in the hope of the surprising the soldier and getting the weapon away from him. Unfortunately, as Duguid came loping across the tarmac half-crouched to present a smaller target, the Yemeni spotted him and fired in his direction. Duguid dived back under cover again.

At this point Duguid saw that the soldier had turned his attention to the wounded casualties who were lying in the open. He began to fire at them, evidently determined to finish them off execution style. In an act of immense personal courage Duguid broke cover again in the hope of drawing the gunman's fire off the wounded. His ruse worked and the soldier immediately began firing at Duguid again, but Duguid's armed escort shot back and wounded the soldier. Duguid saw his chance and charged in and overpowered the gunman. After dealing with the guard, and ignoring the pain from the bullet wound that he had received to his arm, Duguid set about helping the other wounded. The plane had been holed by the fusillade of bullets aimed at it. Aviation fuel was leaking all over the tarmac and the chance of an explosion and a fireball was very great. Duguid, ignoring this peril, set up a triage and applied life-saving first-aid to the wounded. He then made arrangements for the wounded to be conveyed to a local hospital and stayed with them in the vehicle during their journey. Because of his bravery only one man died as a result of the shooting. David Duguid was awarded the Queen's Gallantry Medal in 2009.[34]

Engine revving, a Jeep Cherokee car accelerated towards the entrance to the terminal of Glasgow International Airport at 3.11 pm on Saturday, 30 June 2007. With a loud bang, the vehicle crashed into a barrier that was located in front of the plate-glass entrance doors, damaging both the barrier and the entrance lobby. People turned in disbelief and concern towards what most thought to be a car accident. Curious passengers and airport staff watched as an Asian man climbed down from the Jeep. A police officer rushed across to the scene of the crash, radioing for assistance as he ran, evidently intending to render assistance to the vehicle's occupants. The Asian man had assaulted a bystander seconds before the policeman arrived, and then he immediately punched the policeman, knocking him to the ground. 'I noticed a four-by-four sitting in the middle of the road,' recalled taxi driver, Alex McIlveen. 'Then, as my passenger was paying and getting out, the Jeep rammed into the airport entrance right next to us.'[35] McIlveen watched, amazed, as the man kicked and punched the bystander to the ground before punching the policeman square in the face. 'That's when I saw red. That sort of thing just isn't on.'

McIlveen wasn't the only person 'to see red' as they witnessed what was happening. John Smeaton, a baggage-handler who was having a cigarette break outside the terminal building, witnessed the unfolding drama. He ran towards the Jeep, which by now was on fire. 'All that was going through my mind was I've got to help the policeman, I'm not letting these guys get away with this.' The car was packed with petrol cans and long gas cylinders, which had turned it into a crude but potentially lethal homemade bomb.[4]

[4] The device was basically a large petrol bomb, and when the gas cylinders ignited they produced a flame-thrower effect. It was a very amateurish device, but it still retained huge potential for causing damage.

The Jeep had contained two terrorists intent on wreaking death and destruction at the airport that afternoon. The driver, Kafeel Ahmed, was a medical doctor who worked at the Royal Alexandra Hospital in Paisley and was of Iraqi descent. His accomplice was Bilah Abdullah. Abdullah was soon fighting like a man possessed with several men who had tried to intervene after he had assaulted the police officer, all the while muttering verses from the Koran. Alex McIlveen tried to tackle Abdullah. 'I went for the passenger and managed to skelp him in the face,' he said. 'I followed it up by booting him twice. I kicked him with full force right in the balls but he didn't go down. He just kept babbling his rubbish.'[36]

The driver of the Jeep, Ahmed, was on fire and he crashed out of the car into the terminal building where another policeman sprayed him with a fire extinguisher. Apparently unharmed by the flames, Ahmed jumped up and started fighting everyone as well. 'He [Ahmed] was going crazy, just lashing out at everyone and babbling...in a foreign language the whole time,' said McIlveen. 'I've heard people say since that he was shouting 'Allah!' but I didn't hear that. It just sounded like a lot of crap to me. I ran for the guy and punched him twice in the face with pretty good right hooks.'[37] McIlveen had been joined in trying to restrain Ahmed by John Smeaton, who yelled 'Fucking come on, then,' before kicking Ahmed hard. Smeaton also helped to drag holidaymaker Michael Kerr away from the scene. Kerr had tried to intervene when Abdullah had first hit the policeman. 'I flew at the guy a few times but he wouldn't go down,' recalled Kerr. 'Then he punched me so hard he knocked my teeth out and sent my flying so hard I broke my leg. I landed next to the burning Jeep and thought it was going to explode. That was when John Smeaton dragged me to safety. He's a hero.'[38]

John Smeaton was awarded the Queen's Gallantry Medal in 2008, but Alex McIlveen, Michael Kerr, and another man involved in foiling the terrorist attack, Stephen Clarkson, have so far been denied official recognition by the government. They all did as much as Smeaton in trying to overpower the two terrorists, but it appears that the decision to ignore their contribution may have some political motivations behind it.

Only the day before, in London, another terrorist bomb attack had been foiled by vigilant emergency workers. The attacks have been formally linked with the attack on Glasgow Airport that had occurred on the following day. Two Mercedes-Benz cars had been rigged with petrol cans and gas cylinders and then fitted with a trigger linked to a mobile phone enabling both bombs to be remotely detonated by the terrorists. The first car bomb was left parked outside the Tiger Tiger nightclub in Haymarket. The second was parked in nearby Cockspur Street. It was only by sheer accident that both car bombs were discovered and made safe before they could injure innocent people.

An ambulance had been called to the club during the night to deal with a minor injury to a patron. While the ambulance staff were attending the scene they noticed strong-smelling and suspicious fumes emanating from a Mercedes parked by the kerb. They reported this to the police, who soon established that the car contained a large bomb. An hour later, in Cockspur Street, another Mercedes was ticketed for parking illegally. An hour later the Mercedes was towed to a pound on Park Lane. Staff at the pound also noticed a strong smell of petrol coming from the car and, after being informed that a car bomb had been discovered only a few blocks away they also called the police. A quick inspection revealed another bomb inside this vehicle as well.

The Metropolitan Police bomb disposal team was alerted, and they began the tricky task of making both devices safe. The car outside the Tiger Tiger Nightclub in the Haymarket was left *in situ* while bomb disposal officer Paul Humphrey went to work. He soon discovered that deployment of the tracked disposal vehicle known as a 'wheel barrow' was likely to set the bomb off, so Humphrey decided to manually disarm the device in very cramped and difficult conditions. The wheel barrow is used by both army and police explosives experts, as it allows operators to remain at a safe distance from the bomb while conducting the operation to defuse it. 'For an hour and a half Mr. Humphrey worked alone inside and outside the vehicle, using hand tools to render the device safe,' read his citation in the *London Gazette*. 'This was done in the dark with the aid of only torchlight.' His fellow police colleague, Gary Wright, defused the bomb on the second car, also by hand and in similarly uncomfortable and extremely dangerous conditions. Humphrey was awarded the Queen's Gallantry Medal for his immense courage in the most testing of conditions, and Wright the Queen's Commendation for Bravery.

The men responsible for the attack on Glasgow International Airport and the failed bomb attacks in London were apprehended by the police. Kafeel Ahmed, the driver of the burning Jeep, died of his injuries in hospital shortly after the attack in Scotland. His accomplice, Bilah Abdullah, was later found guilty of conspiracy to murder and sentenced to thirty-two years in prison. Eight other Asians who were resident in Britain, including five doctors working for the National Health Service, were arrested and questioned by anti-terrorism officers, but no further charges were brought.

There is no front-line in the war on terror. The attacks in London and Glasgow and the murder of a police officer in Manchester have shown that the battlefields of Afghanistan and Iraq are not the only places where people are putting their lives on the line to prevent the spread of Islamic extremism. Pakistan is in the vanguard of that war, a Muslim nation bordering Afghanistan with strong historic links to Britain. The old Northwest Frontier of the British Empire in India has become a new battleground in the 21st Century, as Islamic terrorist groups seek to use parts of northern Pakistan as a base and training ground for the fighting in Afghanistan. The Pakistani government has gratefully accepted assistance from the United States and Britain in the continuing fight against the extremists, and Britain especially has been a staunch supporter of Pakistani efforts to turn the tide against al-Qaeda.

One way that Britain has been able to help is in the training of the Pakistani police's anti-terrorism branch. Specialist officers from New Scotland Yard have been sent to Islamabad as instructors, the years of experience gained in combating Irish Republican terrorism in Britain being put to a new use. Detective Superintendent Keith Pearce was one of the Metropolitan Police's senior anti-terrorist officers who helped to investigated the July 2005 London Bombings. In March 2008, he was in Islamabad passing on his experience to his Pakistani counterparts. One lunch time, he was sitting outside a popular Italian restaurant in the city called Luna Caprese when it was targeted by an extremist's bomb. The restaurant was a major draw and meeting place for expatriates, aid workers, foreign intelligence officers and seconded policemen in the city because it served

The Victoria Cross. Since 1856 the VC has been the pre-eminent award for British and Commonwealth gallantry. Since the Second World War only sixteen have been awarded, including to Private Johnson Beharry of the Princess of Wales's Royal Regiment (Queen's d Royal Hampshires) in 2006 for his incredible eroism in Iraq, and posthumously to Corporal ryan Budd of the Parachute Regiment in 2007, who had single-handedly charged the enemy and saved his section from annihilation in Afghanistan the year before.

Inspector Michael Tanner, British Transport Police. He was awarded the Queen's Gallantry Medal in 2004 after tackling a deranged knifeman in Central London three years earlier, and despite being badly wounded. (*Photograph courtesy of Michael Tanner and the British Transport Police*)

The George Cross. Since 1940 the pre-eminent award for civilian gallantry and for members of the Armed Forces for actions that were not performed in the face of the enemy.

Trooper Christopher Finney, The Blues and Royals (Royal Horse Guards and 1st Dragoons). He was awarded the George Cross in 2004 for his actions in saving a wounded comrade whilst under American fighter-bomber attack in Iraq during a tragic 'blue-on-blue' incident.

William Grove, a concerned 84-year-old pensioner who stepped in to stop a violent smash-and-grab robbery at a jewellers shop in Richmond, London, in 2008. His brave actions set off a major debate about the bravery of more recent generations of British people.

Private Michelle 'Chuck' Norris, Royal Army Medical Corps. The 19-year-old Norris rendered emergency aid to a wounded comrade while under sustained enemy fire during an ambush in Iraq, and she became the first woman to win a Military Cross in 2006.

The Military Cross. Created during the First World War as an award for officers only, in 1993 it was extended for award to all ranks of the Armed Services.

Private Luke Cole, a Territorial Army soldier serving with The Mercian Regiment. During an ambush in Afghanistan in 2007 Cole was awarded the Military Cross for his exceptional heroism despite having been seriously wounded.

Sergeant Paul Leigh and Constable Lukmann Mulla, Lancashire Constabulary. For having braved gunfire and petrol bombs to rescue a wounded colleague, the two police officers were awarded the Queen's Gallantry Medal in 2005. *(Photograph courtesy of Lancashire Constabulary)*

The Queen's Gallantry Medal. Created in 1974 and awarded to both civilians and military personnel.

Flight Lieutenant Michelle Goodman, Royal Air Force. Awarded the Distinguished Flying Cross for her gallantry in piloting a rescue helicopter into a battle, dodging mortar fire, small-arms and the threat of anti-aircraft missiles in order to collect a wounded soldier in 2007. She was the first woman to win a DFC.

The Distinguished Flying Cross, Britain's pre-eminent award for gallantry in the air, created in 1918.

Flight Lieutenant Alex 'Frenchie' Duncan, Royal Air Force. Awarded the Distinguished Flying Cross for saving a severely damaged twin-rotor Chinook that the Taliban attempted to shoot out of the sky over Afghanistan in 2008, and thereby saving the passengers and crew.

Constable Elizabeth Kenworthy, Metropolitan Police Service. One of the overlooked heroines of the 2005 London Transport Bombings, PC Kenworthy was made a Member of the Order of the British Empire (MBE) in 2009 for having rendered first aid to bombing victims, and for saving several lives onboard a devastated Underground train. (Photograph courtesy of Charles Green)

Ladies insignia of a Member of the Order of the British Empire (MBE). Women in uniform receive a man's medal.

The Conspicuous Gallantry Cross. The most recent gallantry award created in Britain in 1993, it ranks second behind the Victoria Cross and George Cross Since its introduction, only twenty-nine have been awarded.

alcohol. Pearce, along with several aid workers and some agents from the American Federal Bureau of Investigation (FBI) were dining alfresco when a man lobbed a bomb over a nearby wall where it landed with a thump close to Pearce's table.

With a deafening bang and a shower of shrapnel, diners were flung from their chairs, tables overturned, windows shattered and people lay bleeding and moaning on the ground. Pearce had been struck by shrapnel in one of his eyes, and there was blood oozing down the side of his face and onto his shirt. A Turkish aid worker had been killed instantly by the blast, and eleven other people, including Pearce, were injured. Close to Pearce two FBI agents had been badly wounded. Pearce dragged both of the Americans into the restaurant where he gave them life-saving first aid. Ignoring his own horrendous eye wound, Pearce then ran outside and commandeered a truck. Taking no notice of some American officials who wanted to take the badly wounded FBI agents straight to the US Embassy, Pearce ordered the driver to take the two men to the nearest hospital. This forceful decision saved both of their lives, as the hospital, unlike the embassy, had the proper facilities to deal with their injuries.

Pearce himself, though he had lost the sight in his right eye, refused to be evacuated to a hospital. Instead, he helped to secure the scene and waited to brief the scenes-of-crime officers that soon arrived to investigate the bombing. When Pearce arrived back in London, his eye injury was so bad that the eyeball was eventually surgically removed at Moorfield's Hospital. Pearce's bravery was recognized by the American government. In 2009, at a ceremony in New Scotland Yard, Pearce was awarded the FBI Star by Bureau Director Robert Mueller. The FBI Star is awarded for serious injury sustained in the direct line of duty from physical confrontation with criminal adversaries, an injury inflicted by weapons, gunshot wounds inflicted in the line of duty, or an injury so severe that it would require hospitalization. Pearce was registered disabled after losing his eye. Former Commissioner of the Metropolitan Police, Sir Ian Blair, tried to get Pearce recognition from the British government, but, shamefully, civil servants denied Pearce any award as the men he saved that day in Islamabad were not British subjects. Pearce was awarded the Commissioner's High Commendation, the Metropolitan Police's premier award for gallantry.

This chapter has focused on the threat to peace and stability posed by Islamic terrorism at home and abroad. We should not forget that just over a decade ago Irish Nationalist terrorism posed as big a threat to Britain's peace, and although things have remained quiet in Northern Ireland since the Good Friday Agreement, the potential for a resumption of violence is never far from the surface of the province's turbulent politics. In March 2009 a brief return to the bad old days of 'The Troubles' occurred when the so-called Real IRA launched a sudden and savage attack on the British Army in Antrim.

25 Field Squadron, part of 38 Engineer Regiment, Royal Engineers was based at Massereene Barracks in the town of Antrim, and the unit was preparing to leave for a tour of duty in Afghanistan with 19 Light Brigade which was to replace 3 Commando Brigade in Helmand Province. No-one expected to face death in Northern Ireland in March 2009, and the regiment's members were focused on the dangers and challenges that they would soon by facing in war torn Helmand. On the evening of 7 March, four young sappers, already dressed in desert combats strolled out of the barrack's main gate to meet two men delivering pizzas. 'We knew the situation in Northern Ireland was peaceful and we knew Marc and the boys often sent out for pizzas and Chinese food,' said the mother of Sapper Marc Fitzpatrick. 'The barracks is in fact their home and there was no reason for them to have thought different until it happened.'[39]

The soldiers were all unarmed as they collected their pizzas. Sitting in a blue Vauxhall Cavalier across the street were two Irishmen, each wearing a black balaclava and toting a semi-automatic rifle. A sudden fusillade of shots rang out in the quiet street as the terrorists opened fire at the soldiers and the pizza delivery men. The initial spray of automatic fire felled four sappers and the two pizza delivery drivers, also peppering their cars. Then, in a chilling display of arrogance, the two gunmen climbed out of their vehicle and walked towards the dead and wounded men and fired more shots into them before they turned and ran back to their car and sped away. In total, over sixty shots were fired at the victims. The Northern Ireland Security Guard Service, who since 1999 has been in charge of protecting British Army bases in the province, did nothing to stop the gunmen, even though they themselves were armed. It was the first such attack that they had experienced, and they were slow to react.

Sapper Cengiz 'Patrick' Azimkar, a twenty-one-year-old from Wood Green in North London was dead, along with Sapper Mark Quinsey, aged twenty-three, from Birmingham. The other four men were all wounded. One of the pizza delivery men said: 'The soldiers shouted for us to get down before we even knew what was happening. Then one of the soldiers just threw himself on top of me as the bullets were still firing.' Sapper Marc Fitzpatrick, who saved the Polish driver's life, said that his own life had been saved by the actions of Azimkar. 'If it wasn't for Pat I would not even be here – despite the chaos he was the one who pulled me to the ground and saved my life.'

A few hours later the terrorists' car was found abandoned eight miles away in Randalstown. The *Sunday Tribune*, a Dublin-based newspaper, received a phone call from a caller using a recognized Real IRA codeword. The man claimed responsibility for the attack, and added callously that the pizza delivery men who were also gunned down were 'collaborating with the British by servicing them.' The Real IRA was born out of a split in the mainstream Provisional IRA that occurred in October 1997 as some members found themselves in opposition to Sinn Fein's participation in the Good Friday peace process.

The deaths of Sappers Quinsey and Azimkar were the first army fatalities in the province since 1997, when Lance-Bombardier Stephen Restorick was shot dead by the 'South Armagh Sniper'. Two days after the attack outside Massereene Barracks, PC Stephen Carroll of the Police Service of Northern Ireland was shot dead by a sniper in Craigavon in County Armagh. Former IRA prisoner Colin Duffy and Brian Shivers have been charged with the murders of Sappers Quinsey and Azimkar and are due to stand trial in Northern Ireland.

Sapper Fitzpatrick, from Caerphilly in South Wales, has been honoured by the Polish government for his heroism in saving one of the pizza delivery men. 'He demonstrated huge courage and saved a

Pole's life,' said the head of the Polish National Security Bureau, Aleksander Szczygloon. Fitzpatrick was awarded the Order of Merit of the Polish Republic.

1 'Officer 'should get George Cross', BBC News, 16 April 2005

2 Ibid.

3 Ibid.

4 Ibid.

5 'Hero cop honoured – at last' by John Scheerhout, Manchester Evening News, 6 January 2009

6 '7/7 hero Stoneleigh cop awarded MBE' by Thais Portilho-Shrimpton, Epsom Guardian, 7 January 2009

7 'MBE for Haringey police officer', Metropolitan Police, http://www.cmc.met.police.uk, accessed 19 March 2009

8 Ibid.

9 Ibid.

10 '7/7 hero Stoneleigh cop awarded MBE' by Thais Portilho-Shrimpton, Epsom Guardian, 7 January 2009

11 'MBE for Haringey police officer', Metropolitan Police, http://www.cmc.met.police.uk, accessed 19 March 2009

12 Ibid.

13 '7/7 hero Stoneleigh cop awarded MBE' by Thais Portilho-Shrimpton, Epsom Guardian, 7 January 2009

14 'Tube passenger's MBE for bravery', BBC News, 10 March 2009

15 'London bombings modest hero gets MBE honour' by Bev Creagh, Luton Today, 2 January 2009

16 Ibid.

17 'Light at the end of the tunnel' by Syreeta Lund, Police, February 2006, 12

18 'July 7 bombing hero breaks his silence after MBE honour' by Tony Collins, Birmingham Mail, 31 December 2008

19 Ibid.

20 'Light at the end of the tunnel' by Syreeta Lund, Police, February 2006, 12

21 Ibid: 12

22 Ibid: 12

23 Ibid: 12-13

24 'MBE for London bomb attack hero', BBC News, 31 December 2008

25 'July 7 bombing hero breaks his silence after MBE honour' by Tony Collins, Birmingham Mail, 31 December 2008

26 'MBE for Haringey police officer', Metropolitan Police, http://www.cmc.met.police.uk, accessed 19 March 2009

27 'July 7 bombing hero breaks his silence after MBE honour' by Tony Collins, Birmingham Mail, 31 December 2008

28 'Rookie policeman hero of Tavistock Square', The Daily Mail, 7 July 2006

29 Ibid.

30 'London bombings: Heroes honoured' by Mark Hughes, The Independent, 31 December 2008

31 Ibid.

32 Ibid.

33 'Heroes of 21/7', Panorama, BBC, 9 July 2007

34 The London Gazette, 6 January 2009, Supplement No.1, 113

35 'Bomb hero describes testicles kick', Metro, 4 July 2007

36 Ibid.

37 Ibid.

38 'This is Glasgow. We'll just set aboot ye' by Lawrence Donegan, The Guardian

39 'Devastated sister of soldier murdered in Ulster attacks Real IRA 'cowards' as her brother is laid to rest' by David Wilkes and Anna Machowski, The Daily Mail, 19 March 2009

CHAPTER 7

High Seas Hijack

'Instantly, an excruciating pain hit my left ear. I lay there,
thinking it was the end, until Som, the Master of Arms,
appeared and dragged me across the deck, saving my life.'

Michael Groves QGM

When Sir Thomas Stamford Raffles first set eyes on Singapore he
declared: 'Our object is not territory, but trade,' adding 'Our
commerce will extend to every part [of Asia], and British principles
will be known and felt throughout.'[1] One of the first things the
British did was stamp out the scourge of piracy that would do so
much to damage international free trade. If someone says to you the
word "pirate", the first image that pops into most peoples' minds are
eye patches, peg legs and parrots *a la* Stevenson's *Treasure Island*.
Incredibly, piracy remains a scourge for modern shipping in many
parts of the world and has by no means been consigned to the history
books. Two particular hotspots are off the coast of war-ravaged and
ungovernable Somalia, and through the Malacca Strait connecting
the Indian and Pacific Oceans, just south of Raffles creation of
Singapore. Most of what we use in our modern lives today has been
manufactured in Asia and transported by container ship to Europe.
Ships bringing manufactured goods such as clothing, children's toys,
electrical products and a multitude of everyday products have all
passed through the narrow Malacca Strait off Singapore and sailed
around the Horn of Africa off Somalia to enter the Suez Canal and
the gateway to Europe. This massive volume of trade has meant a
huge increase in piracy through the Strait and around Somalia since

Britain's Royal Navy relinquished full control of the world's oceans after the Second World War. The naval bases from where the once ubiquitous Royal Navy made safe the world's free trade shipping lanes with frigates and cruisers constantly on patrol, places like Singapore and Aden, was closed as the Empire was wound down. In the power vacuum that has followed, many of the newly independent countries are too weak and busy dealing with their own internal problems to be able to police the sea, or too corrupt to care.

The Royal Navy had spent half of the Nineteenth Century sweeping the seas clear of pirates. In the post-Imperial late Twentieth Century the scourge of the seas was allowed once more to prey almost at will upon the merchant life blood of the industrialized world's economies. As yet, no British politician has shown the moral strength to dispatch a naval force sufficient to wipe out the pirate nests. Perhaps, as is so often the case, they are waiting for the Americans to do it for them – forgetting that America's imports come across the Pacific. Individual ships are left to defend themselves as best they can, constrained by international rules that the pirates care nothing for, as politicians in the West apply liberalist attitudes to peoples whose outlook is profoundly illiberal and mediaeval. If history can be seen to be regressing, the issue of piracy in the Twenty-first Century is surely the finest example.

Not only merchant ships ply these dangerous waters, but also cruise liners full of rich, mainly elderly, passengers, and they make especially attractive targets for the dirt-poor pirates. The cruise liners sail unarmed, each captain having to rely on common sense and regular intelligence reports on pirate activity to get his ship safely through the choke points. They are not always successful. One such ship that was assaulted off Somalia was the liner *Seabourn Spirit*, carrying 151 passengers and 161 crew members. The vessel was on the last night of a sixteen-night cruise from Alexandria, Egypt, to Mombasa, Kenya, when she was assaulted on 5 November 2005. She survived due to the courage of only two men – a British police sergeant and former navy man, and a hardy Gurkha.

Michael Groves had served in the Royal Navy for eight years before he joined the police force. Originally from the West Midlands, Groves decided to take a sabbatical as a sergeant from the police after eleven years service and following the break-up of his marriage in

2003. He took a job as Security and Safety Officer with Seabourn Cruise Lines, a company based at Miami, Florida. Sailing on the *Seabourn Spirit*, and providing evidence if needed of the enduring usefulness of ex-Gurkha soldiers in all walks of life, was Som Bahadur Gurung, the ship's Gurkha Master-at-Arms.

The *Seabourn Spirit* was 100 miles east of Somalia on 5 November, when at 5.50am, the ship's chief officer reported a small boat, probably a fishing vessel, off the stern. Groves' job was to protect the liner, and he immediately ran to the stern and peered out into the hazy dawn. 'I saw a boat with about six men in it,' recalled Groves, 'just a few metres away from the ship. My heart started pounding, and they began to fire at me with AK47s.'[2] The Somali pirates were determined to board and capture the big liner and they peppered the ship's side with rifle bullets, evidently hoping that the ship would stop and surrender. 'There was no mistaking the fact they wanted to kill me, so I fell to the ground,' continued Groves. 'All around me, bullets were crashing into the boat.'[3] Groves had no access to real weapons aboard the ship with which to defend himself. Instead, he was forced to rely on a high pressure hosepipe as his first line of defence.

Groves grabbed the hosepipe and stood up, in full view of the pirates, and carefully aimed the nozzle, letting loose a high pressure jet of water directly at them. In the meantime, the captain was moving his passengers, most of whom were completely terrified, into the dining room which, because of its central location, offered them some protection from the automatic rifle fire.

The hosepipe was of only limited use against well-armed pirates, so Groves turned his attention to working the Long-Range Acoustic Device (LRAD), a non-lethal sonic weapon that concentrated sound waves into a laser-like beam that was absolutely deafening to anyone on the receiving end. However, more pirates appeared. 'Then another boat moved to attack us from the other direction,' said Groves. 'One of the pirates was taking aim at me with a rocket launcher. I ran as fast as I could and dived to the ground as the explosion went off over my head.'[4]

When the rocket propelled grenade (RPG) exploded, Groves was injured by shrapnel. 'Instantly, an excruciating pain hit my left ear. I lay there, thinking it was the end, until Som [Gurung], the Master of

Arms, appeared and dragged me across the deck, saving my life.'
During this action, Gurung took over the LRAD, even when another
rocket was launched at the ship. The LRAD position offered no
protection whatsoever to the operator. Unfortunately, Gurung was
clipped by some shrapnel, struck by a rifle bullet and knocked
unconscious just as he was about to turn the weapon on the pirates.[5]
Groves dragged himself back to the LRAD and turned it on the
pirates who had tried to kill him. 'I turned the volume up and I could
see from the pirates' faces the pain it was causing them. About 30
minutes after the attack began, they gave up and we got away.'[6]

After the failed assault, the captain of the *Seabourn Spirit*
abandoned trying to run through the infestation of pirates on the
route into Mombasa and, instead, headed to the Seychelles where the
passengers were landed and the eventful end to their cruise was
finally over. Michael Groves now has poor hearing after the
explosion of the RPG so close to his head, and indeed when he
returned to Britain he failed his police medical and was forced to
leave his career with the force. He also suffered post-traumatic stress
disorder and flashbacks. Groves was awarded the Queen's Gallantry
Medal for repelling the pirates, and Som Bahadur Gurung was
awarded a Queen's Commendation for Bravery[7], both men receiving
their awards together at Buckingham Palace in 2007.

The Italian cruise ship *Melody* was attacked by Somali pirates far
from the African coast in April 2009. The vessel, with a full
passenger list of British holidaymakers, was assaulted 180 miles
north of the Seychelles in the Indian Ocean by eight well-armed
Somalis in a white speed-boat. British passengers were instrumental
in saving the ship and, although they were unarmed, they nonetheless
displayed enormous courage in repelling the boarders as they tried to
scale up the stern of the ship.

The drama began in the early hours of the morning when the
mostly elderly passengers had just finished enjoying a Mozart
concert on the pool deck. 'Everyone heard a cracking sound,'
recalled sixty-six-year-old British passenger Maureen Gawthorp.
'The applause for the musicians died down suddenly and someone
came running in from the open deck and shouted "pirates".'[8] Within
seconds the crew began to shepherd the passengers towards their

cabins, ordering them to stay inside and lock their doors. 'We went to our cabin and we could hear bullets whizzing and clanging as they hit the ship,'[9] recalled Gawthorp.

The pirates, all young Somalis dressed in camouflage uniforms and armed with Kalashnikov AK-47 assault rifles, approached the stern of the white-painted *Melody*, intending to board her using grapnels and scrambling nets. At this point several British pensioners, the most prominent among them being sixty-two-year-old Wyn Rowlands, a retired engineer from Bangor-on-Dee in Wales, picked up deckchairs and began hurling them over the stern directly at the infuriated pirates. 'They started firing like crazy at the ship,' recalled the ship's master, Captain Ciro Pinto. 'They were climbing up, so we reacted.'[10] The pensioners were soon joined by two Israeli security guards who were armed with pistols and some of the crew who unfurled a fire hose. The Israelis fired several shots over the heads of the pirates to try and warn them off while the fire hose was used to douse them. 'They gave up and went off,' said Pinto. The assault was not yet over. Wyn and the passengers and crew may have seen off the pirates, but the raiders continued to follow the ship for twenty minutes. The Somalis plastered the ship with machine-gun fire, bullets whacking off the steel hull, or smashing through windows on the upper decks, forcing passengers and crew to hug the deck for cover. By a miracle, nobody was injured and eventually the pirates gave up the chase and disappeared into the night to hunt for less well-defended prey. The problem of piracy off the Somali coast remains unsolved, and it appears that this problem will get considerably worse in the near future as governments and companies have started paying ransoms to the pirates to get ships and crews returned to them. This naturally only encourages the pirates to yet more bolder assaults on bigger and bigger ships.

1 Arthur Herman, *To Rule The Waves: How the British Navy Shaped the Modern World*, (London: Hodder, 1995), 441-442

2 '*Queen's medal winner relives the trauma of saving cruiser*', The Daily Mail website, http://www.dailymail.co.uk, accessed 25 July 2009

3 Ibid.

4 Ibid.

5 *The London Gazette*, 15 January 2007, Supplement No. 2, 533

6 '*Queen's medal winner relives the trauma of saving cruiser*', *The Daily Mail* website, http://www.dailymail.co.uk, accessed 25 July 2009

7 *The London Gazette*, 15 January 2007, Supplement No. 2, 533

8 '*Hero cruise ship Britons fought off armed Somali pirates with deckchairs and tables*', *The Daily Mail*, 22 May 2009

9 Ibid.

10 '*I fought off gun-toting pirates with deckchair, reveals hero Briton, 62, who foiled cruise ship hijack*', *The Daily Mail*, 29 April 2009

CHAPTER 8

Disaster in the Air

'I turned around and looked at the cockpit and I couldn't
believe what I was seeing. I could hear Allen screaming. All
I wanted to do was make sure he was OK.'

George Francis QGM

'I'm very lucky to be alive,'[1] said world famous Italian jockey
Frankie Dettori from a bed at Addenbrooke's Hospital, Cambridge in
early June 2000. Although he had broken an ankle and had burns and
cuts to his arms, face and head, Dettori had managed to survive a
horrendous plane crash. 'It would certainly seem to be a miracle that
anyone got out of it alive,' said a shocked Inspector Steve Brown,
who investigated the accident for Suffolk Constabulary. Dettori owed
his life to the bravery of his friend and fellow jockey Ray Cochrane,
who had been travelling alongside him when disaster struck.

The two jockeys had boarded a private twin-engine Piper Seneca
aircraft at Newmarket, the famous horseracing town in Suffolk,
bound for Goodwood in West Sussex where both jockeys were due to
ride in races. As the pilot, fifty-two-year-old Patrick Mackey, got the
aircraft off the ground at 12.30 pm something went rapidly and
cataclysmically wrong in a matter of a few seconds. A lick of smoke
was seen from the starboard side of the fuselage. Trouble struck
when the plane was only 300 feet off the ground, and with a
sickening lurch it fell to earth with the pilot desperately trying to
crash land it onto one of the local racecourses. The Piper struck the
ground hard, pin-wheeled across two race courses and burst into
flames as the full fuel tanks ruptured. The wrecked aircraft came to

rest upright but on fire. Inside, Dettori, forty-one-year-old Cochrane and Mackey struggled to free themselves from their seats belts as flames licked around the smashed fuselage. They had only a handful of minutes to escape the rising inferno.

Cochrane struggled to open the cabin door but it would not budge. Instead, he managed to open a small baggage hatch that was located behind the passenger seats and through which he crawled outside. Next, he climbed back into the burning plane and pulled twenty-nine-year-old Dettori, who could not walk because of a broken ankle, out through the same hatch and dragged him to safety. Cochrane returned to the aircraft, determined to rescue the pilot. By this time the fuel fire had fully engulfed the wreck but he could see Mackey trapped in the cockpit. Bravely, Cochrane tried to get near the aircraft but was beaten back by the heat and the flames, suffering burns to his face and his hands.[2] Eventually, he had to give up and retreat from the terrible heat generated by the burning fuselage and Mackey, who had been flying for fifteen years, tragically perished in the inferno.

Dettori immediately called his wife on a mobile phone as he lay on the grass. 'We have had a crash on the July course,' said Dettori, 'and the pilot is dead.'[3] Dettori and Cochrane both praised the pilot, saying that it was Mackey's skill that prevented the falling plane from smashing into a ditch on the racecourse, and killing them all instantly. 'Patrick, the pilot, did a fantastic job,' said Dettori and Cochrane in a joint statement, 'we owe our lives to his skill and courage.'[4] Dettori also owed his life to Cochrane, who had rescued him from the burning wreck. Ray Cochrane received national recognition when he was awarded the Queen's Commendation for Bravery in 2001. He was also awarded the Royal Humane Society's Silver Medal.

John Connell was at work doing some landscaping at a farm in Linwood, Renfrewshire, a few miles from Glasgow. The twenty-four-year-old was used to hearing the drone of aircraft passing overhead from Glasgow International Airport, and he didn't pay much attention. That was until lunchtime on 3 September 1999, when the sound coming from a plane that was passing close overhead did not sound quite right. 'What drew my attention to it was I could hear the engine splutter and then I just heard it cut out and stop,'[5] he recalled afterwards. A life and death struggle was just beginning for those on board the plane as it began a rapid and terminal descent to earth close to where Connell was working.

All had seemed routine when the twin-engine Cessna 402 Titan had taken off at 12.25 pm. Eleven people were on board the Edinburgh Air Charter plane, including two pilots and seven flight attendants who were being flown up to Aberdeen to crew a Boeing 757 charter holiday flight to Majorca that was due to depart later that day. Captain Hugh O'Brien, an Airtours pilot with more than fifteen years commercial flying experience, first suspected something was wrong when the Cessna was at an altitude of about 700 feet. O'Brien was a passenger. He heard a loud thump come from the starboard (right) engine. He and the pilot, John Easson, looked out, but the engine appeared to be working fine. O'Brien then noticed that one of the cockpit gauges was not in its correct setting. Then the plane started to turn and there was a falling sensation. Flight attendant Kevin MacKenzie said that he saw the starboard engine's propeller slow down. 'After the bang the plane continued to rise but as it banked to the right the left wing got higher. It felt wrong and unsafe,'[6] said MacKenzie.

On the ground, John Connell watched as the plane hopped over a line of trees, then one wing dipped down as the plane turned and ploughed into the ground, exploding in a ball of flame. 'I saw an explosion,' said Connell, 'a big ball of flames and smoke. That's when I ran to my tractor to get to the plane.'[7] Before boarding his tractor, Connell, who had been eating his lunch in a field when the plane crashed, called a friend and told him to alert the emergency services. Connell arrived at the scene of the crash to find that the plane had broken up into three pieces, with flames spread over a wide area from the aviation fuel that had poured from wrecked tanks. He immediately saw a man struggling to free himself from the shattered cabin and ran over to assist him. The man was Captain O'Brien.

After helping O'Brien to safety, Connell returned to the burning aircraft and pulled flight attendant MacKenzie clear. For a third time Connell returned to the wreck, and peering inside the cabin he saw flight attendant Derek Morrison was moving, though he was still strapped into his seat. Working quickly, and at considerable personal risk, Connell freed Morrison and dragged him out of the wreck to safety. Unfortunately, everyone else aboard the plane was already dead.

For his selfless bravery in managing to save three lives from that terrible scene of death and destruction, Connell was awarded the Queen's Commendation for Bravery in 2003. He also received a British Red Cross humanity award. Without his decisive intervention the death toll from the tragedy would undoubtedly have been higher.

A fishing boat was in trouble out in the storm-tossed Eastern Atlantic. The weather conditions on the night of 5 March 2001 were appalling, with howling gale force winds that whipped the sea into a roiling turmoil, with huge waves bucking the German fishing boat *Hansa* around like a cork. Visibility was extremely poor; salty spray stung the eyes of the fishermen as they peered out into the inky blackness and prayed for rescue. A distress signal had been sent and intercepted by Her Majesty's Coastguard at Stornoway in western Scotland. The fishermen, nine terrified men, had piled into a life raft when they abandoned their ship. The *Hansa* slipped beneath the black water taking with her six other crewmen who had not managed to get clear before she foundered. The life raft and its soaked and exhausted survivors were bobbing in the ocean some 200 miles off Benbecula in the Western Isles. Their only hope of salvation was the plucky crew of a British helicopter that was soon powering its way through wildly turbulent air out into the Atlantic wastes.

HM Coastguard base at Stornoway is responsible for 3,000 miles of rugged Scottish coastline from Ardnamurchan Point, the westernmost tip of the United Kingdom, to Cape Wrath in the north. Responsibility also stretches far out into the Atlantic, encompassing a search area of 50,000 square nautical miles of some of the most dangerous and unpredictable water in the world. At Stornoway, the Coastguard operate the American-manufactured Sikorsky S61 helicopter. When used by the Royal Navy and RAF it is called the Sea King, a sturdy workhorse of many of the world's navies and air forces for over thirty years. They were the RAFs standard search-and-rescue platforms, and both the RAF and Coastguard operate variants around the coasts of Britain dedicated to saving lives. HRH Prince William has joined one such squadron. The version used by the Coastguard is constructed in America, whereas the military versions are licence-built in Britain by Westland, hence the differing designations. Each carries a crew of four: the captain, co-pilot, winch operator, and winchman.

As soon as the call was received, the four Coastguard crewmen rushed to man their 'chopper'. The big white and red helicopter was soon airborne and headed out into the wild black night. 'It took a long time getting out there in headwinds and bad weather,' recalled a crewman afterwards. 'It was just a matter of minutes we had to do whatever it was we were going to do when we got there.' As they approached the shipwrecked sailors in their life raft the captain realised that he only had enough fuel to remain over the site for twenty minutes before he would have to turn for home. It was going to leave only a small window in which to rescue the German sailors. Added to this worry were the facts that the wind was so strong and the conditions so rough that the pilot would have to position manually the aircraft over the constantly heaving and pitching raft and keep it there – normally the pilot would engage an auto-hover system, but the computer kept disengaging this useful device as the helicopter was thrown around the sky by the strong winds. This made the job of rescuing the survivors even more challenging, and when coupled with the realization that all nine would have to be lifted to safety in only twenty minutes, or else the rescue aborted and the men abandoned to almost certain death, the pressure on the Coastguard crew was enormous. 'They were in a state of shock and it was a terrible scene,' recalled a crewman when he looked down at the terrified faces of the German sailors staring up hopefully at the big helicopter overhead.

The man who would actually rescue the nine terrified Germans was Winchman Chris Murray. He would dangle from the helicopter on a single wire over the storm-tossed sea and try to land on the raft. Murray went straight out over the raft, Winch Operator Julian "Smiler" Grinney paying out the cable as he stood in the open doorway with one hand on the wire while pilot, Clark Broad, and co-pilot, Neil Stephenson, struggled to keep the helicopter steady over the raft. Murray took quite a battering from the sea as he landed on the raft, and at times during the rescue he physically held the raft on station to prevent it from floating off on the disturbed ocean and disrupting the rescue. The sound of the helicopter's engines was deafening, the steady 'whoop, whoop' of the rotor blades was coupled with the shriek and howl of the wind and the crashing of the waves. During the lowering and raising of the winch line, Winch Operator Grinney damaged his shoulder but, ignoring the pain, he kept working.

Winching the German fishermen up two at a time, Murray soon had all nine survivors aboard the helicopter and, with a massive sense of relief Broad turned the chopper for Scotland and home. When the engines were finally shut down on the helipad at Benbecula there was only enough fuel left in the tanks for five minutes flying time – which in real terms meant that the aircraft was practically running on fumes. If they had had to ditch in the roiling sea on the way home, undoubtedly some aboard would have been killed. It was an amazing accomplishment, and a fine example of the day-to-day work undertaken by the Coastguard and RAF Search and Rescue teams around the coast of Britain. Chris Murray received the Queen's Gallantry Medal, while pilots Broad and Stephenson and Winch Operator Grinney each were awarded the Queen's Commendation for Bravery in the Air (QCBA).

Basra Air Station was a vital hub that supplied British forces operating in Iraq. Operated by the RAF, the air station saw continual activity as planes arrived from and departed for Cyprus and Britain, while front-line squadrons of bombers and helicopters operated on sorties around the clock. On 19 July 2004 a Puma helicopter was returning from carrying out a resupply mission to British forces when it crashed on one of the dispersals. After crunching into the tarmac with a sickening impact, the helicopter burst into flames. The three crewmen were trapped inside as small arms ammunition began to 'cook off' like popcorn in a hot pan, and flares exploded as the flames touched them off. The situation was desperate, verging on the tragic.

Thirty-seven-year-old Corporal Darren Mallalieu, an armourer and member of the Visiting Aircraft Servicing Section from RAF Cottesmore in Leicestershire, dropped what he was doing and ran towards the crashed Puma. Completely disregarding his own safety, Mallalieu ventured unprotected into the burning wreckage, even though bullets and flares were exploding all around him. 'This was not an unthinking act,' said Group Captain Phil Osborn, Mallalieu's new commanding officer at RAF Marham, the station he was posted to after returning from Iraq. 'It's the act of somebody who knew well what was going on and still put themselves in harm's way.' He managed to pull two of the badly burned crew to safety, but he could not save the third man. Mallalieu tried several times to reach the last crewman, but he was beaten back by the blaze and the man perished in the flames. 'To me there was nothing heroic in it,' said Mallalieu of his gallant actions. 'I was just intending to get them out and that was it – it was all I had in my mind. I would not stand back and see anybody die.' Darren Mallalieu received the Queen's Commendation for Bravery.

28 August 2004. A light aircraft had lost power from its single engine and was going to crash – the only question was where? Pilot Robert le Page, age fifty-five, was facing a nightmare situation where he had only seconds to decide where to ditch his aircraft as the ground came up at a terrifying rate. His two passengers, forty-one-year-old Andrew Anderson and fifty-five-year-old air traffic controller, David Bougourd, sat rigid in their seats as le Page fought to keep the Socata TB-10 airborne. The plane had just left Bournemouth's Hurn Airport when the engine failed, and the plane was beginning a rapid and terminal descent into the ground. With a massive effort and displaying superb flying skills, le Page managed to crash-land the aircraft in a field, narrowly avoiding ploughing into the crowded Alice in Wonderland theme park that was dead ahead. All three men sat for a few seconds in silence as smoke wreathed around the broken plane and fuel leaked out onto the ground surrounding it.

Former soldier Michael Winstanley had seen the white-painted aircraft smash into the ground as he drove his van alongside the airfield's perimeter fence. Winstanley, now a window fitter, hit the breaks and jumped down from the cab. There was a BANG from the wreck and a lick of flame reared up as the aviation fuel ignited from the shattered tanks. Suddenly, Winstanley saw movement inside the wreck. 'I saw someone climbing out of the window from the left-hand side door,' he recalled. 'I ran over to this person who was struggling to his feet and I led him to safety and laid him down on the road.'[8] Winstanley's modest account does not do his courage justice. The plane was on fire and, when the flames reached the main fuel tanks there would be an explosion. Winstanley, who had served for over thirteen years in the Royal Green Jackets, seeing service in Northern Ireland, Germany and Cyprus, had dived straight into the midst of lethal danger. 'Then I looked up and back towards the aircraft and saw someone else emerging from it via the same window and fall to the ground.'[9] Winstanley ran towards the burning wreckage. 'Mr. Winstanley went back to the burning plane, assisted the second man, by patting out the flames on his clothes, and helped him away from the danger,'[10] read his citation in the *London Gazette*. Unfortunately, the third man on the plane, Andrew Anderson, did not have time to exit the aircraft before it exploded and he was killed.

Winstanley was not initially recognized for his gallantry as he chose to remain anonymous. Instead, another man, window cleaner Nigel Gallimore, falsely claimed that he had saved Bourgourd and Le Page. Gallimore had been one of several bystanders who had certainly assisted Winstanley with looking after the two survivors, but he allowed himself to be feted as a hero when he was nothing of the sort. Winstanley's silence meant that Gallimore was awarded a Queen's Commendation for Bravery and the real hero of the hour was overlooked. Gallimore was given the award based largely on a statement that he had made to the Air Accident Investigation Board, and he had been nominated in good faith by his own father. The truth was revealed at the coroner's inquest into the death of Andrew Anderson that was convened some time later. Gallimore, obviously wrestling with his conscience, admitted in open court: 'A lot of things happened and a lot of questions were asked and in the heat of the moment I probably said things that didn't happen.'[11] Gallimore's admission of lying led the government to rescind his award, and when it emerged that Winstanley was the real hero he was awarded a Queen's Commendation for Bravery in 2007, almost three years after his gallantry went unnoticed, and an injustice was righted.

Thick, acrid choking smoke almost completely obscured George Francis' view through the canopy glass of the cockpit of the shattered jet. He was groggy from the violence of the crash. His pilot was slumped forward in the front seat, unconscious at the controls of the Lockheed Canadair T-33 Shooting Star jet trainer, a large silver aircraft with a distinctive bomb-shaped fuel tank located at the end of each wing. Grabbing the plane's emergency hammer, Francis began to furiously hack at the canopy; he was acutely conscious that time was fast running out.

The day had begun in a quite routine way. The vintage Canadian jet, built in 1953, was owned and operated by the Aircraft Restoration Company based at the Imperial War Museum at Duxford in Cambridgeshire. Francis, an aerospace engineer employed by Zodiac Aerospace of Braintree, Essex, would accompany the aircraft when it attended shows. The T-33 was one of Lockheed's most successful training aircraft, and many have remained in an airworthy condition all over the world. They were originally used to train jet pilots, and for communication, target towing and electronic warfare duties. Piloting the T-33 on 6 September 2006 was highly experienced civilian pilot, Allen Walker. Francis and Walker were due to fly to the Channel Islands, where the aircraft would be displayed at the Jersey Air Show.

The aircraft taxied onto the grass runway at Duxford and lined up for takeoff. As the T-33 hurtled down the grass strip at full throttle, everything appeared to be okay. The plane lifted off, but only managed to stagger about a hundred feet into the air, travelling at 140mph. Suddenly the jet stalled and it started to roll to the left, its wing dipping down, and the aircraft ploughed into the ground nose first. The nose was torn completely off on impact, and the left wing was also sheered off. The 800 gallons of aviation fuel carried on board the jet erupted into a huge fireball that reached over 100 feet into the air as the T-33 cartwheeled along the runway, burst through a line of trees at the end, and broke up into burning debris that was strewn across a recently-cut corn field. The cockpit section of the fuselage survived the heavy impact intact, apart from the missing nose, and had come to rest upright in the field, thick black smoke and dancing flames blanketing up from the burning aviation fuel. Francis and Walker had miraculously managed to survive the crash, but now it looked as though fire and acrid smoke would just as surely kill them.

Forty-eight-year-old Francis knew that he only had a few minutes at most before he was either overcome by smoke inhalation and lost consciousness, or the flames that were dancing around the outside of the cockpit ate their way into the interior and killed him. 'I suppose I acted on instinct more than anything,' said Francis afterwards. 'I couldn't breathe or see properly but I just went on to auto-pilot and acted like a robot. It was almost like there was someone else in my body – a very weird experience.'[12] Francis began battering away at the cockpit Perspex like a man possessed. 'I was completely petrified throughout, but the bottom line is that you have to do what you have to do. It turned out that it took 57 blows with the emergency hammer-knife to break the canopy,' said Francis. 'I really had to use all my might and I think it must have been the adrenaline that gave me the strength.'[13]

Once Francis had cut a hole through the cockpit canopy, some of the noxious smoke vented itself, allowing him to see more clearly. With another massive effort, Francis managed to squeeze out through the hole, breaking some of his ribs in the process. Fire was beginning to engulf the remains of the fuselage and the pilot, Walker, was in a desperate situation, trapped inside the cockpit with no means of escape. Realising the urgency of the situation, now that Francis had saved himself, he set to work saving his friend. 'I turned around and looked at the cockpit and I couldn't believe what I was seeing. I could hear Allen screaming,' said Francis afterwards. 'All I wanted to do was make sure he was OK.'[14] Braving the flames, Francis ran to the front of the aircraft and pulled the emergency canopy jettison mechanism, which blew the canopy clear of the fuselage. Francis quickly reached in and released Walker from his harness and, with another great exertion of adrenaline-fuelled strength, Francis dragged the pilot from the cockpit and pulled him to safety.

George Francis was awarded the Queen's Gallantry Medal for his immense courage in saving Walker in a tremendously dangerous and confusing situation. Air Chief Marshal Sir Glenn Torpy, Chief of the Air Staff, later met and congratulated Francis. 'Although this is a civilian award and Mr. Francis is not a member of the military, his actions demonstrate the type of gallantry I would be proud of in any member of the Royal Air Force,'[15] said Torpy. 'I'm over the moon with it,' said Francis of the award. 'It came as a shock.'[16]

A day of fun turned into a life and death struggle in the skies over Germany in July 2008 when a parachuting competition went horribly wrong. Army Air Corps pilot Garth Greyling was behind the controls of a Britten-Norman Turbo Islander twin-engine aircraft used for parachute training by small groups. The aircraft was at 7,500 feet over Bad Lippspringe and the parachute team had just exited the aircraft using static lines to deploy their parachutes. It was all part of the British Army Parachute Championships held each year. Greyling turned the aircraft about and began to descend towards the airfield's main runway, unaware that a terrible and potentially fatal incident had occurred to one of the parachutists. Major Jeremy Denning was the jump master, and the last to have left the aircraft. Unfortunately, his leg had become caught up with the fifteen foot static line and this had left him trailing under the aircraft by his foot.

As Greyling lined up for his final approach, air traffic control suddenly alerted him to the potential danger. Greyling reacted instantly, immediately climbing the Islander back up to 7,500 feet so that Major Denning would have a good safety margin if he was suddenly released by the line. But Greyling also faced a very serious situation. He was the only person on board the aircraft, as he was flying without a co-pilot. He did not know if Denning was conscious, as normal procedure for a parachutist who finds himself hung up like Denning was to put his hands on his helmet to indicate that you are conscious to the jump master. In this case, Denning was the jump master. The only way to save the Major was for Greyling to leave the aircraft controls, walk back and cut Denning free. 'He [Greyling] trimmed the controls as best he could in the hope it [the plane] would fly without anyone at the controls. He then carried out a dummy run over the dropping zone, and left his seat, making further adjustments to the trim of the aircraft to compensate for the change in weight distribution as he moved around,'[17] said Dick Wilkinson, Secretary of the Royal Humane Society.

Greyling was taking a calculated risk, but he was left with little choice as he could not stay airborne indefinitely, and he could not land with Denning dangling underneath the aircraft. 'Having made all the adjustments he could [Greyling] then carried out a second run over the drop zone and this time left the controls for several minutes to cut Major Denning free.' Denning fell away from the Islander, deploying his reserve chute and floated down safely to the airfield. 'It was possible that any turbulence or the act of cutting the Major free could have put the aircraft in a dive.'[18] For his gallantry in facing an unusual airborne survival scenario Garth Greyling was awarded the Bronze Medal from the Royal Humane Society.

1 *'Miracle' Escape from Plane Crash by Jockeys in England'* by Bill Christine, *New York Times*, 2 June 2000

2 *The London Gazette*, 30 October 2001, Supplement No. 3, 12752

3 *'Dettori 'owes life' to pilot'*, BBC News, 2 June 2000

4 Ibid.

5 *'UK Scotland: Eight die in plane crash'*, BBC News, 3 September 1999

6 *'Pilot describes Cessna crash'*, BBC News, 5 November 2001

7 Ibid.

8 *'Hero honoured for rescue admits faking story'* by Genevieve Roberts, *The Independent*, 11 January 2006

9 Ibid.

10 *The London Gazette*, 15 January 2007, Supplement No.2, 535

11 *'Plane crash 'hero' awarded medal for bravery admits: it wasn't me'* by Richard Savill, *The Telegraph*, 11 January 2006

12 *'Queen's Gallantry Medal for Hero Aircraft Engineer'*, Ministry of Defence Press Office, 6 January 2009

13 Ibid.

14 *'Duton Hill: Hero saves his friend from 'unsurvivable plane crash''*, http://www.thisistotalessex.co.uk, 13 January 2009, accessed 13 July 2009

15 *'Queen's Gallantry Medal for Hero Aircraft Engineer'*, Ministry of Defence Press Office, 6 January 2009

16 *'Dunmow: Aircraft engineer receives Queen's award for bravery'* by Mariam Ghaemi, *Gazette*, 7 January 2009

17 *'Hero pilot let plane fly unaided at 7,500ft as he battled to save parachutist hanging from wheel'*, *The Daily Mail*, 7 December 2009

18. Ibid.

CHAPTER 9

Nerves of Steel

'Normally you would spend three or four hours dealing with
a device like that but we were under fire in the city centre.
The greatest danger is spending time on the ground. I made
it safe in 27 minutes. We only realised how big it was when
we came to move it.'

Staff Sergeant James Wadsworth, Royal Logistic Corps

The Second World War may have ended over six decades ago, but the
detritus of that terrible conflict still has the power to take lives today.
London is littered with unexploded German bombs left over from the
Luftwaffe campaign to rain death and destruction upon British cities
known as the Blitz in 1940-41. The construction of new buildings in
London and many other towns and cities across Britain can be a
hazardous affair, for an unknown number of German bombs of
various sizes lay buried several feet beneath the surface, growing
more unstable with each passing year. It is the job of the army's
Royal Engineers and Royal Logistic Corps to tackle all bomb
disposals across Britain and globally wherever British forces are
deployed, and to assist the emergency services at home.

After several post-Second World War reorganizations, dealing
with unexploded ordnance – aerial bombs, landmines and other
devices like the Improvised Explosive Devices now used extensively
by the Taliban in Afghanistan – is shared between units from two
different parts of the Army. Basically, the disposal of old ordnance,
like German bombs left over from the Second World War and
Argentine landmines in the Falklands, is the responsibility of

Explosive Ordnance Squadrons of the Royal Engineers, who can trace their ancestry back to William the Conqueror. The on-the-spot defusing of newly laid devices on current battlefields, particularly the IEDs laid by the Taliban, is the responsibility of 11 (EOD) Regiment, part of the relatively new Royal Logistic Corps, which was only formed in 1993.

The unit charged with making safe all potential explosive mayhem and death within mainland Britain is 33 Engineer Regiment based at Carver Barracks in Wimbish, Essex. The regiment, the largest in the Royal Engineers, was formed in 1973, but its roots go back to the Royal Engineer Bomb Disposal companies of the Second World War. They were small teams equipped with sandbags, spades and picks that roved around Britain disposing of UXBs (Unexploded Bombs) with a combination of rudimentary tools, a lot of guesswork and nerves of steel. The figures speak volumes of the bravery of these disposers of yesteryear: by the end of the war, the Royal Engineers had disposed of 45,441 aerial bombs, 6,983 anti-aircraft shells and an estimated 300,000 beach mines.[1] Three-hundred and eighty-nine disposers had been killed on the job, and thirteen had been awarded the George Cross for their gallantry, a decoration second only to the VC.

It goes without saying that the men who diffuse bombs for a living have considerable powers of concentration and are not easily rattled. Few jobs, even in the army, place a soldier so close to instant death (or at the very least grievous injury) on such a regular basis, so it is also little wonder that bomb disposal soldiers have been among the most decorated in the army. Sergeant Douglas Leak is one of those men. He grew up in Moffat, in Dumfries and Galloway. On 14 May 2007 Leak, who was thirty-three at the time, was the on-duty bomb disposal officer at Carver Barracks when a call came through from the emergency services reporting a probable unexploded German bomb that had been unearthed in London's Docklands during construction work. Leak and his seven-man team immediately raced down to the capital, ready to make safe whatever they found. Leak was to win a particular regimental accolade in 2007 – the soldier who had made safe the most Second World War bombs in a year, a total of six. It perhaps gives some idea of the volume of unexploded German ordnance that is still buried across Britain that a team of soldiers could be kept busy year on year over half a century after the war destroying these deadly vestiges of conflict.

On arrival at the building site on Roman Road, Leak set about identifying the size and type of bomb that had been discovered. The *Luftwaffe* dropped 250, 500 and 1,000kg bombs – but Leak quickly realized that this mud encased and long-forgotten relic was a 250kg model. If it exploded it had the potential to cause considerable damage up to a mile and a half, and it was a terrible hazard in the midst of a busy modern metropolis. So, Leak's first thought was to minimizing the blast effect if the bomb detonated. Leak and his team constructed earthen ramparts around the bomb to protect nearby buildings and a railway line. He also confirmed that the bomb's detonator was in perfect working order. The Germans built an anti-tamper tremble sensor into their bombs, so that any sharp movements could trigger the detonator. Therefore, it was imperative that the bomb was kept as still as possible during the defusing period.

On day three, with the earthen walls in place, Leak could now address beginning to defuse the bomb itself. The first order of business was to drill a hole into the firing mechanism through which Leak could inject a saline solution that would jam the bomb's working parts. However, that meant Leak crouching over a live bomb for two hours carefully drilling through the casing, knowing all the time that the slightest movement could set the bomb off. If it had gone off Leak would have been instantly vaporized. Once this tricky operation had been completed, Leak then very carefully injected the saline solution into the arming mechanism. Leak retreated 200 metres behind the defensive walls and ordered the next phase of the disposal to commence. A remote control robot, known as a 'Wheelbarrow' was driven up to the bomb.

The Wheelbarrow is a tracked vehicle with a television camera for an eye and a long maneuverable arm to conduct delicate work. It is also armed with a shotgun used to trigger bombs with a single blast. If the bomb detonated, the only thing that would be destroyed would be an expensive robot, and these vehicles had proved their worth on countless occasions before in Northern Ireland and Britain helping to make safe IRA bombs. Originally designed by Lieutenant-Colonel Peter Miller in 1972 for use on the mean streets of Northern Ireland the curious name came about because Miller's original prototype robot was built out of a wheelbarrow and a lawnmower. The lives of many bomb-disposal technicians have been saved by the clever application of technology, the Wheelbarrow being one of the best examples in the business, and a British design that has been extensively copied throughout the world.

The robot was manoeuvred up to the hole in the bomb's casing, and then the arm extended and carefully began cutting the casing so that the explosive could be steamed out. In the back of a van Leak and his team controlled events through a bank of television monitors, the operator driving the robot from a joystick, long wires trailing out from the van towards the vehicle. But then Leak noticed a problem. The robot stopped operating and Leak approached the bomb once more on foot. 'I noticed the explosive inside had started to heat up to the point where it was frying,' said Leak. 'That's dangerous. You don't know if it's going to get hot enough to detonate. I decided to leave it for 20 minutes and go back.'[2] Leak turned his back on the bomb and began to walk back to safety, conscious that the bomb could have detonated. 'That was the long walk,' Leak said afterwards. 'You have to really have a word with yourself.'[3] Leak later calculated that there was over a sixty percent chance that the German bomb would have exploded, so he considered himself very lucky to have survived.

Once everything had been allowed to cool off and settle down, the steaming of the explosive out of the casing continued. Leak and his team gained little sleep over the four days that they were dealing with the bomb, occasionally crashing out in a nearby fire station for a few hours. By 4 am on the fourth day of the operation the mission was completed and the bomb was declared safe. Leak and his team packed up and drove back, exhausted, to Wimbish, where Leak was reunited with his wife and eighteen-month-old twin boys. Just another job and just one of the six German bombs he would deal with that year. Every time he started to tinker with one of those highly unstable and old aerial bombs he did not know if it would be his last job. Being married to a bomb disposal expert is probably almost as stressful as disposing of the bombs themselves. It is perhaps only fitting that Leak, who was promoted to Staff Sergeant shortly afterwards, was awarded the Queen's Gallantry Medal for his leadership and courage of the highest order.

A few years before Leak's exploits in London, on 7-8 January 2002, an equally tense and difficult situation had developed in the town of Lingfield in Surrey. The small town is located close to London Gatwick, one of London's four airports. On 9 February 1943, a lone German raider had dropped a stick of three 500kg bombs over the town. Two had exploded and killed two schoolgirls and two local teachers. The third bomb was never accounted for at the time. This menacing relic of a long past conflict was discovered buried in the soil of a back garden on Mount Pleasant Road in January 2002 when some building work was being carried out. The police and a Royal Engineers bomb disposal team were immediately called in. The police, on army advice, threw up a cordon of 100 metres around the bomb and began to evacuate all of the nearby houses. When Lieutenant Paul Ness, commanding the bomb disposal team, discovered how unstable the bomb was, along with the alarming fact that the bomb's fuse and detonator were fully functioning, he had the cordon extended to 300 metres. The evacuation called for the type of mass organisation of people not seen in the town since the Second World War. Firstly, three evacuation centres were established in the town with enough space to cope with the eventual 500 residents who were forced to spend the night away from their homes. The police also had to reroute all major highways away from the town.[4]

Whilst all this was going on, Lieutenant Ness, closely assisted by Lance-Corporal Dean MacMaster and Sapper Stephen Smith, worked through the night to defuse the German bomb. The device lay only ten feet from the house where it had been discovered, and if it had gone off it would have caused significant damage across a wide area of the town. Ness and his team followed the same procedure that Sergeant Leak later used in London. Holes were carefully drilled into the casing, each vibration taking the men a step closer to their maker. The explosive was not steamed out on this occasion and, instead, the detonator was immobilized and the live bomb was gingerly transported alone by Sapper Smith to a special army range where it was blown up. Unexploded German bombs remain a constant headache for army and navy bomb disposal experts, and as well as aerial bombs the navy is often called upon to deal with old sea mines that are dredged up by fishing trawlers or are washed up on shore. The aerial bombs are usually discovered during building work, as in Lingfield and Docklands, and are normally in areas of dense population and infrastructure. Lieutenant Ness and Lance-Corporal MacMaster were both awarded the Queen's Gallantry Medal for tackling the difficult disposal in Lingfield, and Sapper Smith was awarded a Queen's Commendation for Bravery.

Sometimes, even with modern technology, the worst can happen and bomb disposal experts are killed or horribly injured. The bravery of disposal technicians in dealing with the very modern threat of IEDs in Afghanistan and until recently in Iraq has often been overlooked as journalists and authors have concentrated in the main upon the more dramatic gun battles that regularly rage between British forces and the Taliban.

A soldier who more than deserves the title 'hero' was also involved with bomb disposal and faced his greatest challenge not at home in Britain, but during Britain's turbulent occupation of Iraq. Captain Peter Norton was not a bomb disposal technician *per se*, but rather an Ammunition Technical Officer (ATO) in the Royal Logistic Corps. An ATO is an officer who is involved in all aspects of munitions, including bomb disposal, explosives accident investigation, and the storage, inspection and repair of munitions. The job requires intensive training for sixteen months at the Royal Military College of Science at Shrivenham and the Army School of Ammunition.

Captain Norton, who was born in Margate in 1962, originally joined the Royal Army Ordnance Corps as a private in 1983, he had served in Germany and Northern Ireland and on secondment with the Sultan of Oman's Armed Forces. By 2002 Norton had risen to hold the highest non-commissioned rank in the army, that of Warrant Officer Class 1 Conductor. This rank originated in 1879, when a Royal Warrant established Conductors of Supplies as Warrant Officers, ranking above all other NCOs in the army, including Regimental Sergeant Majors. To attain this rank a Conductor must have been a Warrant Officer Class 1 for at least three years. In 2002 Norton was commissioned as a captain and shortly afterwards found himself serving in Iraq.

On 24 July 2005 Captain Norton, who is married and has two young boys, was second-in-command of the US Combined Explosives Exploitation Cell that was based on the outskirts of the Iraqi capital, Baghdad, when he faced his greatest challenge during his long military career. The unit was formed to help combat the prolific and deadly effective use of IEDs by insurgents in Iraq, and brought together explosives experts from the British and US Armies. They collected IEDs and analysed them to gain precious intelligence data about how the insurgents were constructing them, how they deploy them in the field, plus information about where the explosives and mechanical parts used to make the IEDs came from. This last point often shows how some states are covertly arming Britain's enemies, with Iranian-manufactured parts often turning up in Iraq.

On 30 April 2005, Norton was out in Baghdad investigating the scene of a recent suicide vehicle attack. The vehicle had been packed with explosives, turning it into a giant IED. The calm of the investigation was suddenly shattered. Norton and his team came under attack by insurgents, with two Rocket Propelled Grenades (RPGs) exploding near to him, but Norton remained unfazed and he actually carried on with his job and completed the analysis of the IED vehicle bombing. Another hair-raising exploit occurred just over a week later when Norton was dealing with a supposedly neutralized suicide vest IED, which was packed with explosives and ball bearings. As he was handling the IED, Norton discovered that the detonators were still connected. Without any thoughts for his own safety Captain Norton immediately made the device safe by hand. Then, in the following month, Norton was investigating the site of a recent roadside IED in Baghdad. As he was doing so, he found another IED concealed beside the road. He quickly ordered the American soldiers back and allowed a US Army Ordnance Disposal Team to clear the device. Norton's quick reactions undoubtedly saved the lives of many American soldiers.

On the evening of 24 July Captain Norton was out on patrol in a group of three Humvee lightly armoured vehicles with men of B Company, 2nd Battalion, 121st Regiment. This American formation

130

was part of the Georgia National Guard, the US equivalent to Britain's Territorial Army. They were driving through the Al Bayaa district of downtown Baghdad when they ran straight into an insurgent ambush. Working alongside the National Guardsmen and Norton were two Special Agent Bomb Technicians from the American FBI. Unbeknown to Norton and his team, hostile eyes tracked the patrol's progress, intent on wreaking swift and terrible destruction against the foreign infidel invaders. Norton and his team had been called forward to the site of an earlier IED ambush, where a Humvee had been completely destroyed and four American soldiers killed. A massive IED had been planted by insurgents beside the road, connected to a handheld trigger through what is known as a 'command wire'. The carnage that Norton faced was, as can be imagined, horrendous. Norton coolly took charge and began organizing an investigation in the hope of discovering more information about the first IED and to locate if the command wire was present. Norton went forward towards the devastated Humvee alone, knowing full well that the insurgents often planted secondary IEDs in the hope of killing and injuring would-be rescuers or bomb-disposal technicians who responded to the first explosion.

As Norton carefully surveyed the site looking for a command wire he was suddenly enveloped in a powerful blast. The second IED had been detonated, and this time the weapon had been set off by Norton stepping onto a pressure plate – rather like a land mine. Norton's left leg had been blown off, and he sustained fragmentation injuries to his right leg, to both of his arms and to his lower abdomen. 'When his team came forward to render first aid, he was conscious and lucid and most concerned regarding their safety,' read Captain Norton's citation rather dryly. Norton knew that it was he who had triggered the device, and it stood to reason that more IEDs could be concealed in the vicinity. Laying in a pool of his own blood, minus a limb and studded with shrapnel, Norton refused to allow the American soldiers to render him first aid until he had told them which areas around him were safe so that they could move towards him without risk of triggering another bomb. 'It is typical of the man that he ignored his injuries and regarded the safety of his men as paramount as they administered life saving first aid to him,' continued Norton's citation. The danger to the American soldiers was very real. The next day, bomb disposal experts discovered another IED buried in the ground just thirty feet from where Captain Norton had been blown up, and if he had allowed his team to tramp all over the site while they attended to him would have resulted in another explosion and probably more horrific injuries.

Captain Peter Norton was awarded Britain's highest gallantry award given for actions that are performed not in the face of the enemy, the George Cross. He was also awarded the FBI Star by the United States for his bravery. Despite losing his left leg, he has remained in the army, has been promoted to major and is now studying for an MSc postgraduate degree in Explosive Ordnance Disposal at the army's Cranfield University.

Staff Sergeant James Wadsworth, a twenty-nine-year-old from Over near Cambridge, garnered the unpleasant record of defusing the largest bomb ever found in Iraq in July 2007. Insurgents constructed a bomb containing 120 pounds of high explosives, which they had spray-painted and disguised with rubble until it looked like a stone block. This had been surreptitiously installed outside a hospital close to the main road that led from the British headquarters at Basra Palace to the airport. The bomb was operated by remote control, the intention being to detonate it when a significant British convoy was passing by. The damage that would have been wrought by such a huge bomb in a city centre does not bear thinking about.

Wadsworth had been in the army since he was sixteen years old. A bomb disposal technician with the Royal Logistic Corps, Wadsworth was immediately called in to tackle the huge insurgent bomb when it was discovered. At any moment the bomb could have been triggered by remote control. A bomb of the size and complexity of the one discovered in central Basra would be a time consuming job, requiring the disposal officer to be in constant close proximity to instant death. 'Normally you would spend three or four hours dealing with a device that that,' recalled Wadsworth, 'but we were under fire in the city centre.'[5] Incredibly, Wadsworth was forced to defuse the bomb while bullets flew around him as insurgents launched an attack on the British-occupied buildings in the city centre. 'The greatest danger is spending time on the ground,' said Wadsworth. 'I made it safe in 27 minutes. We only realised how big it was when we came to move it.'[6]

The conditions under which Staff Sergeant Wadsworth and his small team worked that day in Basra were almost intolerable. Under fire and struggling to work in temperatures of 55 degrees Celsius in the shade, Wadsworth was forced to remove his bomb suit and labour on defusing the device without any protection whatsoever, whilst also trying to overcome fatigue that could have resulted in errors. 'Our unit was so busy we hadn't slept for days,' he said. I haven't really told my wife about what I did. You just get on with the job.'[7] Wadsworth had just finished disconnecting the detonator from the bomb when a small light flashed on in front of his eyes – it signalled that a terrorist was trying to detonate the bomb at that moment. Just a few seconds earlier and Wadsworth and many others would have been killed, highlighting just how dangerous and unpredictable the bomb-disposal business is.

'When he defused this bomb he went what the Army call 'beyond duty", said Wadsworth's stepfather Roger Denson, 'because he dragged it back for forensic tests. These can prove very useful to work out where the bombs were from and how they were being put together.'[8] This is something which is also routinely done by British bomb disposal officers operating in Afghanistan. Staff Sergeant Wadsworth was awarded the Conspicuous Gallantry Cross for his extraordinary gallantry and coolness under fire and he promoted to Warrant Officer Class 2.

'To have the mental fortitude and physical stamina to uncover and defuse seven devices is a staggering feat,' read the citation for bomb disposal expert Warrant Officer Gary O'Donnell, who dealt with dozens of IEDs during a tour on the front line of Britain's most recent conflict. Afghanistan has proved to be one of the most challenging war fighting environments faced by the British Army since the Falklands. The Taliban have proved to be extremely capable and brave opponents whose many decades of combat experience against the Soviet Union and each other has meant that Coalition Forces have suffered heavy casualties during operations across this war-torn country north of Pakistan. IEDs have posed as serious a threat to life in Afghanistan as in Iraq, and are used in huge numbers by the Taliban, often in concert with more conventional attacks using small arms and RPGs. Bomb disposal experts have been working at full stretch in appalling conditions trying to deal with the massive IED threat – and sometimes these men have paid the ultimate price. At the time of writing, out of forty-seven British soldiers killed in Afghanistan in 2009, thirty-six died as a result of IEDs. The threat is huge and ever present, and the role of bomb disposal officers as vital as any infantryman or tank in defeating the Taliban extremists who are determined to drag Afghanistan back into the Middle Ages.

In Afghanistan, three main types of IED have regularly been dealt with by army bomb disposal experts. The first is the roadside bomb, detonated by a hidden Taliban insurgent using a command wire. The second is the more sophisticated remote bomb, triggered by a signal from a radio or a cellular phone. The third is the conventional landmine, which is buried and triggered by a pressure plate. The Taliban often use artillery shells as bombs, rigging them with simple detonators and sometimes packing them with fertilizer to increase their explosive power. One further threat to British lives are the tens of thousands of landmines sown by the Soviet Army during their campaigns of the 1980s. In Helmand province during 2008, where most of the British forces are based, army bomb disposal experts made safe 3,276 Taliban IEDs during 2008, more combined than all of the bombs ever planted by the IRA during the Troubles in Northern Ireland. Bomb disposers are daily working at the limits of their endurance, and often tackling multiple devices when extremely fatigued by the sheer pace of the work.

Warrant Officer Class 2 "Gaz" O'Donnell, a Scotsman from Edinburgh, was described by no less an authority than Lieutenant General Sir Graeme Lamb, commander of the Field Army and a former CO of the SAS, as 'bigger than life and as brave as a lion.' O'Donnell had joined the army in 1992, serving initially with the Royal Army Ordnance Corps, and performing tours of duty in Sierra Leone, Northern Ireland, Iraq and Afghanistan with the Royal Logistic Corps. In 2004, when he was a staff sergeant ammunition technician, O'Donnell had passed the 'high-threat operator' test first time round, making him an expert IED bomb-disposal expert. The use of wire and radio-controlled firing devices on IEDs in Iraq and Afghanistan has raised the risk levels for bomb disposal experts to very high levels. They are acutely aware that unlike the conventional buried landmine, these IEDs are triggered by someone watching for the perfect moment to cause the maximum damage. In southern Iraq in 2006, O'Donnell was awarded the George Medal for his 'selflessness and composure in challenging and distressing situations', a good example being the four hours he spent inside a cumbersome bomb-disposal suit working in temperatures hot enough to drive a man crazy deactivating a roadside bomb.

O'Donnell's tour in Afghanistan was incredibly taxing, most bomb-disposal experts dealing with more bombs in one week than many would see in an entire year in Britain. He once disarmed a bomb after it was triggered – not knowing how much time he had until it went off. He also once had to use his fingers to save his own life when trying to diffuse a Taliban landmine. He had raced to the scene where a patrol from the 2nd Battalion, The Parachute Regiment, had discovered a device buried in a track close to their camp at Kajaki. 'The device had a pressure plate. But not like the ones we normally see,' said O'Donnell afterwards. 'The circuit was being held open by what looked like a large clothes peg.'[9] The device was wired to explode when a soldier's weight pushed the peg shut, forcing two metal contacts together. A length of black rubber wrapped around the opposite end of the bomb held the contacts open. The detonator was connected to an 82mm mortar bomb and a Chinese 107mm rocket, giving a total high explosive content of over 2kg. As O'Donnell began gingerly to clear away dirt that was partially covering the device, the rubber band slipped and the contacts began to close. 'I didn't really have time to think, I just had to jam my fingers into the switch.'[10] O'Donnell's hair-raising experiences highlight just how dangerous and unpredictable bomb disposal work is, especially during combat operations in Afghanistan where brave men like O'Donnell are risking their lives, week in and week out, with very little rest.

In May 2008, O'Donnell was called in to diffuse an IED that had been planted close to a Coalition position in the Upper Gereshk Valley in Helmand Province. O'Donnell successfully made the device safe – but he suspected that the Taliban had probably planted several more thereabouts. For nine hours O'Donnell carefully checked the ground. His incredible devotion to duty and investigative talents paid off when he discovered *seven* more bombs that would have wrought terrible loss of life among British forces had they not been found. During those nine hours, O'Donnell worked alone in temperatures of forty degrees. Many of the bombs that he carefully uncovered were fitted with anti-tamper devices, the Taliban hoping to kill British bomb-disposal experts as well as other troops. Even more incredibly, during the painstaking and slow process of identifying and making safe the bombs, O'Donnell was fully exposed to nearby Taliban forces.

In July 2008, a bomb was discovered to be blocking a major convoy route and Warrant Officer O'Donnell was called forward to deal with the threat. A British convoy from the Argyll and Sutherland Highlanders, 5th Battalion, Royal Regiment of Scotland (5 Scots) Battle Group, was forced to halt in an exposed position while O'Donnell went to work diffusing it. Again, the Taliban could have attacked at any time. O'Donnell worked at the side of the road for twenty-four hours, uncovering a total of eleven devices that would have devastated any convoy that had passed by. One of the devices was controlled by a command wire, meaning it could be remotely detonated and, as O'Donnell approached it the concealed Taliban triggered the device. Fortunately O'Donnell survived because the bomb failed to detonate fully, but the enormous dangers faced by men like O'Donnell were blatantly clear to everyone.

Tragically, in September 2008, Gary O'Donnell was killed when he tried to approach yet another IED, so that he could clear a path through for his comrades. The bomb was blocking the route for a 5 Scots convoy that was trying to move to the west of the small town of Musa Qaleh. During his final tour in Afghanistan O'Donnell had defused a total of over fifty IEDs. Warrant Officer O'Donnell was married with four children, and the youngest child was born only nine weeks before O'Donnell was killed in Afghanistan. 'He was a larger-than-life character,' said his widow Toni. 'He loved his job. He did what had to be done.'[11] For his incredible and sustained acts of bravery, O'Donnell was posthumously awarded a second George Medal (displayed as a bar on the ribbon of his first award). It was the first time in twenty-seven years that someone had been awarded the George Medal twice, the last recipient being, not unsurprisingly, another army bomb disposal expert named Peter Gurney. Gurney gained his first medal in Northern Ireland in 1973 and the second diffusing an IRA bomb on Oxford Street in central London in 1981.

'It was his passion and he took immense pride in making places safer for other people,' said O'Donnell's commanding officer, Lieutenant-Colonel David Wilson. 'The danger to his own life rarely seemed to affect him. If it did, he kept it to himself. He was a real character, and a natural leader of men, his smile giving assurance to the less experienced or more anxious.'[12] Being awarded the George Medal twice was some consolation for a life lived and ultimately sacrificed in trying to help others. 'You cannot describe the feelings I have. I am so proud of him,' said Toni O'Donnell when she was informed of her husband's honour. 'He would be chuffed about this...I'll tell the children about him. He was a brave man. A big man.'[13] His citation from the Ministry of Defence stated what could be the job description for all bomb-disposal experts: 'He [O'Donnell] repeatedly placed himself in immense personal danger and saved an untold amount of lives with his skill and selfless determination.' Another senior Army officer was moved to write of O'Donnell: 'What he used to do was ridiculously brave. He went far beyond the call of duty.

1 *Fact File: 33 Engineer Regiment*, BBC News, 28 March 2003, add website info.
2 '*Bomb hero soldier is honoured by Queen*' by Elizabeth Hopkirk, *Evening Standard*, 2 July 2008
3 Ibid.
4 '*WW II bomb safely detonated*', BBC News, 8 January 2002
5 '*My stomach was torn open...so I tucked my shirt in and kept shooting: Amazing stories of the selfless heroes of Afghanistan*' by Matthew Hickley and Paul Harris, *The Daily Mail*, 7 October 2008
6 Ibid.
7 Ibid.
8 '*Rare honour to Basra bomb hero*' by Damion Roberts, *Cambridge News*, 9 May 2008
9 '*George Medal winner killed in Helmand was father of four*' by Jerome Starkey and Kim Sengupta, *The Independent*, 13 September 2008
10 Ibid.
11 '*Bomb disposal expert blown up by Taliban awarded second George Medal as 178 heroes are honoured for Bravery*' by Matthew Hickley, *Daily Mail*, 6 March 2009

12 'Warrant Officer Gary O'Donnell: selfless soldier and George Medal recipient', *The Times*, 18 September 2008

13 '*Bomb disposal expert blown up by Taliban awarded second George Medal as 178 heroes are honoured for Bravery*' by Matthew Hickley, *Daily Mail*, 6 March 2009

14 '*Hero gets 2nd George Medal*' by Tom Newton Dunn, *The Sun*, 5 March 2009

CHAPTER 10

The Last Place on Earth

'Then I got shot again. I looked at my stomach and it was cut
open, so I tucked my shirt in to keep it together and kept on
firing until more lads from the platoon arrived.'

Private Luke Cole, The Mercian Regiment, 2008

'People keep running down our teenagers but it is a lot of
rubbish. The youth of today are volunteers who chose to
come and serve and they chose to be brave. Courage is not a
feat it's a brutal application of will power and they have it in
abundance.'

Lieutenant General Graham Lamb,
Commander Field Army, 2008

The typical experiences of a young infantry officer serving a tour of
duty in Afghanistan can perhaps be summed up by those of Major
Tom Biddick of the Royal Anglian Regiment during the summer of
2007. After the death of the battalion's first soldier on the tour,
Private Chris Gray, Biddick, a company commander, launched a raid
that killed twenty-two Taliban fighters during intense close quarters
combat. In June, Biddick was traveling in the front of a Viking
armoured vehicle when it ran over a mine. Corporal Daz Bonner,
who was sitting in the back, was killed. Major Biddick later led his
company on a epic twelve-day trek behind enemy lines where they
eliminated a major Taliban sanctuary in heavy fighting, killing an
estimated seventy-five of the enemy. The intense combat operations

completed by Major Biddick and the other members of the Royal Anglian's battlegroup in 2007 are not unusual and demonstrate that British soldiers are experiencing some of the heaviest fighting undertaken by the British Army since the Korean War and paying a heavy price in casualties. Biddick was awarded the Military Cross for being 'fearless in combat' and showing 'exceptional leadership skills.' Biddick was one of several officers and men of the battalion decorated for their gallantry. 'The medal is an absolute honour, as was the privilege to command an infantry company in combat,' said Biddick. 'As a battle group we had one of the most successful and aggressive tours of duty in recent times and it's right and proper that that has been recognised.'[1]

It is not just officers who are winning a reputation for bravery and daring on the battlefield but more junior soldiers are also being increasingly called upon to lead by example and one of the extraordinary developments to have emerged from Afghanistan is the steady stream of stories of young men, most barely out of their teens, who have taken command when their leaders have been hit, and rallied the men to incredible feats of bravery. Many other junior soldiers have exercised huge resources of initiative while under fire and performed immense acts of courage to save their mates from certain death and injury. This is the generation of young people so often derided by the media. Lieutenant General Graham Lamb, Commander Field Army, raised the point that the courage shown by British troops on operations against the Taliban in Afghanistan was a testament that Britain's youth, when properly trained, are as good as their forbears.

The war in Afghanistan began on 7 October 2001. It was a reaction to the attacks that had shaken the United States on September 11th. US intelligence had long identified the Taliban government of Afghanistan as the main supporters and suppliers of the militant Islamist terrorist coalition known as al-Qaeda, headed by the notorious Osama bin Laden. The British government, faithful to the Special Relationship that had been so important to the two nations since the Second World War, contributed significant combat forces alongside the Americans aimed at ousting the Taliban from power and freeing the Afghan people from tyranny. It has been one of the most controversial decisions taken by a Britiah government in a long time, and the outcome of the deployment still remains difficult to predict.

The aims of the invasion, as stated by President George W. Bush and Prime Minister Tony Blair, was to locate bin Laden and other al-Qaeda leaders who were believed to be hiding out in Afghanistan, and to remove the Taliban from power in Kabul and set up a democratically elected government. The second of these aims was rapidly achieved when Kabul was secured, but then things began to slip rapidly into chaos and conflict. The American-imposed 'democratic' government of President Hamid Karzai in Kabul remains unpopular across the country, each area having its own tribes and regional leaders. The scourge of the warlord has not been eliminated by toppling the Taliban and flooding the country with foreign troops; neither has Afghanistan's reliance on heroin production to prop up its poor and underdeveloped economy. The Taliban still controls large stretches of the hinterland today, and has engaged American, British and Coalition forces in almost continuous fighting for the best part of a decade, with neither side actually achieving very much. The cost to the British has been a steady stream of casualties and a slow turning of the public against the war. Most people do not understand why British forces are fighting in Helmand Province, or what they are fighting for, and politicians struggle to give real answers to these important questions.

The current operation in Afghanistan is supposed to be a NATO one. A basic principle of NATO is that 'an attack on one country is deemed to be an attack on all and should be opposed by all. The September 11th attack was clearly an attack on the United States. But, the American operations in Afghanistan are only being substantially supported by Britain, with reasonable support also coming from Canada. There are twenty-eight countries in NATO, mostly in Europe. The big controversy in Britain is that the remaining European countries are only sending token forces to Afghanistan and, then, only to the more peaceful regions. This craven attitude leaves the British bearing the majority of the European casualties and the financial costs.'

Two military operations are currently being run simultaneously in Afghanistan. Firstly, there is the American-led Operation 'Enduring

Freedom' that is focused on combating the Taliban throughout the eastern and southern areas of the country, especially those provinces bordering Pakistan (the old British Empire's North West Frontier). The second operation is the International Security Assistance Force, run by Nato and tasked with securing Kabul and its environs.

The British government has been slow to appreciate how difficult it is to win a war against the Afghans. A quick glance at the military misadventures of the British Empire in Afghanistan demonstrates a sorry catalogue of defeats and humiliations in a country with essentially mediaeval infrastructure and some might argue an essentially mediaeval people. Listed below are the occasions in which British forces have either invaded Afghanistan or fought battles along its borders, and for which service and campaign medals were issued. It is, as can be seen, a very long list, but any lessons that Britain learned from all this death and destruction appear to have been conveniently forgotten by politicians in the 21st century.

1839-42 – First Afghan War
1878-80 – Second Afghan War
1894-95 – Waziristan
1901-02 – Waziristan
1908 – Northwest Frontier
1919 – Afghanistan
1919-21 – Waziristan
1921-24 – Waziristan
1925 – Waziristan
1930-32 – Northwest Frontier
1935 – Northwest Frontier
1936-37 – Northwest Frontier
1937-39 – Northwest Frontier
1939-45 – Northwest Frontier
2001-present – Afghanistan

The British Army is short of men, equipment and helicopters. This situation has been deliberately created by constant defence reviews that have reduced the numbers of infantry battalions. The responsible politicians have, ironically, continued to commit British forces to wars all over the world. The situation has become so bad that the Reserve Forces are being called upon in ever increasing numbers to plug the gaps in the ranks of the regulars. The Territorial Army now accounts for nearly a quarter of the army's strength. Part-time warriors are leaving their civilian jobs and serving in Afghanistan, facing death and destruction in common with their regular colleagues. Some have already paid the ultimate price.

Like many members of Britain's military reserves, Lance-Corporal Matthew Croucher of the Royal Marines Reserve volunteered to serve in Afghanistan with his regular colleagues, helping to make up the shortfall in men experienced by Britain's overstretched and under-funded military. Croucher, who was born in 1984 in Solihull in the West Midlands, had joined the Royal Marines in November 2000. He was a regular marine until November 2005 when he transferred to the Royal Marines Reserve and took employment in civilian life. Before going to Afghanistan, Croucher had already completed three tours of duty in Iraq with 40 Commando. Croucher was certainly no stranger to fierce and high intensity action. When he was stationed at Forward Operating Base (FOB) Inkerman in Helmand Province in 2007 he displayed immense courage under fire. On 9 November, Croucher's troop had become involved in a fierce exchange of fire with Taliban insurgents. One marine was down with a serious wound to the chest, but the medic was unable to reach him to render first aid as he was himself pinned down by heavy enemy fire. Croucher had crawled forward to the wounded man and, for twenty minutes, he had applied emergency first aid to the marine while Taliban bullets had cracked overhead or kicked up spurts of dirt and dust around them. Croucher had saved the man's life and disregarded his own in doing so. Croucher was later involved in an accident where his leg was broken but, after intensive treatment in England, he had volunteered to return to Afghanistan as soon as he was medically fit.

On 11 February 2008 Croucher was a member of the elite Commando Reconnaissance Force tasked with being the eyes and ears of 3 Commando Brigade in Helmand. He was part of a four-man patrol tasked with stealthily searching some Afghan compounds for bomb-making materials used by the Taliban to manufacture Improvised Explosive Devices or IEDs. The lethality of IEDs had become legendary both in Iraq and Afghanistan and targeting the bomb makers and their workshops has become a vital Coalition task, as IEDs have continued to take a heavy toll of lives.

Croucher and his comrades were operating at night in almost complete darkness, as they carefully crept through a dirty, mud-walled compound of the type that form most of the towns and villages in Afghanistan. Croucher was in the vanguard, at the head of the single column of marines, with the Patrol Commander about five metres behind, and two other marines similarly spaced out behind him, weapons at the ready. The commander had just given the order to begin extracting back towards a pre-arranged rendezvous with the rest of the Reconnaissance Force. As Croucher crept forward he suddenly felt a wire brush against his legs just below his knees, the wire going tight before Croucher could stop his forward motion, and then suddenly slack. With a dropping sensation in his stomach, Croucher heard a metallic ping and then the thud of something heavy landing in the dirt at his feet. He realized immediately that he had sprung one of the oldest types of booby-trap used in warfare, the tripwire grenade. A hand grenade had been concealed beside a doorway, and a wire connected to the grenade's round metal pin had been strung across the void. Apply enough pressure to the wire and the pin was pulled out of the grenade. When a booby trap like this is activated, the grenade's arming handle flies off and the fuse begins to wind down towards detonation with a hiss. How long before the grenade explodes is simply determined by how many seconds the fuse was manually set at, and Croucher had no way of knowing that. 'With extraordinary clarity of thought and remarkable composure,' read Croucher's citation, 'he shouted 'Grenade', then 'Tripwire' in an attempt to warn his comrades to find cover before the grenade exploded.'[2] He and his comrades were completely exposed, with no cover available in the few remaining seconds before the grenade went off. 'In an act of great courage, and demonstrating a complete disregard for his own safety, he threw himself on top of the grenade, pinning it between his day sack, containing his essential team stores, and the ground.'[3] Croucher pressed his body down onto the grenade, believing that he was about to die. He pulled up his legs and wrapped his arms around them.

With a loud bang and a dense cloud of dust the grenade detonated. 'It felt like someone had run up to me and kicked me in the back really hard, along with a loss of hearing, ears in extreme pain and a throbbing head,' recalled Croucher. 'Then body started aching and there was a smell of burning. Total disorientation.' Remarkably, Croucher survived with only superficial injuries, his day sack absorbing most of the explosion and shrapnel. Croucher had been thrown some distance by the detonation and the pack had been ripped from his back. His body armour and helmet were studded with grenade fragments. The pack contained a large lithium battery used to power the patrol's electronic countermeasures equipment, and this had burst into flames. Amazingly, Croucher refused to be evacuated for treatment and instead, sore, bruised, partially deaf and somewhat singed, he continued to do his job.

His amazing courage in trying to save the lives of his comrades, while clearly prepared to lay down his own to do so, meant that Matthew Croucher was awarded the George Cross. When he was informed of the award, Croucher said simply: 'There are a lot of other heroic acts which go on in Afghanistan which go unnoticed.' As with so many incredibly brave and courageous people, Croucher's humility shone through. He was one of only 404 people to have received the award, and one of just twenty-one living recipients.

The Parachute Regiment had been established on the orders of Winston Churchill in 1940, and first seen action a year later during the dark days of the Second World War. Within a few short years the Paras had built for themselves a reputation for boldness, courage and tenacity that it had taken the line regiments hundreds of years to acquire, winning immortality during the D-day invasion of Normandy in 1944 with the daring capture of the Merville gun battery that threatened the British invasion beaches. Later that same year Paras stubbornly held Arnhem Bridge against overwhelming attacks from the crack *Waffen-SS* troops as the vanguard of Operation 'Market Garden', the largest airborne operation mounted when three airborne divisions, including one British, had dropped into occupied Holland to secure the route for a planned British armoured thrust into the heartland of Germany and end the war early. The operation was a costly failure, but the Paras had covered themselves with glory. The Paras had last jumped into action in their traditional role during the 1956 Suez Crisis, when they had captured Gamil Airfield in Egypt, during the Anglo-French operation attempting to recover control of the Suez Canal which the Egyptians had recently nationalised without paying compensation to the British and French shareholding governments. That operation failed after American opposition to it. They had served with distinction and some controversy in Northern Ireland throughout The Troubles, where they had earned wide counter-insurgency experience that would later prove invaluable in Afghanistan, and won glory for themselves, and two Victoria Crosses, during the 1982 Falklands War where they had proved once again that they were, in the words of their motto, *Utrinque Paratus* – Ready for Anything. None of the three Para battalions had served in the Gulf War in 1991 but the Paras had been deployed to Iraq in 2003 where they had patrolled and guarded locations but had seen no fighting. Afghanistan was to prove quite different.

The 3rd Battalion, The Parachute Regiment (3 Para) had a gruelling tour of Helmand Province in 2006 under the command of Lieutenant-Colonel Stuart Tootal. They had been dispatched originally to provide security during reconstruction efforts; specifically the protection of the vital Kajaki Dam hydroelectric station, but their tour had rapidly degenerated into a struggle for survival as the Taliban launched some of the heaviest attacks yet seen by British troops in Afghanistan. One incident in September 2006, outside the town of Kajaki, has entered regimental legend for the bravery displayed by many of the participants, and for the tragic and controversial death of one of them.

At noon on 6 September 2006, a 3 Para patrol set out from Observation Post (OP) Normandy located on a hill above the town of Kajaki to investigate the possible sighting of Taliban fighters. A group of Taliban had boldly set up a vehicle checkpoint on the edge of the town and they were fleecing drivers of their cash at gunpoint. Normally, when the British spotted Taliban moving about in the open the Fire Support Group (FSB) would engage them with mortars or machine-gun fire. On this occasion it was not possible to open fire as the Taliban were mixed up with civilians in the town and they knew that they were relatively safe from attack.

Lance-Corporal Stuart Hale of Support Company requested permission to move closer to the Taliban with his sniper rifle, in the hope of picking off their leader. Permission was granted, and Hale set off down the dusty hill. When Hale arrived near the bottom of the hill he jumped over a narrow dry river bed – and into a world of hurt. Suddenly finding himself lying on his back, stunned and with dust and debris raining down around him, he 'looked down and saw that he was missing a finger. His leg was twisted at a weird angle and there was a stump where his foot should have been. He had stepped on a mine.'[4] Half a mile away, at OP Athens, another small post keeping watch over Kajaki, the men of the Mortar Platoon heard the mine explode. Corporal Mark Wright began calling for medics and stretcher bearers; and nine men were quickly assembled and started down their hill towards where Hale lay helpless and exposed. When the medics arrived, they quickly dosed Hale with morphine for the pain, applied tourniquets his leg and gave him fluids intravenously. Wright decided that hauling Hale up the hill on a stretcher over the rough ground would probably result in him bleeding to death, so instead Wright got on the radio and requested a casevac helicopter. Wright and his men could see a flat area of ground, ideal for use as an improvised landing zone (LZ), just fifteen yards from their position, and Wright and Corporal Stuart Pearson began clearly a route to it from Hale's position, probing the ground with their bayonets for hidden mines. They marked the route with tape and the men safely carried Hale over to the LZ.

So far the rescue was going according to plan. Corporal Pearson returned along the marked path towards the site where Hale had been wounded and where several of the men were waiting, intent on collecting a water container. Suddenly there was another loud explosion and Pearson was thrown to the ground. He had stepped on another mine that had been overlooked during the rush to get Hale to the LZ. Pearson lay badly injured only a few yards from the other men, but everyone realized that any further movement could trigger other, as yet unseen, mines. Pearson strapped a tourniquet around his own shattered leg and injected himself with morphine to help alleviate the pain.

One and a half hours after the initial explosion that had badly injured Lance-Corporal Hale a big RAF twin-rotor Chinook helicopter roared overhead. The aircraft unfortunately lacked a winch, so it would have to land on the LZ, which was in the middle of a minefield. Corporal Wright realized that the huge downwash from the Chinook's rotors would dislodge stones, and probably

147

trigger more mines, let alone the weight of the chopper actually landing. He desperately waved the chopper off before it set down but, as he shielded his eyes from the massive dust and sand cloud whipped up Wright knelt down. His knee settled unknowingly onto another mine, and the detonation badly wounded Wright in the left upper chest, face, neck and arms. Lance-Corporal Alex Craig, a Para-trained medic with the Royal Army Medical Corps, was struck in the chest by shrapnel from the mine. Private Dave Prosser of the Mortar Platoon went to Craig's assistance. Even though he was wounded and bleeding badly, Craig set off to walk back up the hill, unaided, to the British position.

In the meantime, Lance-Corporal Paul Hartley, another Para medic, decided to try and reach Wright. He took off his medical pack and flung it to the ground in front of him, using it as an unorthodox mine detector as he slowly moved towards the grievously injured NCO. By this method Hartley successfully reached Wright without tripping any more mines. Fusilier Andy Barlow, who was on attachment with 3 Para from his parent regiment, the Royal Regiment of Fusiliers, was standing nearby and he took a single step backwards in order to give Hartley more room to treat Wright – and triggered another mine. Barlow's left leg was studded with shrapnel, some of which also hit Private Prosser. Realizing that he was quite badly hurt, Prosser jammed a field dressing into the hole in his chest and wrapped another around the wound in the hope of stemming the bleeding. He recalled that he 'started first-aiding myself with what I could find. I had blood pissing out of my chest and everywhere.'[5]

At Camp Bastion, the 3 Para HQ, their commanding officer, Lieutenant-Colonel Tootal, requested that American Blackhawk helicopters be dispatched immediately to rescue the stranded Paras. The American choppers, unlike their British equivalents, were equipped with winches so that they could hover over the minefield and pick up the wounded men rather than risk touching their wheels down. It was another example of how the British were trying to fight a modern war without the correct equipment, whereas the Americans were well-supplied. Tootal's superiors in the city of Kandahar informed the Colonel that he would have to wait a long time for the American choppers; it would be three hours after the first mine exploded before two Blackhawks started towards Kajaki.

While the men waited in the baking heat, Corporal Wright kept up their spirits with jokes, and they chatted about home and Wright's forthcoming marriage. Eventually, after a seeming eternity lying out in the open, Wright and his colleagues heard the reassuring sound of two Blackhawk helicopters fast approaching. Two specialist US Air Force aircrew Senior Airman Jason Broline and Staff Sergeant Cameron Hystad, came down the winch cables with a scoop stretcher and started picking up the wounded. Lance-Corporal Hale went first, followed by Wright and the others. After collecting all of the wounded, the Americans then rescued all of the unwounded British soldiers as well. Wright was flown directly to an LZ at the Kajaki Dam where he was transferred to a waiting RAF Chinook. The intention was to fly him to the main British hospital at Camp Bastion for emergency treatment, but twenty-eight-year-old Wright died of his wounds during the flight. He was later posthumously awarded the George Cross. Paul Hartley, the army medic, received the George Medal, and Corporal Pearson the Queen's Gallantry Medal. The two American airmen who risked their lives saving the British wounded were each awarded a Queen's Commendation for Bravery in the Air.

Fusilier Damien Hields was one of thousands of young men for whom the British Army had been their whole teenage and adult life. Hields had joined up when he was sixteen, and when his greatest test as a soldier arrived in the summer of 2007 he was twenty-four years old and married with a young family. Hields, from Denbigh in North Wales, along with the 1st Battalion, The Royal Welsh (Royal Regiment of Wales) had been posted to the second city of Afghanistan, Kandahar, in the south of the war-torn country. Patrols from 1 Royal Welsh, under the command of Lieutenant-Colonel Huw James, was involved in several operations around Kandahar, assisting other ISAF nations in operations aimed at killing Taliban insurgents, and also disrupting the region's endemic and highly profitable heroin trade, heroin that very often ended up on the streets of Britain. Hields and part of 1 Royal Welsh were returning to Kandahar on 3 June from an operation 100 miles north in the province of Uruzgan, where they had been assisting Dutch peacekeepers. A long convoy of desert tan Land Rovers snaked along a dusty track that wound its way through a parched valley, the vehicles loaded up with hot and tired British soldiers who were looking forward to getting back into the safety of their base in the city after a challenging mission. Unbeknown to the 1 Royal Welsh patrol, the fifty soldiers travelling in the convoy were about to drive straight into a carefully prepared killing ground. Concealed in positions on either side of the valley were upwards of 150 Taliban fighters waiting in silence, dressed in their traditional dishdasha robes and turbans, many wearing Chinese-made webbing and ammunition pouches. They were well-armed, sporting the usual Taliban weapons of choice – AK47 assault rifles, AKM machine-guns (the Soviet equivalent of the reliable British General Purpose Machine-Gun), and the ubiquitous RPG-7 rocket propelled grenade launchers that had proved so effective against British and Coalition vehicles in Afghanistan and in the war in Iraq. The Taliban also had a few Russian 82mm mortars ready to lob high explosive bombs down onto the British convoy when the time came to spring the trap.

The first the British knew of the presence of the Taliban was a sudden loud explosion from the head of the convoy and a huge cloud of black smoke that brought all of the vehicles behind shuddering to a screeching halt. The lead Land Rover had triggered a land mine that had been carefully laid by the Taliban to stop the convoy and the vehicle had been thrown on to its roof by the impact of the massive blast. Seconds later, while the boom of the explosion still echoed off the valley walls, hell broke loose as the insurgents launched their assault. From both sides of the valley, small-arms fire erupted from a multitude of positions, as bullets whined and cracked around the British vehicles, kicking up spurts of sand and dust and thumping into the Land Rovers like hail onto a tin roof. These were followed by the sudden WHOOSH of an RPG rocket, a white vapour trail marking the launcher's position, as they flew in the direction of the halted convoy, detonating with a loud bang and a shower of white-hot shrapnel and shards of razor-sharp rock.

Fusilier Hields was operating a grenade machine-gun, an enormously potent weapon that was loaded with a box containing thirty-two individual grenade rounds. It enabled an operator to lay down a considerable volume of fire onto any target. Hields realized that he needed to suppress the huge volume of Taliban fire that was raking the convoy, and the grenade machine gun appeared to be the perfect weapon to take on an enemy who was partially concealed amongst the rocks of the parched and desolate valley. The RPG is an old but, nonetheless, potent weapon, especially when fired at infantry in the open, or at the soft-skinned or lightly-armoured vehicles used by the Coalition Forces in Afghanistan. It has also proved effective against helicopters. An American twin-rotor Chinook had been shot down by a lucky hit from an RPG rocket in June 2005, with sixteen soldiers being killed.[6] The Americans earlier lost several Blackhawk helicopters to RPGs during their failed operations to restore order and government in the city of Mogadishu in Somalia in 1993.

Fusilier Hields soon pinpointed one of the positions from which the grenades were being launched. He began by firing a few ranging shots until he was sure he had identified the RPG firing point. 'Then I switched to automatic fire,' recalled Hields. 'I emptied a box onto the position and you could see all the dust and smoke flying about where they hit. After that no fire came back from that position and I moved on to the next one.'[7] Hields was fully exposed to the furious Taliban fire all the time he operated the grenade machine-gun, but he was so focussed on knocking out the enemy firing positions that he barely noticed the bullets that cracked past him or impacted against the sides of his Land Rover with menacing regularity. He had silenced the first enemy position, 'and I moved on to the next one,' recalled Hields, 'One or two rounds until I got onto the target, and switch to automatic and empty the box.'[8] It may have been overkill, but it was working.

The Taliban soon realized that enormous punishment was being inflicted upon their forces by a lone British soldier operating a fearsome new weapon. They soon directed much of their fire towards Hields' Land Rover, RPGs and machine gun and rifle bullets whooshing and cracking past Hields, a blizzard of lead battering the Land Rover or ricocheting away across the valley floor. Hields was wreathed in dust and smoke as he continued to pour a deadly and accurate fire from his grenade machine-gun, silencing one enemy position after another. Suddenly, as Hields was in the process of bending down to retrieve yet another box of grenades from inside his Land Rover, he crumpled against the gun and fell back into the vehicle. 'I felt a sharp punch in the kidneys on my right side,'[9] said

Hields. When he looked at the wound he could see a bullet hole in his body armour and a little blood. His driver dragged him clear of the vehicle, which was taking a terrific pounding from the concentrated Taliban fire. 'There were so many holes in it [Hield's Land Rover], it was like a teabag,'[10] commented Hields' commanding officer, Lieutenant-Colonel James, when he saw it after the battle.

In another feat of incredible bravery a female medic, twenty-six year old Lance-Corporal Carley Williams jumped to her feet and dashed headlong through the storm of enemy fire to assist Hields, ignoring the screams of her fellow male soldiers to stay down. 'They saw one round actually pass between my legs,'[11] said Williams of the few moments of madness that ensued. Fortunately, it turned out that Hields had only been lightly wounded. The bullet 'had smashed a rib and gone out of me again without touching any internal organs which was very lucky,'[12] said Hields. Later Hields gave more details of his injuries, demonstrating just how lucky he had been. 'I got shot in the chest, it went through my ribs, smashed my rib cage and straight back out, but I got up and carried on fighting.'[13]

Before the Taliban bullet had knocked him down, Hields had single-handedly managed to destroy seven Taliban positions. 'Fusilier Hields showed extraordinary courage under intense fire,' said Colonel James. 'His actions allowed his patrol to come out of the ambush in which they were outnumbered by three or four to one and probably saved a lot of lives.'[14] Hields only stopped fighting when the effects of his wound began to take hold. 'I carried on, but then I collapsed in lots of blood and the driver got me out.'[15]

Hields was awarded the Military Cross for his gallantry, and the Nato Meritorious Service Medal.

Equal in status to the Navy's Distinguished Service Cross, the Military Cross is given to officers and (since 1993) Other Ranks of the British Army in recognition of '...gallantry during active operations against the enemy.' It was originally created in 1914 to cope with the huge numbers of brave actions performed by officers in the First World War. Lance-Corporal Williams, who made the valorous dash of mercy through a hail of lead and shrapnel, was awarded the Joint Commanders' Commendation. Hields swiftly recovered from his wounds after being evacuated by helicopter, along with many more seriously wounded men, and he was back with his company a month later on operations in Afghanistan.

As we have seen earlier in this chapter in the case of Royal Marine Reservist Lance-Corporal Matthew Croucher, not only professional soldiers are finding themselves in the thick of the action in Afghanistan and the heaviest fighting the British Army has experienced since the Korean War, but because of chronic under manning in most units, part-timers from the Reserves are in the front-line as well. The Territorial Army used to put up with a lot of stick from the regulars, often derisively being described as 'weekend warriors' or 'Saturday night soldiers'. But many of the Reservists bring with them from civilian life much needed skills, for examples civilian doctors and nurses serving with the Army Medical Services. Since the end of the Cold War, the TA has seen its operational focus change dramatically from simply providing a second line of defence for mainland Britain against a feared Soviet invasion to supporting the regular army wherever it is deployed on equal terms. Most of those who go on operations are volunteers, leaving behind civilian jobs and their families to serve their country. Several have lost their lives, and some have covered themselves in glory and greatly improved the image of the TA across the military world in the process.

Afghanistan has witnessed quite large-scale TA deployments. All of the infantry regiments in the Army (excluding the Foot Guards and the Royal Gurkha Rifles), have at least one TA battalion based in the counties from which their regular battalions recruit. Individuals and sometimes formed units from the TA battalions often join the regular battalions in the field to help make up the numbers and to gain operational experience. The Mercian Regiment is typical of this arrangement. The regiment was formed in 2007, part of the government's apparently incessant reorganization of the infantry that has witnessed the creation of ever bigger regiments, and the sad loss of so many historical units. The Mercian Regiment was formed from three regular regiments and one TA unit.

Private Luke Cole was twenty-two years old and in civilian life he was a forklift truck driver. He had originally joined the West Midlands TA unit, which after 2007 became the 4th Battalion,

Mercian Regiment. Cole had enthusiastically volunteered to go overseas with the regulars to Afghanistan, and was seconded to the 2nd Battalion in war-torn Helmand Province. The battalion was involved in many serious firefights with the Taliban in and around dusty little towns whose names have come to symbolize the Afghan conflict: Garmsir, Sangin, Lashkar Gar and the strip of agricultural land known as the Green Zone that lies along the banks of the Helmand River.

2 Mercians undertook a seven-month tour between March and October 2007. On 8 September elements of the battalion took part in a major operation to push the Taliban out of compounds in villages around the town of Garmsir. The Mercians were the spearhead of Operation 'Pechtaw', which was designed to push the Taliban in Helmand Province towards the Pakistani border. Ironically it was the battalion's final mission before they would return to Britain. Private Cole was one of eight soldiers forming a night patrol from A Company when he and his comrades came under fierce Taliban attack. The men had already christened their mission 'Operation Certain Death' as they faced advancing into the heart of Taliban country where they would be heavily outnumbered. They moved through a landscape of bombed-out compounds and buildings, the whole area criss-crossed with stagnant drainage ditches. Private Cole took a bullet through the leg. 'It took us all by surprise,' he said. 'Within seconds I was shot in the leg – the force of the bullet broke my leg.'[16] The bullet shattered five inches of bone. 'The pain didn't hit me at the time', recalled Cole. 'I thought it was a flesh wound. But I looked down and it was a mess, to be honest. I knew it was serious but I thought, 'This can't be the way I go out.' So I carried on. I could see muzzle flashes of enemy weapons in a ditch behind some trees so I kept shooting and gave my mates first aid when I could.'[17]

Twenty-five-year-old Private Johan Botha, a South African, had been hit and killed during the initial contact with the Taliban, and incredibly the Taliban fighters were trying to grab Botha's body as a trophy. The patrol commander, Sergeant Craig Brelsford, determined to prevent this from happening. Brelsford, a twenty-five-year-old from Nottingham, led a team of men to recover Botha's body. They nicknamed themselves the Spartans, and ran forward into a storm of bullets and RPGs, closer to within fifteen yards of the Taliban positions.

Most people, on getting seriously wounded, would wait for assistance and first aid, but not Private Cole. Instead, he continued to return fire at the enemy with his SA80 rifle. Other member's of Coles' patrol had also been hit, including Private Sam Cooper who lay injured and bleeding in the dirt. Cole crawled forward whilst under intense Taliban fire to try to give aid to Cooper. Cole exposed himself to the bullets that were smashing down all around him. 'I crawled along the ground and started to put a bandage around Cooper. But then I got shot again,' recalled Cole. 'The bullet went into my hip and through my stomach.'[18] This second wound was horrific. 'I looked at my stomach and it was cut open,' said Cole, 'so I tucked my shirt in to keep it together and kept on firing until more lads from the platoon arrived.'[19]

Apparently undeterred by his serious wounds, Private Cole continued with his self-appointed mercy mission. 'I kept firing at the enemy and trying to help Cooper.'[20] Cole also managed to radio a situation report to his platoon commander, twenty-five-year-old Lieutenant Simon Cupples. At this point Lance-Corporal David Chandler came to drag Cole away for medical attention. Even when evacuation was available, Cole refused to go until the more seriously injured Cooper had been taken first. 'The next thing I knew I was waking up at Selly Oak Hospital [in Birmingham].'[21] Two of his comrades were dead, and six others, not including Cole himself, had been injured in the intense battle with the insurgents. Sergeant Brelsford had been killed when he had run forward to place his body between the Taliban fire and the wounded in an act of incredible bravery. He was posthumously awarded the Military Cross. Lieutenant Cupples had come forward to rescue both the wounded and recover the bodies of the dead. 'It was asking a lot of the blokes to run forward into enemy fire like that,' recalled Cupples afterwards. 'But they did it because their mates were out there. When you live and serve with your men like that it creates a very special bond. You would do anything for those guys. That's what drove the soldiers forward.'[22] Cupples was awarded the Conspicuous Gallantry Cross.

Another TA soldier who served with Cole in Afghanistan

remarked on the intensity of the fighting. Lieutenant Aaron Browne, a twenty-nine-year-old teacher, received a Mention in Despatches for his bravery under fire. 'I came close to dying so many times I've lost count,' he said later. 'There was some very intense moments and the experience will live with me forever.'[23] Notwithstanding his experiences in Afghanistan, Browne planned to transfer from the TA to the regular army.

Because of the injury that he sustained, Private Cole has been left unable to walk without the use of a stick. When he was informed that he had been decorated for his gallantry, he said simply: 'At the end of the day I was just doing my job.'[24] Luke Cole was only the third Territorial Army soldier to be awarded the Military Cross in the past fifteen years. Back in Wolverhampton, Lieutenant-Colonel Ivan Yardley, commanding officer of the 4th Battalion, paid his own tribute to Private Cole. 'I have known Luke for a number of years and he has always struck me as a calm, intelligent, professional soldier...Pte Cole has shown the ability of the Territorial soldier to operate alongside his regular counterparts as a part of that fighting unit.'[25] Undoubtedly, Britain's citizen soldiers will remain in the vanguard of combat operations for many years to come.

Corporal Bryan Budd was an elite soldier in an elite unit. In August 2006, A Company of the 3rd Battalion, The Parachute Regiment (3 Para) was based in the small town of Sangin in the southern Afghan province of Helmand. The British, as part of NATO's International Security Assistance Force (ISAF) were supposed to be assisting the Afghan army and police with reconstruction and training efforts throughout the region, but the Para battle group had been sucked into sporadic fighting with local Taliban insurgents, who were keen to eject the British invaders from their homeland and reassert their totalitarian control over the local population. Bryan Budd was a member of the Pathfinder Platoon, an elite group of Paras whose task was more usually to drop in ahead of the rest of the battalion to conduct reconnaissance, mark out drop zones or conduct independent offensive operations in advance of the forward edge of the battle area. The Pathfinders had already been in continuous contact with the Taliban when they were besieged for fifty-two days in the town of Musa Qala after trying to assist trapped and surrounded Afghan National Police.

On 20 August, Budd and his platoon found themselves tasked with holding a small and isolated outpost known as a 'platoon house' in the dusty town of Sangin, while engineers blew holes in a compound 500 metres away. For months, Sangin had daily been attacked by the Taliban. On 20 August, three rifle sections, totaling twenty-four men, were out on patrol. They were spread out in a cornfield where visibility was limited because the corn was standing head high. Corporal Budd, in the vanguard, suddenly observed four Taliban insurgents approaching his section at a distance of fifty metres. A battle was clearly in the offing.

Budd signaled to his section using hand signs and organised the men into a flanking manoeuvre designed to cut the four Taliban off. The Paras quietly took up positions along the edge of the cornfield, but as they did so the Taliban observed this movement and opened fire. Suddenly, more automatic fire started to cut through the corn from another small group of Taliban who were firing at the British from behind a dried mud wall further back. Within seconds, one of Budd's men had been shot through the shoulder and another was struck in the nose. Budd quickly appraised the situation and realized that his section was being concentrated on by the Taliban and, unless he did something quickly, his men were going to die. In an act of enormous selfless courage, Budd suddenly stood up, fully exposing himself to the enemy fire and charged off alone into the cornfield, firing his SA80 rifle on full automatic mode at the Taliban fighters. Budd disappeared, but the rest of the section noticed that the Taliban fired suddenly slackened off and the section was able to pull back out of the immediate danger and get their casualties treated.

Corporal Budd remained unaccounted for after the rest of A Company went into action against the Taliban in the area in a attempt to locate the brave NCO. Apache gunships and RAF Harrier jets also plastered the Taliban positions, and the insurgents soon gave up and withdrew. An hour after he had charged the Taliban single handed, Budd was found lying beside three dead Taliban fighters. He was badly wounded, unconscious and appeared to have no pulse. The company sergeant-major took Budd's body back to the platoon house on a quad bike, but it was evident that Budd was dead. The commander of 3 PARA, Lieutenant-Colonel Stuart Tootal, said that

Budd was an 'outstanding leader.' His professional manner 'inspired confidence in all who worked with him.' Budd had 'died doing the job he loved, leading his men from the front, where he always was. He was proud to call himself a paratrooper and we were proud to stand beside him.' Budd's widow Lorena collected her husband's Victoria Cross from the Queen at Buckingham Palace on 7 March 2007.

The 1st Battalion, The Royal Irish Regiment deployed to Afghanistan as part of 16 Air Assault Brigade for a tour between March and September 2008. Three members of the battalion were awarded the Conspicuous Gallantry Cross (CGC), an award that is only one step below the Victoria Cross. All three men were decorated for their role in mentoring the Afghan National Army (ANA), a task that often involved British soldiers going into battle against the Taliban alongside their ANA charges. It is a vital task to try and make the ANA a more professional and competent force that can one day perhaps take over the job of combating the Taliban almost entirely alone, and then Coalition forces can finally leave Afghanistan. The three men awarded the CGC were mentoring different groups of ANA and they were involved in separate, but equally bloody, firefights with the Taliban.

Lance-Corporal Jone Toge, who was originally from Fiji and was on his second tour in Afghanistan, was awarded the CGC after taking command of the Operational Mentoring Liaison Team that was supporting the ANA north of the town of Musa Qaleh in Helmand Province after his commander had been wounded by Taliban fire. 'We were the only ground troops in the area, so we got the order to secure the high ground and get sight of a village where the Taliban were operating from,' recalled Toge. The ANA with Toge as mentor moved up to the village in two Warrior armoured vehicles. Suddenly, the vehicles came under a blizzard of RPG fire. 'The commander of the other Warrior got hit, so they withdrew back,' said Toge. 'We were left there alone, out in the open. Then we got hit.' The Warrior was badly damaged after taking half a dozen RPG strikes. Some of the ANA troops had already been moving forward on foot when the RPGs began to hit home and many were wounded. Toge, inside the Warrior, was dazed. 'I was out for about ten seconds,' said Toge. 'It was like in the movies – I had the radio strapped to my head, and I remember the commander asking, 'what's wrong, what's happening out there.'"

Toge could see that some of the ANA were wounded. 'They were screaming. One had a neck and shoulder injury,' recalled Toge. 'I knew I had to extract the casualties – that was my priority. So I went with the ANA medic – we crawled forward, got the guys, pulled them back and patched them up.' All the while Toge and the medic were saving the ANA soldiers they were under intense automatic and RPG fire and fully exposed to the enemy. The second objective of the ANA patrol that Toge was with was to secure the high ground before the village. Toge radioed for another Warrior to pick up the ANA wounded and take them back for treatment. 'We had our eyes on the enemy in the village. Literally, I was looking at them and their eyes were looking at me, and we were firing into each other – it was kind of weird.' Toge led the ANA troops in fighting off the Taliban forces and securing the area. His leadership and heroism were vital in permitting a second team to capture the entire village.

Acting Sergeant Alwyn Stevens was a section commander who was working alongside two other British soldiers mentoring ANA troops in the field when their patrol was ambushed by the Taliban. 'We came under heavy enemy fire from three different sides and they were moving to surround us,' recalled Stevens, 'so I took a team and pushed out to the flank and managed to engage them before they engaged us.' Stevens' quick and aggressive actions meant that his ANA team was able to escape an encirclement without taking any casualties. It is expected that, in the field, British soldiers will step in and lead ANA units in combat operations. Mostly, quite junior British NCOs have to take over from ANA commanders and direct combat operations and make decisions normally reserved for junior officers on the field of battle, and the British Army's emphasis on developing junior leaders' initiative skills has been proved time and again in fierce combat. The third CGC winner, Corporal Robert McClurg, demonstrated how well British soldiers mentoring ANA detachments performed under fire.

'I joined the Army three weeks after I left school when I was 16,' said McClurg. 'I always wanted to be in the Army – it is a career for me. There is nothing else I would want to do.' In Afghanistan in 2008 Corporal McClurg stepped in and took command of a group of ANA soldiers, and continued to lead them through six hours of combat with the Taliban. 'Suddenly, his group was fired upon and took casualties, including the ANA commander, who became ineffective. Undaunted, McClurg rallied his force, directing and leading a series of frontal and flanking assaults over a series of six hours. McClurg's intervention turned the battle.' What is all the more remarkable about Toge, Stevens and McClurg was the fact that they were commanding foreign troops, and were unable to speak the language of the men that they were leading in battle.

In October 2008 the 2nd Battalion, The Princess of Wales's Royal Regiment (Queen's and Royal Hampshires) were serving in southern Afghanistan. The battalion had seen constant operations against the Taliban, including plenty of close-quarter fighting. In a particularly fierce engagement Lance-Corporal Colin Spooner acted with conspicuous heroism when his patrol was ambushed and found itself cut off and surrounded inside a small Afghan compound. Twenty-two-year-old Spooner braved massive enemy machine gun and rocket fire to pass commands on to his men because the barrage of Taliban fire, which also included mortar bombs, was so loud that the men could not hear instructions that were being issued to them through their ear pieces. Spooner acted as a runner, passing on verbal instructions to the pinned-down sections from the patrol commander, sprinting between positions that were under intense Taliban fire. Spooner managed to make several trips between the positions, even though bullets, rockets and shrapnel flew past him in all directions. Suddenly he was felled by a mortar bomb than detonated close to him. Spooner was launched into the air by the blast, and his legs and groin were peppered by razor-sharp shards of shrapnel. Incredibly, although Spooner was concussed and bleeding from the painful blast injuries to his lower body, he got back onto his feet and continued with his job. In total, Spooner had thirty-two pieces of shrapnel embedded in his body. 'I realised I'd been hurt and I got dragged into a building and treated. I carried on giving orders.'[26] When the patrol, numbering nineteen men, was ordered to withdraw, Spooner, though he was in great pain, refused a stretcher because he knew that four men would be required to carry him, and that was four less rifles holding the Taliban at bay. Instead, Spooner hobbled along on his bleeding legs for several hundred yards as the patrol withdrew under fire until his mates were eventually able to load him onto a vehicle for medical treatment. 'That's what did most of the damage [to his body], but I'd do the same again.' For his astounding devotion to duty and courage, Colin Spooner received the Military Cross from The Prince of Wales at Buckingham Palace.

Lightning fast reactions are sometimes the only thing between living and dying in the war in Afghanistan. One British serviceman has exemplified this when he managed to save thirty of his comrades in a breathtaking display of pure bravery and dash. Sergeant Noel Connolly, a forty-one-year-old veteran Royal Marine, was serving with Plymouth-based 42 Commando, part of 3 Commando Brigade, in Kandahar Province in November 2008. The brigade tour lasted until March 2009, and included much fighting in Helmand Province as well.

Connolly, who hailed from Manchester and had originally joined the Marines in 1987, was a troop sergeant. His men had occupied an abandoned school and had set up a watch on traffic running along the nearby road. Connolly was standing close to the school when he noticed out of the corner of his eye an Afghan riding a motorcycle towards the Marines. 'I told my lads to expect a bomber,' recalled Connolly. 'The motorcyclist looked lost. He turned the bike around up the track and came back.'[27] Connolly was by now fully alerted to the Afghan's suspicious behaviour and he quickly ordered two marines to accompany him to investigate. 'I had no idea if he was the bomber. The only way of finding out was to challenge him,' said Connolly. Sergeant Connolly stepped into the road and shouted at the Afghan in Pashto, ordering him to stop. 'He stalled the bike and started pushing it away from us,' said Connolly. 'He stopped, straddled it and turned to face us. As I got to within ten metres, there was a loud crack from halfway down the bike.'[28] The Afghan was indeed a suicide bomber. 'That's when I saw a small toggle switch had been fitted to his handlebars. As soon as he went for the toggle again I rushed him. I grabbed him by the front of the shirt and hauled him off.'[29]

The frame of the motorcycle was later found by bomb disposal experts to contain 154 pounds of high explosive. It the bomb had been triggered many of the marines in the school would have been killed or injured. 'I'm not brave,' said Connolly afterwards, 'Someone had to stop him.'[30] The bomber was handed over to the Afghan Police and later sentenced to eighteen years in prison.

Sergeant Connolly, who has two children and whose wife is serving in the Royal Navy, was most concerned that his eighty-one-year-old mother was not told about his heroics. 'He doesn't talk about what happens when he's away,' said Connolly's sister. 'Our mum is a devout Catholic and has been praying every day since he has been away. Noel wrote telling her everything was quiet and he wasn't in the danger zone because he didn't want to worry her.'[31] It has been announced by the Ministry of Defence that Sergeant Connolly will in due course receive the Military Cross for his courageous actions.[32]

Able Seaman 1st Class Kate Nesbitt rose from cover and dashed headlong through a withering Taliban crossfire to reach a British soldier who lay bleeding in the dust from a ragged bullet wound to the neck. Nesbitt, a Royal Navy medic was serving on attachment with the 1st Battalion, The Rifles on operations in the Marjah District of Helmand Province when her patrol was ambushed by the Taliban. The soldiers were subjected to intense automatic rifle fire and RPGs that whooshed overhead and impacted all around them. Several men were wounded. Nesbitt dashed seventy yards through Taliban fire to help Lance-Corporal John List, who had been badly wounded, and she proceeded to treat him for forty-five minutes while Taliban fire erupted all around them. 'I heard "man down, man down" on the radio and I knew I was needed,' recalled Nesbitt. 'I got the location details and just sprinted.'

'I felt the impact go through my jaw, and the next thing I knew I was on my back,' said twenty-one-year-old List. 'I thought that was it. Then Kate appeared from nowhere, reassuring me everything would be OK. Kate says to be called a hero is too much. I say it could never be enough.'[33]

'When I first saw him [List], I didn't think he was going to make it. A round had gone through his top lip, ruptured his jaw and come out through his neck. He was struggling to breathe and choking on his own blood.' Nesbitt worked fast to save List's life. 'Bullets were whizzing around my head and shoulders and hitting the ground all around us. The Taliban knew they'd got someone and they were targeting us.' Nesbitt comes from a service family, her father having served in the Royal Marines, one brother currently serving in the navy aboard HMS *Ocean* and another training as a commando medic.

Nesbitt, who was only twenty-one at the time, repeatedly left cover to render first aid to her wounded comrades, placing herself directly into the line of fire several times. 'Able Seaman Nesbitt's actions throughout a series of offensive operations were exemplary,' reported the Ministry of Defence. 'Under fire and under pressure her commitment and courage were inspirational and made the difference between life and death.'[34] Nesbitt was one of fourteen members of 3 Commando Brigade who were awarded the Military Cross, and the first woman in the Royal Navy to receive this high gallantry award. Nesbitt's case demonstrates that, in modern warfare, women are increasingly playing a vital front-line role supporting the fighting troops. Able Seaman Nesbitt was only the second woman to receive the Military Cross, the first having been won by another medic in Iraq, Private Michelle Norris of the Royal Army Medical Corps in 2006. British women are seeing combat in increasing numbers, and proving themselves every bit as courageous as their male counterparts.

Another woman lauded for her courage under fire, and who may receive a bravery award, was Lance-Corporal Sally Clarke of the Royal Army Medical Corps. A medic attached to the 2nd Battalion, The Rifles, she was on a patrol south of Sangin in June 2009 when it was suddenly ambushed by the Taliban. The patrol had come across an anti-tank mine, which they were in the process of dealing with, when Taliban insurgents suddenly popped up from behind a nearby wall and fired two RPGs at them. One of the grenades actually bounced off one of the soldier's equipment, and both detonated with deafening explosions, spraying molten metal over a wide area. Seven members of the patrol were wounded.

Lance-Corporal Clarke, who was twenty-two and from Cheltenham, was one of these wounded in the attack, with dozens of shards of shrapnel embedded in her back and shoulder. Even though she was in great pain she immediately started treating the wounded. 'I ran to the most seriously injured first,' she recalled. This was Corporal Paul Mather, the Forward Air Controller. 'It hurt like hell, but once the explosions stopped and my hearing came back, I managed to climb through a ditch towards a group of soldiers treating other casualties,'[35] he recalled. 'Cpl Mather had taken wounds to his left bicep and had very bad shrapnel wounds across the lower part of his body,' said Clarke, 'one of the pieces had torn a fist-sized hole through his skin.'[36] Clarke treated all seven wounded soldiers, helping also to assist them to a helicopter landing site where they were evacuated for treatment in the hospital at Camp Bastion. Clarke, however, refused to board the helicopter, even though she was badly wounded. 'I didn't feel like my injuries were bad enough to go back to the hospital, particularly as I was the only medic on the ground at the time.'[37] Her professionalism and devotion to her comrades were astounding, considering that she had been peppered by shrapnel and was in considerable pain. 'It was pretty scary but it's my job to do it,' Clarke said afterwards.

The bravery of Royal Air Force, Royal Marine and Army Air Corps helicopter pilots in Afghanistan is another feature of the war that is often overlooked. Without the helicopters the troops could not be moved around, be supplied and the wounded extracted for treatment. More helicopters are needed in Afghanistan than the armed forces currently can deploy, and those that are there are the vital workhorses of the war on terror. The chopper pilots and crews face incredible risks and deadly situations on a virtually daily basis as the Taliban often deliberately target British helicopters.

Flight Lieutenant Alex "Frenchie" Duncan, a thirty-two year old Chinook pilot from 27 Squadron, based at RAF Odiham in Hampshire, was transporting the provincial governor of Helmand Province, Gulab Mangal, from the town of Musa Qala to the capital Lashkar Gar in May 2008. The RAF fly helicopters very low across the Afghan countryside in an effort to prevent the Taliban from having time to engage them with ground fire, but it does happen nonetheless with alarming regularity. Duncan was following a dried-up riverbed when the Chinook was struck by a hail of heavy machine gun fire as RPGs sailed past it.

'We were flying at 140 knots (160 mph) at 20ft,' recalled Duncan, who is married with two young children. The Taliban were aware that Governor Mangal was aboard the Chinook, and killing him would have been a major coup for them. In the words of Frenchie Duncan 'they were going to try and take us out.'[38] The first intimation Duncan had of trouble was when they flew over a parked vehicle. Duncan had maneuvered the big chopper so that his rear gunner could engage the vehicle, but suddenly the Chinook jolted and pulled up to the right. 'I had done nothing to the controls and wondered what had happened. Then one of the crew shouted 'We're hit'. For a second I thought 'Oh shit, we're going in'. Then I tried the controls and they responded. I said 'Right, we've getting out of here.'[39] The Chinook swerved up over a ridge and narrowly avoided colliding with a tall radio transmitter at the summit. Duncan did not realise that he and his crew had had a very lucky escape indeed, for the tail rotor blade had a hole torn in it, Duncan had lost part of his hydraulic system and automatic flight control system. 'I was going to put us down straight away because I thought we may crash at any second. But we were still in Taliban territory and if I landed we would have been killed by the enemy. So I decided to try and carry on.'[40] The nearest safe British base was thirty minutes flying time, but Duncan made it.

When Duncan and his crew stepped down at the base and started to examine their aircraft they were stunned by how lucky they had been. An RPG had gone straight threw the rear rotor without exploding. If it had the Chinook would have crashed. 'All the blood drained away from our faces,' recalled Duncan. 'I got out and had a look at the back rotor blade and started swearing a great deal.'[41] Six days later and Duncan and his crew were back in action, this time bringing in reinforcements for Paras fighting a fierce engagement with the Taliban. Duncan made two runs through intense ground fire. Afterwards, he said it was 'like a night in Berlin in World War Two. Everything was going up, rocket-propelled grenades, heavy machine-guns, the lot.' The first RPG narrowly missed taking out the cockpit. 'It was so close I could see the purple fizz coming out of the back of it and I instinctively lifted my legs up off the controls.' Duncan's flight commander called: 'Black Cat 223 [Duncan's call sign], are you OK.' Duncan replied laconically 'Shaken not stirred.'[42]

Alex Duncan received the Distinguished Flying Cross for his aerial courage and daring.

Marine Sam Alexander had been shot in the head just hours before he performed a spectacular feat of bravery in Helmand Province. 3 Commando Brigade sent units into Helmand Province to conduct Operation 'Abii Toorah' (Blue Sword) that was designed to interrupt the flow of Taliban reinforcements entering Helmand. Over two days the marines were involved in heavy skirmishing with the Taliban, during which Alexander had taken a bullet to the head. By a stroke of luck, Alexander's helmet had saved his life, the bullet becoming lodged in the lining. Just a few hours later, Marine Alexander and his section were ambushed by heavily armed Taliban who opened up on the marines from inside a compound. Within the space of a few seconds the section commander, a corporal, had been shot twice, and other members of the section had gone forward through the storm of lead to rescue him.

Marine Alexander, who was twenty-six, picked up a General Purpose Machine Gun (GPMG) and peppered the Taliban position with several belts of bullets to cover his mates. As he fired he advanced on the Taliban, seemingly oblivious to the heavy fire being directed at him as he strode towards the enemy firing the machine gun from the hip. The Taliban were only about forty-five feet away, but the heavy concentration of fire that Alexander put down had some effect. When he ran out of ammunition for the GMPG, Alexander tossed it and instead drew his 9mm pistol and began firing at the Taliban until he had exhausted all of its ammunition. He fired the weapons 'despite being completely exposed to heavy and accurate enemy fire,' and the Taliban eventually fled from their position, pursued by other marine units that had come up in support. For his gallantry, Sam Alexander received the Military Cross. His father, Stuart, sailing correspondent for *The Independent* newspaper, said of his son's courageous actions: 'Every father hopes to have a son who will excel and Sam has achieved that. He is anxious to underline that he regards this award as being as much for his comrades as it is for himself. He is part of a team and they all look after each other.'[43]

The fighting in Afghanistan is very often up close and personal. Some British soldiers have even had to resort to the use of that oldest of infantry weapons, the bayonet. One such was Lieutenant James Adamson, a twenty-four-year-old platoon commander in the Argyll and Sutherland Highlanders, 5th Battalion, The Royal Regiment of Scotland. One day in 2009 he was commanding two eight-man sections that were operating against the Taliban in the infamous Green Zone of Helmand Province. Adamson was constantly moving between the two sections that were spread out along a river bank opposite a large maize field. 'The Taliban kept probing us,' recalled Lieutenant Adamson, who comes from the Isle of Man. 'Myself and Cpl. Fraser 'Hammy' Hamilton were wading down a river which connected the two positions.'[44] Corporal Hamilton ran straight into a young Taliban fighter who was armed with a Soviet KPM machine-gun, a weapon similar to the British General Purpose Machine Gun. 'There was an exchange of fire and Hammy fired off all his ammunition and then the weight of fire coming from the Taliban forced him under the water.' By now, another Taliban fighter had joined his comrade in attempting to outflank the British positions. Adamson caught up with the pinned-down Hamilton. He quickly spotted one of the Taliban. 'He was only three or four metres away. I shot him with a burst from my rifle which was already set on automatic – he went down straight away and I knew I had him. Hammy said I shouted 'have some of this' as I shot him but I can't remember that.'[45]

The second Taliban fighter who was armed with the KPM machine-gun was dealt with swiftly and decisively by Lieutenant Adamson. Realizing that his rifle magazine was empty, Adamson reacted fast. 'I either waited vital seconds changing the magazine on my rifle or went over the top and did it more quickly with the bayonet – I took the second option. I jumped up over the river bank. He [the Taliban] was just over the other side, almost in touching distance. We caught each other's eye as I went towards him, but by then, for him, it was too late. There was no inner monologue going on in my head, I was just reacting in the way I was trained.' It was either kill or be killed. 'He was alive when it went in – he wasn't alive when it came out – it was that simple,' stated Adamson. The young lieutenant quickly picked up the KPM and slung it over his shoulder to deny its use to the enemy. 'Then we had to wait for more of my men to join us. We thought there could be more Taliban about and we were waiting for more to come out of a big field of maize which came right up to the river we were wading through.'[46] After the rest of his men arrived, they took stock of the situation. 'One of my men, Corporal Billy Carnegie, reached us, looked at the two dead Taliban on the ground and then saw blood on my bayonet and said 'boss, what the fuck have you been doing?'' James Adamson received the Military Cross for his gallantry.

1 '*Medals awarded to honour brave soldiers*' by Thomas Harding, *The Telegraph*, 7 March 2008

2 *Citation for the George Cross: Lance-Corporal Matthew Croucher*, Ministry of Defence, http://www.mod.uk, accessed 15 May 2009

3 Ibid.

4 Patrick Bishop, 3 PARA, (London: Harper Perennial, 2008), 245

5 Ibid: 247-248

6 Ibid: 67

7 '*Military Cross for hero of ambush*' by Michael Smith, *The Sunday Times*, 9 March 2008

9 Ibid.

9 Ibid.

10 Ibid.

11 Ibid.

12 Ibid.

13 '*Prince William visits Cardiff and presents the Prince William Cup*', The Prince of Wales, 8 November 2008, http://www.princeofwales.gov.uk, accessed 15 July 2009

14 '*Military Cross for hero of ambush*' by Michael Smith, *The Sunday Times*, 9 March 2008

15 '*Prince William visits Cardiff and presents the Prince William Cup*', The Prince of Wales, 8 November 2008, http://www.princeofwales.gov.uk, accessed 15 July 2009

16 '*Pride of the Midlands – the magnificent seven of the Mercian Regiment*' by Emma Cullwick, *Birmingham Mail*, 7 March 2008

17 '*My stomach was torn open…so I tucked my shirt in and kept shooting: Amazing stories of the selfless heroes of Afghanistan*' by Matthew Hickley and Paul Harris, *The Daily Mail*, 7 October 2008

18 '*Pride of the Midlands – the magnificent seven of the Mercian Regiment*' by Emma Cullwick, *Birmingham Mail*, 7 March 2008

19 '*My stomach was torn open…so I tucked my shirt in and kept shooting: Amazing stories of the selfless heroes of Afghanistan*' by Matthew Hickley and Paul Harris, *The Daily Mail*, 7 October 2008

20 '*Pride of the Midlands – the magnificent seven of the Mercian Regiment*' by Emma Cullwick, *Birmingham Mail*, 7 March 2008

21 Ibid.

22 '*My stomach was torn open…so I tucked my shirt in and kept shooting: Amazing stories of the selfless heroes of Afghanistan*' by Matthew Hickley and Paul Harris, *The Daily Mail*, 7 October 2008

23 '*Pride of the Midlands – the magnificent seven of the Mercian Regiment*' by Emma Cullwick, *Birmingham Mail*, 7 March 2008

24 Ibid.

25 '*TA soldiers gets Military Cross*', Ministry of Defence Press Office, 7 March 2008

26 '*Heroic Selby soldier Lance Corporal Colin Spooner presented with Military Cross by Prince Charles for his courage during a Taliban ambush in Afghanistan*' by Richard Harris, *The Press*, 28 November 2009

27 '*Marine saved 30 comrades by rugby-tackling a suicide bomber then told sister: 'Don't tell mum, I don't want her to worry*' by Jaya Narain, *The Daily Mail*, 10 September 2009

28 Ibid.

29 Ibid.

30 '*How I rugby tackled a Taliban suicide bomber*' by Tom Newton Dunn, *The Sun*, 16 April 2009

31 '*Marine saved 30 comrades by rugby-tackling a suicide bomber then told sister: 'Don't tell mum, I don't want her to worry*' by Jaya Narain, *The Daily Mail*, 10 September 2009

32 '*Marine who saved 30 comrades by tackling suicide bomber to receive Military Cross*' by Alastair Jamieson, *The Telegraph*, 10 September 2009

33 '*Medic becomes first woman in Royal Navy to be awarded the Military Cross after tending to soldier under Taliban fire*', *The Daily Mail*, 28 November 2009

34 '*Pride of the fleet: Afghan war medic is Navy's first woman to win the Military Cross*' by Matthew Hickley, *The Daily Mail*, 11 September 2009

35 '*Pictured. Heroic female medic who ignored shrapnel embedded in her shoulder to save SEVEN soldiers during Taliban ambush*', *The Daily Mail*, 3 September 2009

36 '*Riddled with shrapnel, but still she saved seven comrades from Taliban*' by James Woodward, *The Independent*, 3 September 2009

37 Ibid.

38 '*RAF pilot wins Distinguished Flying Cross*' by Michael Smith, *The Times*, 8 March 2009

39 Ibid.

40 Ibid.

41 Ibid.

42 Ibid.

43 '*Military Cross for Marine who charged at Taliban*' by Cahal Milmo, *The Independent*, 10 September 2009

44 '*Officer who fought Taliban with his bayonet after running out of ammunition is awarded the Military Cross*', *The Daily Mail*, 13 September 2009

45 Ibid.

46 Ibid.

47 Ibid.

APPENDIX 1

A Guide to British Gallantry Awards

Currently, the British government awards several decorations and medals for gallantry and distinguished service. Divided into twelve levels, there are fifteen individual decorations, medals and insignia available to both civilians and service personnel. Some date from the Victorian period, others from the Second World War, while some are more modern. All of them were designed to reward acts of gallantry based upon strict criteria determined by the government. Some of the awards are restricted to the military only, and some civilian awards can be given to members of the armed forces for brave actions that have not been performed in the face of the enemy. All are awarded sparingly, with many of those honoured being personally invested by the Queen or the Prince of Wales at special investiture ceremonies held at Buckingham Palace throughout the year.

Before the Second World War, very few medals existed to reward civilian courage and gallantry. The oldest was the Albert Medal, named for Queen Victoria's consort, established in 1866 and awarded in two classes for saving life at sea or on land. The 1st Class was replaced in 1949 by the George Cross, and the 2nd Class was discontinued in 1971. In total, the Albert Medal was awarded 568 times. The only other civilian gallantry award was the Edward Medal, named for King Edward VII, and introduced in 1907 for award to miners and quarrymen who had endangered their lives in rescuing their fellow workers. In 1909 the medal was extended to acts of bravery by all industrial workers. It was awarded a total of 583 times, but only twice to women. The 1st Class was replaced by the George Cross in 1948 and the 2nd Class discontinued in 1971. The Medal of the Order of the British Empire for Gallantry (known as the Empire Gallantry Medal) was introduced in 1922 as the highest civilian award for gallantry, and was also open to military personnel. Before it was revoked and replaced by the George Cross in 1940 it was awarded a total of 112 times.

Up to the Second World War most gallantry awards were reserved for servicemen but all this changed when civilians found themselves in the front lines for the first time as the German *Luftwaffe* pounded Britain's cities and U-boats prowled its coastline and shipping lanes. King George VI and his government responded by introducing several new gallantry awards for ordinary civilians, the most prominent among them being the George Cross. Though intended primarily as awards to civilians, most could also be given to personnel of the three armed services for acts of courage performed 'not in the face of the enemy'. Today, there are seven medals and decorations available to reward those British men and women, from all walks of life, who have performed acts of great courage in their everyday lives or professions.

Apart from decorations and medals specifically created to recognize bravery and/or distinguished service, one of Britain's orders of chivalry is often used to reward people from all walks of life where a particular bravery award is not deemed appropriate. The insignia of a Member of the Order of the British Empire (MBE) has been used to reward courage, most notably heroes from the London transport bombings in 2005, six of whom received MBEs in 2009. The British Empire Medal with Oakleaves was awarded between 1958 and 1974 until it was replaced by the Queen's Gallantry Medal.

The complete abolition of the BEM was a long overdue reform because the BEM had been awarded to those whose occupation or social status did not rank as high as those of MBE recipients. It was a long overdue abolition of class distinction in the rewarding of gallantry and meritorious awards that was eventually completed by Prime Minister John Major in 1993.

Commonwealth countries such as Australia, Canada and New Zealand have introduced their own honours, decorations and medals replacing most of the old Imperial awards, though some countries continue to award and/or to recognize British bravery awards today, such as Britain's remaining Overseas Territories and smaller Commonwealth nations like Papua New Guinea and the Cook Islands. In the case of the Cook Islands and the Bahamas, these two countries have continued to award the British Empire Medal for Gallantry, even though it is no longer used in mainland Britain.

Britain's gallantry awards that are currently in use in 2010 are, in order of precedence, as follows:

1. THE VICTORIA CROSS

Instituted by Queen Victoria on 19 January 1856 and awarded for '...most conspicuous bravery, or some daring or pre-eminent act of valour or self-sacrifice, or extreme devotion to duty in the presence of the enemy.' The VC takes precedence over all other bravery awards and orders of chivalry in Britain and the Commonwealth, and, as such, it is the pre-eminent award available. Since its foundation shortly after the Crimean War only 1,357 have been awarded and since 1945 just sixteen. All VCs are cast from the same lump of bronze, taken from the cascabel of a Chinese cannon captured from the Russians at the Siege of Sebastopol in 1854. Recently, Australia, Canada and New Zealand introduced their own version of the VC for award to their citizens, but the cross is identical to the British version and is cast from the same lump of metal (the only difference being the Canadian version where the inscription 'For Valour' has been changed to the Latin 'Pro Valore' to accommodate Canada's two official languages of English and French). The first person thus awarded was Corporal Bill Apiata who received the Victoria Cross of New Zealand in 2007 for his actions when serving with the New Zealand SAS in Afghanistan in 2004.

Description: bronze cross pattee, 41mm high and 36mm wide, bearing on the obverse a crown surmounted by a lion and the inscription FOR VALOUR. The reverse is plain and engraved with the name of the recipient and the date of the action. The VC is suspended from a crimson ribbon.

2. GEORGE CROSS

The pre-eminent award for civilian gallantry was created by King George VI on 24 September 1940, when Britain was under direct aerial attack from the Germans. Awarded only sparingly, it is given for acts of the highest gallantry and ranks equal in status to the Victoria Cross, and may be given to service personnel for acts of the highest bravery not performed 'in the face of the enemy'. It replaced the Empire Gallantry Medal. Since its introduction the George Cross has only be awarded 161 times. The citation states the medal may be given for "acts of the greatest heroism or of the most conspicuous courage in circumstances of extreme danger." It may be awarded posthumously.

Description: plain silver cross, 48mm high and 45mm wide, with a circular medallion in the obverse centre depicting an effigy of St. George and the Dragon, surrounded by the words FOR GALLANTRY. The angles of each limb of the cross contain the Royal Cypher GVI. The reverse is plain and engraved with the name of the recipient and the date of the award. The George Cross ribbon is dark blue.

3. Conspicuous Gallantry Cross

Instituted following John Major's review of the British honours system in 1993, the CGC is awarded for '…an act or acts of conspicuous gallantry during active operations against the enemy.' The introduction of the CGC was intended to remove the distinction of rank that existed between awards for bravery, the CGC replacing both the Distinguished Conduct Medal and the Conspicuous Gallantry Medal (Naval and Air Force) as a second level award to other ranks and ratings, and the Distinguished Service Order (DSO) as an award to officers for gallantry (the DSO has been retained as an award for outstanding leadership). Since 1993, the Conspicuous Gallantry Cross has been awarded on only thirty-seven occasions (up to 2009).

Description: silver cross patee imposed on a wreath of laurel, with the Royal Crown in a circular panel in the obverse centre. The ribbon is white with blue edges and a red central stripe.

4. Distinguished Service Cross

A third level military decoration that was reserved for naval officers only until 1993 when it was opened to ratings also. Originally created as the Conspicuous Service Cross in 1901, the name was changed to the DSC in 1914. Since 1945 fewer than 100 DSC's have been awarded.

Description: plain silver cross with rounded edges measuring 43mm in height and width. The obverse has a circular centre with the Royal Cypher of the reigning monarch. The reverse is plain. The ribbon consists of three equal stripes of dark blue, white and dark blue.

Military Cross

Equal in status to the Navy's DSC, the Military Cross is given to officers and (since 1993) other ranks of the British Armed Forces in recognition of '...gallantry during active operations against the enemy.' The Military Medal, a former third level decoration for other ranks, was discontinued in 1993. The Military Cross was created in 1914.

Description: 46mm in height and 44mm in width, the Military Cross is an ornamental silver cross with straight arms terminating in broad finials decorated with imperial crowns. The reverse is plain with the recipients name and the year of issue engraved on the lower limb of the cross. The ribbon is three equal parts of white, purple and white.

Distinguished Flying Cross

Another third level bravery award, this time primarily awarded to officers and men of the Royal Air Force and Royal Marine air squadrons, the DFC was created on 3 June 1918 shortly after the RAF was formed. Since 1993 other ranks have been eligible for the award of this medal, the Distinguished Flying Medal having been discontinued. The DFC is awarded for '...an act or acts of valour, courage or devotion to duty whilst flying in active operations against the enemy.'

Description: cross flory with the horizontal and bottom bars terminated with bumps, and the upper bar with a rose. The obverse features aircraft propellers superimposed on the vertical arms of the cross and wings on the horizontal arms. The centre contains a laurel wreath around the RAF monogram surmounted by an Imperial Crown. The reverse features the

Royal Cypher in the centre and the year of issue engraved on the lower arm. The ribbon is diagonal alternate stripes of white and deep purple.

5. AIR FORCE CROSS

Awarded for '...an act or acts of valour, courage or devotion to duty whilst flying, though not in active operations against the enemy.' The AFC has been awarded to both officers and other ranks since 1993, the Air Force Medal having been discontinued, and it was established in 1918 at the same time as the DFC.

Description: silver cross 60mm high and 54mm wide, representing aircraft propeller blades, with wings between the arms. The obverse depicts Hermes riding on the wings of a hawk holding a laurel wreath. At the top of the upper arm is the royal crown, while the other three arms bear the Royal Cypher of the reigning monarch. The AFC ribbon is diagonal alternate stripes of white and red.

6. GEORGE MEDAL

Instituted on the same day as the George Cross, the George Medal is awarded for acts of great civilian bravery, and can be awarded to military personnel whose courageous acts must not have been performed in the face of the enemy. Since 1977 it has also been awarded posthumously. Since 1940, just over 2,000 have been awarded.

Description: circular silver medal of 36mm diameter. The obverse depicts the crowned effigy of the reigning monarch and a legend. The reverse shows St. George on horseback slaying the dragon on the coast of England, with the legend THE GEORGE MEDAL around the top edge of the medal. The ribbon is red with five equally spaced thin blue stripes (the blue taken from the George Cross).

7. QUEEN'S POLICE MEDAL FOR GALLANTRY

This medal has virtually fallen into disuse. It is awarded only posthumously to police officers who have performed "acts of exceptional courage and skill at the cost of their lives." Introduced on 19 May 1954 to replace the King's Police Medal, since 1977 this medal has been rarely awarded. Recipients today normally receive the George Cross, George Medal or The Queen's Gallantry Medal instead. A Queen's Police Medal for Distinguished Service is regularly awarded for different criteria.

Description: circular silver medal 36mm in diameter. The obverse depicts the effigy of Queen Elizabeth II. The reverse depicts a figure holding a sword and a shield surrounded by the inscription FOR GALLANTRY. The ribbon consists of three silver stripes and two wide blue stripes, each silver stripe having a thin red stripe running through it.

8. QUEEN'S FIRE SERVICE MEDAL FOR GALLANTRY

Both Gallantry and Distinguished Service versions of the Queen's Fire Service Medal exist. The medal for gallantry is rarely awarded, and as with the Sea Gallantry Medal and Queen's Police Medal for Gallantry, recipients have instead been awarded the George Cross, George Medal or Queen's Gallantry Medal so this medal is considered to be virtually redundant. The Queen's Fire Service Medal for Gallantry is only awarded posthumously to firefighters for "acts of exceptional courage and skill at the cost of their lives." This award was introduced at the same time as the Queen's Police Medal.

Description: circular silver medal 36mm in diameter. Identical in design to the Queen's Police Medal. The ribbon is red with three yellow stripes and a single blue stripe running through each yellow stripe.

9. SEA GALLANTRY MEDAL

This is a unique award among British honours and decorations. Officially the Board of Trade Medal of Saving Life at Sea, the Sea Gallantry Medal is the only bravery award currently issued under the authority of Parliament, rather than the Crown. It was first struck in 1855, and since 1903 the medal has been designed to be worn. Since 1952 only 26 have been awarded, the last in 1989, as the acts of bravery that merit this medal normally attract instead the George Cross, George Medal or The Queen's Gallantry Medal today.

Description: circular silver medal 36mm in diameter. The obverse contains the crowned effigy of the reigning monarch and the Royal Cypher with the words AWARDED BY THE BOARD OF TRADE

FOR GALLANTRY IN SAVING LIFE. The reverse shows a man clinging to a spar and beckoning to a lifeboat. The ribbon is scarlet with two narrow white stripes.

10. QUEEN'S GALLANTRY MEDAL

Instituted by Queen Elizabeth II on 20 June 1974 to replace the British Empire Medal with Oakleaves, the Queen's Gallantry Medal is awarded to both civilians and military personnel (for actions not in the face of the enemy) for exemplary acts of bravery. Fewer than 600 have been awarded.

Description: circular silver medal 36mm in diameter. The obverse shows the crowned effigy of the reigning monarch. The reverse image consists of an Imperial Crown above the words THE QUEEN'S GALLANTRY MEDAL in four lines, flanked by laurel sprigs. The ribbon is three equal stripes of dark blue, pearl grey and dark blue with a narrow rose pink stripe in the centre.

11. MENTION IN DESPATCHES

If a subordinate officer or soldier performs a noteworthy action that is mentioned in a report (despatch) from a senior commander to his superiors, that soldier is said to have been 'mentioned in despatches.'

Description: a certificate and a silver oak leaf worn on the ribbon of the service medal issued to soldiers who served in a conflict. If no medal was awarded the insignia is worn on the left breast of dress uniform.

12. QUEEN'S COMMENDATION FOR BRAVERY

This award is open to both British subjects and the citizens of foreign nations for bravery entailing risk to life and meriting national recognition.

Description: a certificate and a spray of laurel leaves, silver for civilians and bronze for military personnel, worn on any associated campaign medal, or if no medal issued, pinned to the left breast.

13. QUEEN'S COMMENDATION FOR BRAVERY IN THE AIR

Awarded for gallantry performed in the air that was not in action with the enemy entailing risk to life, and meriting national recognition.

Description: a certificate and a silver RAF eagle worn on any associated campaign medal, or if no medal issued, worn pinned to the left breast.

THE MOST EXCELLENT ORDER OF THE BRITISH EMPIRE

Although this is part of the Orders of Chivalry, the insignia of the lowest grade of the Order of the British Empire has occasionally been awarded for bravery, especially where the criteria for established bravery awards have not been specifically met and there was a desire to recognize individual heroism. The Order was established by King George V in 1917, and the motto is 'For God and the Empire'.

The Order is divided into five levels: Knight Grand Cross or Dame Grand Cross (GBE); Knight Commander (KBE) or Dame Commander (DBE); Commander (CBE); Officer (OBE); and Member (MBE). Only the first two grades carry knighthoods. The Order is divided between a Civil and a Military division.

Description: The insignia of the MBE is a silver cross patonce, the obverse showing the heads of King George V and Queen Mary, the reverse George V's Royal and Imperial Cypher. The cross is suspended from a rose-pink ribbon with pearl-grey edges.

Honours and Awards for the London Bombings of 7 and 21 July 2005

NEW YEAR HONOURS 2006

THE MOST EXCELLENT ORDER OF THE BRITISH EMPIRE

COMMANDER (CBE)

Julie Dent, Southwest Strategic Health Authority, London

Peter Hendy, Transport For London

Tim O'Toole, (Honorary award as a US citizen)

OFFICER (OBE)

Deputy Commissioner Roy Bishop, London Fire Service

Deputy Assistant Commissioner Peter Clarke, Metropolitan Police

Martin Flaherty, London Ambulance Service

Major Muriel McClenahan, Salvation Army

Alastair Wilson, Royal London Hospital

Member (MBE)

Commander Chris Allison, Metropolitan Police

Dallas Ariotti, Guy's and St. Thomas's Hospitals

David Boyce, Transport For London

John Boyle, Transport For London

Alan Dell, Transport For London

John Gardner, Transport For London

Peter Hendry, Transport For London

William Kilminster, London Ambulance Service

Inspector Glen McMunn, British Transport Police

Inspector Stephen Mingay, British Transport Police

Roy Parry, Transport For London

Julia Peterkin, Royal London Hospital

Constable Deborah Russell-Fenwick, British Transport Police

Peter Sanders, Transport For London

Angela Scarisbrick, National Health Service

Peter Swan, London Ambulance Service

Jim Underdown, London Ambulance Service

Roy Web, London Ambulance Service

Queen's Police Medal for Distinguished Service

Detective Superintendent Douglas McKenna, Metropolitan Police

Detective Superintendent John Prunty, Metropolitan Police

New Year Honours 2008

Queen's Gallantry Medal

Angus Campbell, London Fire Service

NEW YEAR HONOURS 2009

THE MOST EXCELLENT ORDER OF THE BRITISH EMPIRE

MEMBER (MBE)

Tim Coulson

Stephen Hucklesby

Constable Elizabeth Kenworthy, Metropolitan Police

David Matthews, Transport For London

Gerald McIlmurray

Antonio Silvestro

QUEEN'S COMMENDATION FOR BRAVERY

Adrian Heili

Lee Hunt, Transport For London

APPENDIX 3

Awards of the Royal Humane Society

The Royal Humane Society was founded in London in 1774, and now has branches in Australia, Canada and New Zealand. It was originally founded as 'The Society for the Recovery of Persons Apparently Drowned', the aim being to artificially resuscitate those who had perished in water. The earliest Royal Humane Society building was the Receiving House in Hyde Park, on the banks of the Serpentine where many people drowned every year. It was constructed on land donated by King George III. The society distributed money-rewards, medals, clasps and testimonials to those who had saved or attempted to save, drowned people. This was later extended to all cases of exceptional bravery in trying to save lives, and although cash rewards are no longer made, medals and testimonials continue to be awarded. To date, the RHS has made over 85,000 awards since 1774. Famous recipients of bravery medals have included Tsar Alexander I of Russia, the engineer Isambard Kingdom Brunel, lifeboat heroine Grace Darling, author of the novel *Dracula* Bram Stoker, explorer David Hempleman-Adams and Olympic swimmer Duncan Goodhew. The current patron of the RHS is HM The Queen, and HRH Princess Alexandra is the President and presents many of the awards.

The medals awarded by the RHS are the same dimensions and style as official British service medals. Each medal has its own distinctive ribbon and design. They may be worn by recipients in the same manner as state medals, though on the right breast, not the left. All the medals show the insignia of the RHS on the observes.

STANHOPE MEDAL

Established in 1873, this is the most prestigious medal awarded by the RHS. It is named for Captain Chandos Stanhope, RN, who was famous for saving lives during the 19th century. The medal, made of gold, is presented annually to the most outstanding existing medal winner across all RHS organizations in Britain, Australia, Canada and New Zealand.

The ribbon consists of a central wide blue stripe, flanked by a thin yellow stripe, and a dark green outer stripe.

SILVER MEDAL

Established in 1775, the medal, made of silver-gilt, is awarded to recipients who have placed themselves in extreme personal danger, carried out a very long and arduous rescue or returned repeatedly to a highly dangerous situation.

The ribbon consists of a thin central yellow stripe, flanked by two wide blue stripes, then a thin white stripe along the edges.

POLICE MEDAL

This silver-guilt medal was established in 2000 to recognize police bravery. It is rewarded to the police officer who has performed the most outstanding act of heroism during the preceding year.

The ribbon consists of three equal stripes of blue, yellow and blue.

BRONZE MEDAL

Established in 1837, the Bronze Medal is awarded to people who have put their own lives at great risk to save or attempt to save someone else. The ribbon is dark blue.

Sources and Selected Bibliography

BOOKS

Ahmed, Nafeez Mosaddez, *The London Bombings: An Independent Enquiry*, Gerald Duckworth & Co. Ltd, 2006

Ashby, Philip, *Unscathed: Escape from Sierra Leone*, Pan Books, 2002

Beattie, Doug, *Task Force Helmand: A Soldier's Story of Life, Death and Combat on the Afghan Front*, London, Simon & Schuster Ltd, 2009

Beharry, Johnson, *The Barefoot Soldier*, Brown Book Group, 2006

Bishop, Patrick, *3 PARA*, Harper Perennial, 2008

Brown, Gordon, *Britain's Everyday Heroes*, Mainstream Publishing, 2007

Brown, Gordon, *Courage: Eight Portraits*, Bloomsbury Publishing Plc, 2007

Cawthorne, Nigel, *Heroes: Winners of the Victoria Cross*, John Blake Publishing Ltd., 2007

Collins, Dan, *In Foreign Fields: Heroes of Iraq and Afghanistan in Their Own Words*, Monday Books, 2008

Croucher, Matt, *Bullet Proof*, London: Century, 2009

David, Saul, *Military Blunders: The How and Why of Military Failure*, London: Robinson, 1997

De la Billiere, Peter, *Supreme Courage: Heroic Stories from 150 Years of the VC*, Abacus, 2005

Fowler, William, *Operation Barras: The SAS Rescue Mission Sierra Leone 2000*, Phoenix, 2005

Hennessey, Patrick, *The Junior Officers' Reading Club: Killing Time and Fighting Wars*, London: Allen Lane, 2009

Herman, Arthur, *To Rule The Waves: How the British Navy Shaped the Modern World*, London, Hodder, 2005

Hunter, Chris, *Eight Lives Down*, London: Corgi Books, 2008

Kemp, Patrick and Hughes, Chris, *Attack State Red*, London: Michael Joseph, 2009

Kiley, Sam, *Desperate Glory: At War in Helmand with Britain's 16 Air Assault Brigade*, London: Bloomsbury Publishing Plc, 2009

Lewis, Damien, *Operation Certain Death*, Arrow Books Ltd, 2005

Senauth, Frank, *A Morning of Terror: The London Bombings on July 7th 2005*, Outskirts Press, 2007

Tootal, Stuart, *Danger Close: Commanding 3 PARA in Afghanistan*, London: John Murray, 2009

Turner, John Frayn, *Awards of the George Cross 1940-2005*, Leo Cooper Ltd., 2006

White, Rowland, *Phoenix Squadron: HMS Ark Royal, Britain's Last Top Guns and the Untold Story of Their Most Dramatic Mission*, London: Bantam Press, 2009

NEWSPAPERS AND PERIODICALS

Birmingham Mail

Cambridge News

Daily Mail

East Anglian Daily Times

Epsom Guardian

Gazette (Colchester)

Guardian

Hertfordshire Mercury

Independent

Liverpool Echo

London Evening Standard

London Gazette

Luton Today

Manchester Evening News

Metro (London)

New York Times

Police

Richmond & Twickenham Times

The Sun

Sunday Times

Sunderland Echo

The Telegraph

The Times

Yorkshire Evening Post

PAPERS

Evoe, Patrick J., *Operation Palliser: The British Military Intervention into Sierra Leone, A Case of a Successful Use of Western Military Interdiction in a Sub-Saharan African Civil War*, MA Dissertation, Texas State University – San Marcos, 2008

WEBSITES

BBC News, bbc.co.uk/news

Daily Mail, www.dailymail.co.uk

Lancashire Constabulary, www.lancshire.police.uk

Metropolitan Police, www.cmc.met.police.uk

Ministry of Defence, www.mod.uk

Panorama, www.bbc.co.uk/panorama

Police999, www.police999.com

Prince of Wales, www.princeofwales.gov.uk

Princess of Wales's Royal Regiment (Queen's and Royal Hampshires), www.army.mod.uk/infantry/regiments/3479.aspx

This Is Total Essex, www.thisistotalessex.co.uk

Index

Adamson, Lt. James, 168
Alexander, Marine Sam, 166
Al-Qaeda, 20, 140
Anderson, Andrew, 118-119
Anderson, Jade, 76-77
Archer, PC Jeremy, 32-33
Armiger, Derek, 12-13, 14
Apiata, Cpl. Bill, 48
Ashby, Maj. Phil, 21-24
Azimhar, Spr. Cengiz, 103

Bangura, Lt. Musa, 24, 25, 27
Barlow, Fus. Andy, 148
Bartlett, CSM Harry, 29
Beard, LAC Martin, 68-69
Beckley, Dep. Ch. Con. Rob, 13
Beharry, Pvt. Johnson, 49-55,
    59
Biddick, Maj. Tony, 139-140
Blair, Comm. Sir Ian, 101
Blair, PM Tony, 20, 25, 83, 84,
    140
Bonner, Cpl. Daz, 139
Botha, Pvt. Johan, 154
Bourgourd, David, 118-119
Brawley, George, 94
Brelsford, Sgt. Craig, 154
Broad, Clark, 116-117
Brown, Lt. Aaron, 155-156

Brown, Gordon, 91
British Army:
  Divisions:
1st Armoured Division, 47
  Brigades:
    1 Mechanised Brigade, 47, 50
    7 Armoured Brigade, 47
16 Air Assault Brigade, 47, 56,
    158
19 Light Brigade, 102
  Regiments:
Argyll & Sutherland
    Highlanders, 5th Battalion,
    Royal Regiment of Scotland,
    136, 167
Army Air Corps, 66, 122
Black Watch, 42
Blues and Royals, 56
Life Guards, 56
Light Infantry, 22
Mercian Regiment, 153-154
Parachute Regiment, 20, 21, 26-
    30, 48, 145-146, 156
Princess of Wales's Royal
    Regiment, 46, 49-50, 64, 160
Queen's Royal Lancers, 50
Rifles, 66, 163
Royal Anglian Regiment, 21,
    139-140
Royal Gurkha Rifles, 153

Royal Irish Regiment, ix, 21, 24-25, 158
Royal Regiment of Artillery, 21
Royal Regiment of Fusiliers, 50
Royal Welsh, 149-150
Royal Welsh Fusiliers, 50
Special Air Service Regiment, 20, 21, 25-26, 27-30
Corps:
Royal Army Medical Corps, 26, 46, 148, 163
Royal Engineers, 57, 58
Royal Logistic Corps, 124-125, 129-130
Operations:
Barras, 25
Palliser, 20
Pechtaw, 154
Telic, 47, 69
Brims, Maj.-Gen. Robin, 47
Budd, Cpl. Bryan, 49, 60, 155-157
Burgess, Fl.-Lt. Timothy, 29
Burns, 2nd Officer Peter, 29
Burridge, ACM Brian, 47
Burton-Garbett, Arthur, 94
Bush, Pres. George W., 140

Caines, Cpl. Martin, 64-65
Calder, Maj. Nick, x
Camp, Lt. Tony, 24
Campbell, Angus, 93-94
Carnegie, Cpl. Billy, 168
Carroll, PC Stephen, 103
Chandler, L-Cpl. David, 155
Chiswell, Maj. James, 29
Clarke, L-Cpl. Sally, 163-164

Clarkson, Stephen, 98
Cochrane, Ray, 112-113
Cole, USS, 96
Cole, Pvt. Luke, 153-155
Connell, John, 113-114, 115
Connelly, Sgt. Noel, 161-162
Cooper, Pvt. Sam, 155
Coulson, Tim, 86-87, 90
Coulton, PC Richard, 41-42
Cradden, Capt. Liam, 27, 28
Craig, L-Cpl. Alex, 148
Crisp, PC Matthew, 42, 44
Crompton, Anthony, 11-12
Croucher, L-Cpl. Matthew, 143-145, 153
Cunnington, PC David, 38-39
Cupples, Lt. Simon, 155

Davies, PC Jonathan, 36-37
Dawes, Cpl. Simon, 28
Denning, Maj. Jeremy, 122-123
Dettori, Frankie, 112-113
Douglas, Emma, 76
Duguid, David, 96-97
Duncan, Fl.-Lt. Alex, 164-166
Dutton, Brig. Jim, 47

Easson, John, 114

Federal Bureau of Investigation, 101, 132
Finney, Tpr. Christopher, 56-59
Fitzpatrick, Spr. Marc, 102, 103, 104

Flynn, Cpl.-of-Horse Mick, 57, 59
Francis, George, 119-121
Fuery, Capt. Evan, 29

Gardner, Beth, 76
Gawthorp, Maureen, 109-110
Goodman, Ft.-Lt. Michelle, 66-67
Gray, Pvt. Chris, 139
Gray, PC Richard, 42-44
Greenall, PC Robert, 71-72
Greyling, Garth, 122-123
Griffiths, Sean, 79
Grinney, Julian, 116-117
Grove, William, vii-ix, x
Groves, Michael, 107-109
Gurung, Som Bahadur, 108-109

Hale, L-Cpl. Stuart, 146-147, 149
Hamilton, Cpl. Fraser, 167
Hamilton, Thomas, 43
Hansa, 115-116
Hartley, L-Cpl. Paul, 148, 149
Hayden, Cpl. David, 68-69
Heili, Adrian, 88
Hellyer, PC Jeanne, 79
Hields, Fus. Damien, 149-152
Hucklesby, Stephen, 88, 91
Hull, L-Cpl-of-Horse Matty, 58
Humphrey, Paul, 99-100
Hunt, Lee, 88-89
Hussein, Saddam, 47, 51, 61

James, Lt.-Col. Huw, 149, 152
Jones, Lt.-Col. Herbert, 48
Jones, Nigel, 7-9

Kabbah, Pres. Ahmed Tejan, 19
Kallay, Foday, 24-30
Karzai, Pres. Hamid, 140
Kenworthy, PC Elizabeth, xi, 85-86, 91
Kerr, Michael, 98
Kwok Man Fan, 5-7

Lamb, Lt.-Gen. Graham, 140
Lane, Janet, 1-2
Leak, Sgt. Douglas, 125-128
Leigh, PS David, 40-41
Le Page, Robert, 118-119
Lingard, Maj. David, 22
Lomas, PC David, 40-41
Lynch, Owen, 9-10

Macarthy, Alison, 91
MacFarlane, Sqn. Ldr. Iain, 29
Mackenzie, Kevin, 114-115
Mackey, Patrick, 112-113
MacMaster, L-Cpl. Dean, 128-129
Mahdi Army, 50-51
Mallalieu, Cpl. Darren, 117-118
Marshall, Maj. Alan, 24-25, 27-30
Marshall, PS Ian, 74-75
Matthews, A. Capt. Danny, 28, 29
Matthews, David, 87, 91

Maybanks, Mark, 94
McClurg, Cpl. Robert, 159-160
McConnell, Sgt. Stephen, ix-x
McIlveen, Alex, 97, 98
McKay, Sgt. Ian, 48
McMunn, Insp. Glenn, 87-88,
    89-90
Melody, 109-110
Miller, Michael, 77-78
Moore, Reserve Constable
    Robert, 37-38
Morrison, Derek, 114-115
Moyes, Capt. Allan, 30
Mulla, PC Lukmann, 40-41
Murray, Chris, 116-117
Murray, Vicky, 73-74

Nesbitt, ABS1 Kate, 162-163
Ness, Lt. Paul, 128-129
Norris, Pvt. Michelle, 46, 65,
    163
Norton, Capt. Peter, 129-132
Nyazika, Stephen, 9-10

Oake, DC Stephen, 81-82
O'Brien, Hugh, 114
O'Donnell, WO2 Gary, 133-137

Page, Col. Sgt. Ian, 46
Panther, PC Gary, 41-42
Pardoe, Jason, 78-79
Pearce, Christopher, 9-10
Pearce, Det. Sup. Keith, 100-
    101
Pearson, Cpl. Stuart, 147, 149

Pennington, Andrew, 8-9
Police Forces:
  Avon & Somerset Police, 11
  British Transport Police, 34,
  85, 89
  Cheshire Constabulary, 42
Devon & Cornwall Police, 2
Greater Manchester Police, 82
Lancashire Constabulary, 40
Metropolitan Police, 36, 81, 85,
  99
Northumbria Police, 76
Police Service of Northern
    Ireland, 37
  Suffolk Constabulary, 4, 112
  West Mercia Police, 42, 44
  West Yorkshire Police, 41
Priest, Fl.-Lt. Jonathan, 29
Prosser, Pvt. Dave, 148
Purvis, PC Darren, 76-77

Quinsey, Spr. Mark, 103

Raffles, Sir Thomas, 106
Rathmell, Dr. Andrew, 59-60
Restorick, L-Bdr. Stephen, 103
Revolutionary United Front, 19,
    20-21, 22, 23, 24-30
Richards, Brig. David, 20
Righton, Michael, 72-73
Roberts, Neil, 2
Rowland, Lt.-Com. Paul, 22
Rowlands, Wyn, 110
Royal Air Force:
  27 Squadron, 164

63 Squadron (Queen's Colour Squadron), 68
78 Squadron, 66
RAF Benson, 66
RAF Cottesmore, 117
RAF Lynham, 91
Royal Fleet Auxiliary:
  Fort Austin, RFA, 20
  Sir Percivale, RFA, 24, 29
Royal Marines:
  3 Commando Brigade, 47, 102, 143, 161
  40 Commando, 143
  42 Commando, 20, 161
  Royal Marines Reserve, 143
  Special Boat Squadron, 26
Royal Navy:
  Amphibious Ready Group, 20
  Chatham, HMS, 20, 26
  Illustrious, HMS, 20
  Marlborough, HMS, 96
  Ocean, HMS, 20, 163

Samsonoff, Capt. Andrew, 22
Sankoh, Foday, 19
Seabourn Spirit, 108-109
Scorey, Linda, 15-16
Scott, DC Mark, 4-5
Seery, Michael, 12
Sheard, Pvt. Julian, 28
Shepherd, Fl.-Lt. Paul, 29-30
Shott, Leslie, 16-17
Sierra Leone People's Party, 19
Silvestro, DC Antonio, 85, 86, 91, 98
Sindall, SSgt. Andrew, 57, 59
Smeaton, John, 97, 98

Smith, Fus. David, 61-63
Smith, Spr. Stephen, 128-129
Spooner, L-Cpl. Colin, 160-161
Staniforth, Wing Com. Craig, 91
Stephenson, Neil, 116-117
Stenson-Pickles, DC Stephen, 4-5
Stevens, ASgt. Alwyn, 159
Stevens, Comm. Sir John, 33
Stevens, Linda, 15-16
Stuart, Maj.-Gen. Andrew, 47-48
Swindells, DC Michael, 39-40

Tanner, Insp. Michael, 34-35
Thompson, Tpr. Mark, 48
Thornes, DCI Sheila, 44
Tinion, Bdr. Bradley, 29
Toge, L-Cpl. Jone, 158-159
Tootal, Lt.-Col. Stuart, 146, 148, 157
Torpy, ACM Sir Glenn, 121
Trussell, Barbara, 10-11

Ulla, Mohammed, 16-17

Vause, Rfn. Stephen, 66, 67

Wadsworth, SSgt. James, 131-132
Walker, Allen, 120-121
Walker, PC Ashley, 92
Walton, PC Matt, 40
West Side Boys, 24-30
Williams, L-Cpl. Carley, 152

Winstanley, Michael, 118-119
Woodhouse, PC Nick, 32-33
Wornham, Jeffrey, 77-78
Wright, Gary, 99-100
Wright, Cpl. Mark, 147, 148, 149

Yardley, Lt.-Col. Ivan, 156

Zambellas, Capt. George, 29
Zimonjic, Peter, 91